MISSISSIPPI
FIDDLE TUNES
AND SONGS FROM THE 1930s

MISSISSIPPI FIDDLE TUNES

AND SONGS FROM THE 1930s

Harry Bolick and Stephen T. Austin

University Press of Mississippi / Jackson

www.upress.state.ms.us

The University Press of Mississippi is a member
of the Association of American University Presses.

First printing 2015

∞

Library of Congress Cataloging-in-Publication Data

Bolick, Harry.
Mississippi fiddle tunes and songs from the 1930s /
Harry Bolick and Stephen T. Austin.
pages cm. — (American made music series)
Includes index.
ISBN 978-1-4968-0401-3 (cloth : alk. paper) — ISBN 978-1-4968-0407-5
(pbk. : alk. paper) — ISBN 978-1-4968-0402-0 (ebook) 1. Folk music—
Mississippi—History and criticism. 2. Fiddle tunes—Mississippi—History
and criticism. 3. Ethnomusicology—Mississippi. 4. Folk music—Mississippi.
5. Fiddle tunes—Mississippi. I. Austin, Stephen T. II. Title.
ML3551.7.M6B65 2015
781.62'130762—dc23   2015019112

British Library Cataloging-in-Publication Data available

CONTENTS

PREFACE

My interest in discovering the fiddle music of Mississippi began in the 1970s with reissues of commercial 78rpm records of Mississippi string bands and fiddlers made from in the late 1920s and early 1930s. From England, Tony Russell listed them all; along with interviews, photos, and descriptions of the bands and fiddlers in his magazine *Old Time Music* no. 20 (spring 1976). That issue became my roadmap in locating copies of those tunes so that I could learn them. My next revelation was the 1987 LP *Great Big Yam Taters,* which contained some of the WPA field recordings made in 1939 accompanied by excellent liner notes. Eventually my search for the rest of those 1939 field recordings led me to the American Folklife Center at the Library of Congress. While there, I discovered that the photos from 1939 were archived in Jackson, Mississippi. When I travelled there, to my great surprise I discovered a treasure trove of 1936 WPA fieldwork. Dismayed by the scarcity of information about the sources and their music, I have searched for any information to provide more contexts for these mysterious tunes. The essay contained in the first part of this book is the result of that effort.

A selection of the fiddle tunes collected by the WPA in 1936 and 1939 was originally intended as a small part of a larger WPA book on Mississippi folk music. Sadly, the Federal Arts projects engaged in that work were defunded and disbanded before their efforts came to fruition. The collected materials were archived. The book in your hands contains transcriptions of *all* of the fiddle tunes from those collecting efforts, many more than would have been included in the planned WPA book.

In piecing together the story of how the WPA came to collect fiddle tunes in Mississippi, a story whose events all happened before my birth, I was deeply dependent on the work of the collectors, the contributions of the families of the source musicians, the work of other authors in the field, and the work of the institutions that did the original collecting and studied and preserved it. I am grateful to them all. The detective work has been delightful, the search rewarding, and the music enlightening. My contribution with this book essentially has been editorial in nature, pulling together the facts and the source material to present to the reader.

Many friends, colleagues, and family have encouraged and helped me in bringing this book into being, and they deserve to be thanked here for sharing their patience, expertise, collections, and skills: Greg Adams, Andy Kuntz, Kerry Blech, Elsie Berryhill, Lynda Brister, Ken Bloom, Mary Connor, for her great detective work in locating descendants of the 1939 sources, Pat Conte, Joyce Cauthen, Celeste Frey, Ann Hoog of the American Folklife Center at the Library of Congress, Jeff Place of the Smithsonian/Folkways Rinzler Archive, Tony Russell, Brian Slattery, Ruby Brown Smith, and Julia Marks Young and Anne Lipscomb-Webster at the Mississippi Department of Archives and History. I need to acknowledge Steve Austin's exacting, superlative work in bringing the transcriptions of Halpert's 1939 fiddle tunes to life. I asked him for help and he graciously took the lead for those tunes. A useful transcription is far closer to reading the mind of the source than just documenting what was recorded. I join all those interested in the musical heritage of Mississippi in gratefully acknowledging the work of the many named and unnamed WPA workers who collected the music presented here. My deepest thanks go to my wife, Patricia Schories, for understanding and encouraging me all through this long process.

This stage of my research into the fiddle music of Mississippi is now complete; however, my interest continues. As more information comes to light, perhaps due to the publication of this book, I will share it via my website: www.mississippi fiddle.com.

If fans or family members have home recordings of Mississippi fiddlers that they would like to share, I would be most honored to be contacted via my website.

I have made recordings containing my versions of some of the most interesting tunes in this collection. That project is available from my website.

A set of mp3s created from the notation software playback of all of the 1936 tunes in this book are posted at my website.

I am working with Document Records on a project to issue all of the 1939 Halpert fiddle recordings; check my website for more information.

INTRODUCTION

Over a hundred fiddle tunes, many of them unique, and thousands of songs were collected and notated in manuscript form throughout a large part of the state of Mississippi in the summer of 1936. The roughly 130 field workers employed by the Works Progress Administration (WPA) were novices, the amount of duplication considerable, and the quality and the notation of the music collected quite variable. There are beautiful tunes, tantalizing fragments, and some frustratingly opaque notation. But as a body of work, it is an unparalleled and fascinating snapshot of vernacular music as heard in Mississippi in the early part of the recorded era. Until now, the music has been unpublished and forgotten, available only by visiting the Mississippi Department of Archives and History.

In the summer of 1939, Herbert Halpert and Abbott Ferriss followed an itinerary based on contacts made and previous collecting done by local WPA field workers. Carrying a state-of-the-art disc recorder, they toured the state recording 144 fiddle tunes and a larger number of songs. A map of their trip is in Appendix A. Their recordings and field notes were archived at the Library of Congress, and for many decades only a handful were published. In 1987 forty-three of the best of the fiddle tunes from that trip were published in an LP, *Great Big Yam Potatoes*.

The intent of this book is to revive this neglected music by bringing it to the attention of musicians and scholars, putting it in an historical context, and making both the music and the collectors' notes accessible.

In the first part of this book, "Collecting Folk Music in 1936 and 1939," I trace the effect of a chance event and the power of definition. Early folklore scholars held to a romantic vision of their work as saving the remnants of dying culture. By the time of the fieldwork in Mississippi, the term *folklore* was beginning to be understood as a study of ongoing cultural adaptation. Defining folklore seems to be a scholarly abstraction. But how can you find something until you define what you wish to locate? For example, when African American folklore was defined as spirituals or blues, many black fiddlers were passed over. The collecting efforts of the 1930s were triggered by previous events. What if a student at the University of Mississippi had not piqued Professor A. P. Hudson's curiosity by reciting a local ballad? Without Hudson's pioneering work, who would have located the singers and musicians? What if there had been no polio outbreak in Mississippi in 1936 and the music teachers employed by the Federal Music Project (FMP) of the WPA were not set to collecting folk music? The politics of the WPA, the personalities involved, the evolving ideas, and the accidents of history have combined and conspired to allow this fascinating collection of fiddle tunes to survive.

To make the collected music accessible to musicians, the second part of this book contains transcriptions of all the fiddle tunes that were collected in 1936 and new transcriptions of all of the 1939 Halpert fiddle recordings. Steve Austin and I made the new transcriptions in the hope that they will help revive otherwise unknown tunes and aid in deciphering the recordings where they are available. Recordings generated from the 1936 manuscripts are posted at www.mississippifiddle.com to provide access to the tunes for those who prefer to learn by ear.

While we are very fortunate to have the transcriptions of the tunes collected in 1936, we know very little about the performers. In many cases all we have is the source's name and home county. Often it is unclear if it is the collector or the source to which the tune is attributed. However, in 1939 we have a complete reversal. Abbott Ferriss of the Federal Writers' Project in Mississippi not only took extensive and literate notes but also diagrams of home floor plans, drawings, and beautiful photographs. Some of his character descriptions rival his photographs in revealing the subject. I could not resist including them in this book adjacent to the source's tunes.

Of all the sources that contributed tunes to the WPA's collecting efforts in Mississippi, only one fiddler, John Alexander Brown, had his music collected in both years. All of his collected tunes are included here.

In addition to the fiddlers whose repertoires were documented in the WPA projects, there is a fiddler who was not included but whose music was an integral part of Mississippi fiddling in that era. Alvis Massengale was a fiddler documented in several eras. In 1930 he recorded four tunes on two 78rpm records with his band, the Newton County Hillbillies. He was interviewed in 1939 as part of the research preceding Halpert's trip and a list of his repertoire was collected. Researcher Gus Meade rediscovered him in the 1970s and made tape recordings. In preparation to have him appear

in the 1974 Festival of American Folklife in Washington, D.C., Howard Marshall also made field recordings. Lists of his repertoire, a photo, and four transcriptions of his tunes are in Appendix B.

As a group, African American fiddlers of the era unfortunately were underrepresented in the 1936 and 1939 projects. Instructions given to the field workers for collecting from African American and Caucasian sources were quite different and are included as illustrations in the essay. Most pertinently, there was no direction to collect fiddle tunes from African American sources. And yet, there seem to have been eight 1936 African American sources for fiddle tunes: Allen Alsop, Jim Gooch, E. Thomas, Annie Lee, Henry McClatching, Charlie Addison, Sam Freeman, and Josephine Compton. Of these, the tunes from Allen Alsop are the most distinctive. In 1939 Herbert Halpert did not record any fiddle music from African American sources, although he did record many performances by African Americans of other styles of music. It is particularly frustrating that he did not record Allen Alsop.

Fiddle tunes are the focus of this book, but in the Mississippi state archive there were more than three thousand songs collected in notation in 1936, and Halpert recorded more songs than fiddle tunes in 1939. Songs from minstrel shows and popular sheet music were numerous in the 1936 collection, as were ballads, cowboy, gospel, and children's play songs. Some songs seem to have been learned from radio or 78rpm recordings, such as Gene Autry's 1932 hit "That Silver Haired Daddy of Mine." Many were collected multiple times from multiple sources, such as the twenty-two versions of "Tell Mother I'll Be There" and the nine versions of the Georgian folk song "Dark Eyes," recorded by Django Reinhardt in 1940. I have included a small number of songs in this book to point the way to the larger body of songs that remain unpublished. I have left the work of reintroducing the remaining songs for some one else to pursue.

One fascinating aspect of rediscovering the tunes was finding that their melodies often are unrelated to what someone conversant with old-time fiddle music would expect to hear associated with the tune's title. Fiddle tunes are made from common building blocks, a musical DNA consisting of a body of phrases, grammar, floating verses, and titles. In this collection a contemporary fiddler will recognize parts of some of the tunes. However, it is as though some mysterious force of geography had dissolved the structure of the tunes that migrated to Mississippi, and reconstituted them from that primordial soup. The names of the fiddle tunes in this book are familiar: "Billy in the Lowground," "Sugar in the Gourd," "Forked Deer," "Soldier's Joy," and others, but the melodies are often unexpected.

In my mind, this propensity for reshaping tunes is the defining trait of Mississippi old-time fiddling. For example, compare three "Fisher's Hornpipes" in this book. The first, from Mr. N. Odom, is fairly true to the standard versions of the tune, two standard melodies of the eight measures and repeat pattern. Second, examine the Alvis Massengale version for its more individual structure of a seven-measure first phrase followed by a nine-measure second phrase. Finally, there is Stephen B. Tucker's rather radical and, I think, inspired reconstruction of the tune in eleven and one-half measures with a succeeding part of almost six measures.

The fiddler Charles Smith perhaps best described one way this reshaping occurred in Norman Mellin's interview with him for *Mississippi Folklife* magazine in 1999: "We had an old record player, but I never did learn much fiddle music from it. Most of what I picked up was by hearing someone else play. That's probably the reason that most of what I play I don't play right. I'd hear it and have to wait until I got home to play it. When I couldn't remember it all, I'd have to fill in the gaps."

In other Southern states, when tunes are "crooked"—that is, with parts not constructed in units of four or eight measures—the bit that makes the tune "crooked" is usually a note held too long or not long enough, or an extra repeated phrase. In Mississippi the "crooked" tunes tend to be complete musical thoughts expressed in an unusual number of measures. They do not violate the rule so much as ignore it.

Considering the fieldwork done in 1936 and 1939, along with commercial 78rpm recordings of the 1920s and 1930s in Mississippi, a much fuller picture of fiddling in Mississippi emerges. Traditional, certainly, but greatly reshaped to suit the very local individual tastes and desires. A good friend has suggested in explanation that "There must be something in the water."

—Harry Bolick, May 2014

HOW THE BOOK IS ORGANIZED

This book is in two main sections. The first section, "Collecting folk music in 1936 and 1939," puts these collecting projects into a historical context and explains how they were conceived and carried out.

The second section, "The Music," opens with a short essay explaining our approach with the transcriptions and contains 329 tunes. They are organized into a group of 180 collected in 1936; a second group of 145 collected in 1939; and four tunes in Appendix B. The 1939 section has a subsection at the end for banjo tunes, which is preceded by a short essay explaining banjo tablature. I have listed all known repertoire of a source along with photos and biographical information where available. Most of this information comes from the 1939 field notes. Tune-specific information follows the tune's title above the music notation.

Appendix A contains two maps. The first shows the stops on Halpert's 1939 recording trip; the second shows the geographic distribution in Mississippi of field collecting in 1936, 1939, 1970s, and commercial recording from 78rpm era with a list showing the distribution of the individual musicians.

Appendix B contains four tunes, collected in the 1970s, and biographical information of fiddler Alvis Massengale.

Appendix C contains an account of a 1936 fiddle contest in Hazlehurst.

Appendix D contains a listing of tunes in alternate tunings.

Roadside stop. Photo by Abbott Ferriss, 1939, courtesy Mississippi Department of Archives and History.

Roadside stop. Photo by Abbott Ferriss, 1939, courtesy Mississippi Department of Archives and History.

MISSISSIPPI
FIDDLE TUNES
AND SONGS FROM THE 1930s

Recording session at the Walker house; note the cable on the floor. Photo by Abbott Ferriss, 1939, courtesy Mississippi Department of Archives and History.

PART 1

Collecting Folk Music in 1936 and 1939

Folksongs of Mississippi and Their Background

A. P. Hudson's book *Folksongs of Mississippi and Their Background,* published in 1936, remains the major collection of folk songs from the state to this day. It also served as a catalyst to the events that added to the documentation of fiddling in Mississippi. The late 1920s and early 1930s had seen the commercial record industry's efforts in Mississippi accumulate about 185 fiddle recordings from the state. Field collecting in the summers of 1936 and 1939, building on Hudson's efforts and contacts, documented another 331 fiddle tunes.

Arnold Palmer Hudson (1892–1978) was a Mississippi native, born in Palmer's Hall in Attala County, Mississippi. As a freshman at the University of Mississippi in 1908, Hudson was inspired by his English teacher Ebner C. Perrow's interest in collecting folk songs. Perrow at that time was preparing a number of songs for publication in the *Journal of American Folklore.* However, moving from inspiration to action took fifteen years. Hudson began teaching in the English department of the University of Mississippi in 1920. Three years later, during his English

class teaching English and Scottish ballads, one of his students, Wessen M. Crocker, recited several songs. Crocker stated that his cousin, Mrs. G. V. Easley, knew many more. In 1925 Hudson and Crocker visited Mrs. Easley at her farm and collected twenty-five ballad texts. Shortly thereafter two of his students, T. A. Bickerstaff and Lois Womble, collected more texts.

His interest in folk song growing, Hudson gave a lecture, "A Patch of Mississippi Balladry," during the 1926 summer session at the University of Mississippi, which generated interest and donations of ballads collected by students. Newspaper coverage of the lecture generated "a number of communications from widely scattered sections of the state,"[1] including ballad texts.

In the fall, Hudson taught a seminar course in the folklore of Mississippi where his eight students collected several hundred ballads. The following year nine students added about 500 more songs. In the spring of 1927, Hudson founded the Mississippi Folk-Lore Society, which never grew beyond twenty-five members and published only one collection, *Specimens of Mississippi Folklore,* later largely absorbed into *Mississippi Folk Songs and Their Background.*

Ballad singers: Mrs. Bickerstaff, Mrs. Lillian Bickerstaff Pennington, Miss Hellums, Mrs. Audrey Hellums, and Miss Eri Douglas, state director, FWP. Tishomingo, May 11, 1939. Photo by Abbott Ferriss, courtesy Mississippi Department of Archives and History.

Hudson's approach to documenting folk song was editorial. Instead of working from primary written sources, as had many previous scholars, he utilized his students to do the bulk of the actual collecting. The focus was primarily on survivals of English balladry among white people in Mississippi.

In his book, Hudson utilizes early census reports to describe the settlers and therefore their music's cultural origins. He points to patterns of migration to suggest that the bulk of settlers in early Mississippi were of English cultural background, with a small percentage of Scots and even fewer Irish. He traces them as part of the ongoing westward migration starting with the offspring of residents of the well-settled states of Virginia, North and South Carolina, Georgia, and Alabama. He notes the large numbers of slaves but does not factor them into his calculations. He ignores their music as well.

Publishing was certainly on Hudson's mind in 1927. One hundred pages of "Ballads and Songs from Mississippi" appeared in the *Journal of American Folk-Lore* (Vol. XXXIX, no. 152, 1927), which also allocated thirteen pages to Harvard's preeminent folklore scholar, Professor George Lyman Kittredge, discussing two of the songs. The idea of a larger work was forming in Hudson's mind, and he approached Professor Kittredge about it, writing him: "If Harvard University Press brings out the volume, I am afraid you will have to take my judgment about some little matters of inclusion and exclusion, for in these ballad books (of which Harvard University Press makes something of a specialty) the Syndics rather lean on me."[2]

Hudson's collecting work in Mississippi folklore ended in 1930 when he received his PhD from the University of North Carolina and moved there to teach as associate professor of English.

Ballad singers: Mrs. Mae Wesson, Ila Long, Theodosia Bonnet Long, Birmah Hill Grissom. May 8 or 9, 1939. Photo by Abbott Ferriss, 1939, courtesy Mississippi Department of Archives and History.

Due to the financial constraints of the Depression, publication of *Folk Songs of Mississippi and Their Background* was delayed until 1936, when the University of North Carolina Press published it. The book in its published form contains 157 songs and ballads, many with multiple versions listed, but in text only, without musical notation. Its 321 pages also contain chapters on Mississippi history, ballad communities, and singers. Much attention is paid to aligning the ballads with versions from Francis Child's epic work of scholarship, *The English and Scottish Ballads*.

Hudson was well aware of the limitations in publishing a book of folk song without musical notation. In a 1937 letter of advice to a Florida English teacher on how to go about collecting folk song, he said: "If it is at all possible, musical notation of the song or ballad should be secured. Interest in the musical side of folk song is decidedly on the increase."[3] His 1937 publication (with

George Herzog, "one of the first scholars to be called an ethnomusicologist"[4]), *Folk Tunes from Mississippi,* rather modestly attempted to diminish that failing with its publication of forty-five melodies:

> The following folk song tunes were collected from white people in Mississippi between the years of 1923 and 1930. . . . The notations were made by sundry obliging friends and acquaintances, some of whom were trained musicians but most of whom knew only the elements of musical notation. For the merits or shortcomings of the notations I am not qualified to offer either praise or apology. I am uncritically grateful to each and every one of my helpers.[5]

A young Alan Lomax, then twenty-three years old, wrote a very critical review of Hudson's *Folk-songs of Mississippi and Their Backgrounds* at the end of 1938, attacking Hudson for his defense of southern class structure where the "privileges of a superior order were more or less conceded." He further argued that the songs were presented out of social context with no mention of the informant's poverty or that folk songs were still being made up. Lomax saw folk music is a living tradition, whereas Hudson's framing of folk as static and ancient reeked of Francis Child's outdated idealization of the "folk." A few months after that review, in the summer of 1939, Alan and John Lomax stopped in North Carolina to see A. P. Hudson. They were conducting a courtesy call to inform him that they would be collecting in his "turf" and to ask for his advice and support as they were planning some recording in his area.

That same year, Charles Seeger of the FMP in Washington reviewed the Mississippi music manuscripts collected in 1936, work that was based on songs and contacts from Hudson's *Folksongs of Mississippi and Their Backgrounds.* Excited by the richness of that collection, Seeger proposed the summer expedition that recorded Mississippi fiddlers.

Hudson continued to teach folklore and English romantic literature at the University of North Carolina until his retirement. In 1952 he edited (with H. M. Belden) two volumes of the *Frank C. Brown Collection of North Carolina Folklore.* He edited *North Carolina Folklore,* the journal of the North Carolina Folklore Society, from 1954 to 1963.

Hudson had the only folk recordings available on campus on a small shelf in his office, which he used to illustrate his course. Admittedly there were few recordings available in the early fifties, but in his class Hudson made no distinction between the recordings of the Kingston Trio, John Jacob Niles, and opera singers performing "folk" as art song or Lomax field recordings of actual ballad singers. A University of North Carolina graduate student in 1953 described attending A. P. Hudson's course "The English Ballad": "When he played these pieces in class, Hudson listened as raptly to the over-artful renditions of Dyer-Bennet as to the classic traditional performances of Horton Barker."[6] That grad student, Daniel W.

Patterson, took over the ballad course on Hudson's retirement in 1968 and began building on Hudson's small shelf of records. Eventually the library at the University of North Carolina became the home of the John Edwards Memorial Collection, one of the premier sources of documentation and recordings for early country music in America. Hudson's papers and recordings were one of the first folk collection donations to the university.

Roosevelt and the Depression

Everybody in Washington from the Roosevelts on down was interested in folk music . . . They were the first prominent Americans to ever spend any money on it.
—Alan Lomax[7]

These were tumultuous times. The stock market finally bottomed out on July 8, 1932, after the 1929 crash. Bank closings started in February 1933 in Louisiana and spread to other states. There was increasing panic heading toward the inauguration. Farmers were rioting. All twelve Federal Reserve banks closed. Banks in forty-three states had closed; there was only limited business or restricted banking. President Herbert Hoover did nothing. Eight days after his inauguration, Franklin Delano Roosevelt gave the first of his "fireside" speeches, claiming that there is "Nothing to fear but fear itself" and promising action. The next day, Monday, the banks reopened. America was ready for dramatic changes.

Roosevelt turned to Harry Hopkins, with whom he had worked when governor of New York, for ideas and action to put people back to work. Together they put into place a series of short-term programs to create work, with an alphabet soup of acronyms: NRA, FERA, RS, and CWA. Funding varied wildly from year to year as the administration shifted programs and priorities to navigate the economy and the anti–New Deal opposition.

The Federal Emergency Relief Administration (FERA) was a temporary first attempt to relive the crisis by administering direct relief. But, as Harry

Afro-American church gathering. Photo by Abbott Ferriss, 1939, courtesy Mississippi Department of Archives and History.

Hopkins saw it, there were two major flaws. First, $6.50 per week was not enough money to live on. Second, applying for relief required a humiliating "means test" of providing proof that one was indeed destitute. Hopkins firmly believed, based on his previous relief administration experiences in New York, that most people would rather work than take handouts. Charity abused their dignity, but there is no shame in work. Moreover, workers could retain or develop new skills and the nation could benefit from the results of the work.

When the FERA expired unemployment remained high, and along with it the need for government assistance. By executive order Roosevelt then created Works Progress Administration, again headed by Harry Hopkins, who directed that it "shall be responsible to the president for the honest, efficient, speedy and coordinated execution of the work relief program as a whole, and for the execution of that program in such manner as to move from the relief rolls to work on such projects or in private employment the maximum number of persons in the shortest time possible."[8]

In the midst of a mighty effort to get America back to work, Roosevelt, in stark contrast with Hoover, found it useful to focus attention on poor whites and minorities that were suffering the most from the Depression. Folk music became one more tool, celebrating the strength and resiliency of the "Forgotten Man" and emphasizing cultural unity and collective action.

Folk music was encouraged in programs throughout the New Deal, but also invited directly into the White House for concerts nine times during the Roosevelts' time in residence. Alan Lomax was invited by Eleanor to sing privately for Franklin Roosevelt in their home. The high point for New Deal folklorists was the state visit in May 1939 by the King and Queen of England. Charles Seeger was involved in programming of a performance arranged by Eleanor Roosevelt. Marion Anderson, Kate Smith, and Lawrence

Dinner on the ground, New Hope Baptist Church, May 21, 1939. Photo by Abbott Ferriss, 1939, courtesy Mississippi Department of Archives and History.

Tibbett performed classical and light pop. Alan Lomax sang cowboy songs and the Coon Creek Girls string band from Kentucky performed with the Soco Gap Square Dance Team.

The WPA Federal Arts Projects

Hell, they've got to eat, just like other people.
—Harry Hopkins, 1934[9]

Early in 1935, the Emergency Relief Appropriation Act passed with $4.8 billion in funding. From this, the WPA was created in May 1936, with Harry Hopkins as its head. In August the Federal Number One project was created as the umbrella organization for the four federal arts programs: the Federal Music Project (FMP), the Federal Arts Project (FAP), the Federal Theater Project (FTP), and the Federal Writers Project (FWP). Hopkins

had deep experience in "relief" organizations and had seen firsthand the damage to the human spirit and dignity caused by charity. He saw to it that the overriding imperative of the WPA was to put people to work; work to resuscitate, to rebuild the human capital of Depression-era America. People need to work, even artists.

A tiny part of the total WPA efforts, in 1936 the arts programs of Federal One spent about $40 million and employed 40,000 (vs. over three million in WPA overall) but generated most of the bad press. They were easy targets for the anti–New Dealers. People were literally starving; who needed art or theater, music or writing?

Of the four federal arts projects, the writers and music projects were the most involved with folk music, particularly in Mississippi.

Each of the arts projects was shaped by the personalities of the directors. Before coming to head the Federal Writers Project, Henry Alsberg had a wide variety of experience to draw from; lawyer, foreign correspondent, assistant to the ambassador to Turkey, editor, playwright, Jewish relief worker in Russia. Lacking in administrative skills, he somehow managed to exude authority.

One of his first problems was finding directors for the state projects in all fifty states. Some states just did not have writers, much less writers he could work with. Worse yet, in the beginning there was no idea of what they should be writing. In larger cities where there were numbers of writers, many had leftist or communist leanings. The inter-office political arguments were ferocious. Many had drinking problems. People were on the payroll, but what were they supposed to be writing? Alsberg was politically savvy enough to realize that he needed to have results to show for the expenditures, and it needed to be for the "public good." Simply funding creative writing would invite attack. The answer came in the form of travel guides for each state. Other kinds of projects also were carried out, such as local histories, ex-slave interviews, and folktale compilations. Hundreds of books and pamphlets were eventually produced. But many months went by before the Music Project had anything to show for it efforts, thus giving its critics ammunition.

From the very start of the FWP, in response to the Alsberg-distributed manual of instructions, folklore was being collected. As it began to pile up in Washington, Alsberg realized he needed someone knowledgeable to sort it out, and in 1936 he turned to John Lomax as the National Advisor of Folklore and Folkways. For a year Lomax gathered Negro lore, recorded a large number of folk songs, and wrote instructions for the interviewers of ex-slaves. The interviews were later compiled and edited by B. A. Botkin into *Lay My Burden Down: A Folk History of Slavery* (1945).

The 1930s were particularly grim for professional musicians. Preceding the Depression, the new technologies of movie soundtracks, radio, and records conspired to eliminate most of the jobs that had been filled by classically trained musicians. Theatres, restaurants, hotels, pubs, and funerals all quickly embraced inexpensive canned

music. Worse yet, popular tastes were changing quickly. Interest in and opportunities for classical music were declining. The spotlight was moving to jazz and swing. The American Federation of Musicians estimated that in 1933, 12,000 out of 15,000 union members in New York and two-thirds of the musicians in the country were out of work. Due to the dire need, the FMP was the first of the arts projects begun.

The FMP started slowly, with employment in November 1935 of less than a thousand. But at its peak in 1936 there were 15,842 workers, musicians, educators, and score copyists on the payroll. This made the FMP the largest of the arts programs, and by that standard the most successful. As with the entire WPA, putting the unemployed back to work was complicated by the need to not compete with those who still had jobs. To avoid competing with private teachers, the 6,000 FMP music teachers could only teach those who could not pay. There was no shortage of pupils: fourteen million were taught composition, theory, history, appreciation, and conducting for choral or instrumental groups. There was also group instruction in folk dancing and folk music for adults and children.

Nikolai Sokoloff, the national director of the FMP, had been a child prodigy, a conductor of San Francisco Philharmonic, and the director of the Cleveland Orchestra. Schooled in European traditions and composers, Sokoloff was unwavering in his belief that spreading "good music" would "elevate" American culture. Music that did not measure up to his exacting standards was not worthy of his support. He stated: "We know that we could not suddenly take away the accustomed music diet of a community so we studied and shared with our groups the least obnoxious of their favorites. We sang their songs and listened to their prodigies. But all the time we were working up to a different type of song to supplant the spurious 'popular' music."[10] Sokoloff's stated goals for the FMP were to provide employment for musicians on relief, to establish high standards, to classify musicians, to stimulate community interest, to educate the public, and (most importantly in terms of the programs' survival) to show government fighting the Depression.

In accepting the job, Sokoloff knew that he and the project would be fighting to survive and would be attentively monitored by WPA critics for any misstep, radicalism, or anti-American influence. He needed allies. He created advisory councils enlisting support from some of the country's most prestigious musicians of the time, the American Federation of Musicians Union (AFM) and even the president of the four-thousand-member National Federation of Music Clubs. The AFM was not an easy association to make as the bulk of its membership performed popular and dance music. Few of its 105,000 members in 1936 were classical musicians. The FMP compromised with the AFM on hiring practices and pay, and the AFM provided political cover for the FMP. The AFM had and enforced a policy against political radicalism by members. Of all of the federal arts projects, the FMP had the least amount of controversy.

Sokoloff's bias for classical music over all other forms had a practical disadvantage. As Joseph Webber, president of the AFM, argued, previous to the Depression orchestras and classical performances only sustained about a thousand professional musicians in the whole country, and the need for employment and the WPA's goals for assistance far exceeded that minority. He could see no reason that Sokoloff's hopes for a renaissance of classical music was likely or would be of use in solving the unemployment problem. But in the face of resistance and opposition, Sokoloff persisted in his pursuit of (in the words of New York City FMP director Lee Pattison) "a permanent audience for the support of really good music in this country."[11] Initially the FMP was well regarded, as it provided employment and quality low-cost music to local communities. But the near-exclusion of vernacular music from the FMP had its critics. When the New Deal political coalition began to weaken in 1936, conservative rural and anti–New Deal legislators forced cutbacks and investigations. There were charges of communist supervision.

Under Sokoloff, FMP was able to do little with folk music collecting or performance. The Federal Writers Project was more open to collecting folklore. However, under pressure, the FMP did support some folk festivals. Harry Hopkins requested that the FMP promote a national folk festival; though the FMP did not follow through on his directive, a few local festivals such as the American Folk Song Festival near Ashland, Kentucky, received some assistance from FMP. In early 1936 Jean Thomas in the Kentucky unit organized a folk performing unit, the Kentucky Mountain Minstrels, and collected "some two hundred folk songs and fiddle tunes."[12] Sokoloff would not let the performing group be promoted, and it was disbanded in July. Folk projects under the FMP tended to be of short duration and limited in resources. The exception was in New Mexico. Operating from 1936–41, it collected, transcribed, and disseminated folk music, songs, and dances of the old Spanish West to teachers throughout the state and printed five publications.

And then there was the summer of 1936 in Mississippi.

The 1936 Federal Music Project in Mississippi

For a few months in the summer of 1936, over one hundred music teachers became folk music collectors, amassing well over 3,500 versions of songs and fiddle tunes. Unlike other collections made by trained folklorists working alone, the collection they brought back would contain a bit of everything: parlor music from the 1890s, songs from then-recent 78rpm records, gospel songs, a Russian folk song, fiddle tunes, minstrel-show songs, cowboy songs, and children's songs. Their instructions were to collect songs of certain types, although no mention was made of documenting anything about the informant and his thoughts about the music. This was progress away from Kittredge's vision of "The text is the thing." In 1936 we have interviewers in the field gathering both text and music—and yet, for some of that music we do not even know the source's name. The work of these interviewers now resides in the Mississippi Department of Archives and History. Maps showing the geographic distribution of their work appear in Appendix A.

When the FMP project in Mississippi first got under way in early 1936, however, its primary mission was to employ musicians in teaching and performing, not in collecting songs and tunes. Jerome Sage, the Mississippi state director for the Federal Music Project, had her hands full. She was new to the job, and in fact the whole organization was new and the rules were changing rapidly, as funding and direction were modified by national and state politics. It was a large undertaking, consisting of about 130 music teachers, a ten-person orchestra in Jackson, a five-person entertaining unit in Meridian, a four-person Negro mixed quartet in Jackson, and six administrative positions. To help her manage the enterprise spread out over forty counties with poor transportation and communications, she had two district directors and three secretaries. Many letters were handwritten. Bulletins and a few important letters were typed. What should have been the small effort of getting blank music books was difficult and snared in bureaucracy. Simple communications failures could be very time consuming, as noted by Miss Jerome Sage in her directive to state workers in her April 23, 1936 bulletin:

It has come to my attention that workers on the Federal Music Project are not adhering to systematic schedules. . . . In visiting some of the projects in the state it has happened in several instances that I would find no one on the project at the time it was scheduled in the district office to be in progress. You can readily see that if the State or the District Supervisor drives from twenty-five to fifty miles to observe classes in instruction, it is rather disconcerting to find that these classes meet the next day instead of the day scheduled.[13]

With only nineteen performers on the payroll in Mississippi, the main employment opportunity became teaching music classes. Author Milton Meltzer elaborates: "In Mississippi alone, the project reached 70,000 people across 40 counties, evoking such an intense response to music that the sale of secondhand pianos shot up."[14] Federal instructions on teaching mandated that the FMP not compete with private music instructors; thus the FMP could only offer lessons to those unable to pay for lessons. All music programs were required to have local sponsors, such as the American Legion, YMCA, YWCA, etc. The local sponsors would often provide space and political cover as proof of community support.

From the very beginning of the FMP in Mississippi in early 1936, there was some small thought given to collect folk music. Jerome Sage wrote in her report:

Many of the "River" songs that are peculiar to the state are being written down for the first time and we plan to have a booklet of these tunes which will be placed in the Department of Archives and History. The custom prevails among the Negroes in the Delta section of the state of assembling on the levee of the Mississippi River to sing to "Ole Man River" when he threatens to go on a rampage in the spring of the year. These songs have a peculiar plaintiveness and spring partly from superstition and partly from the Negro's implicit faith that "God will roll all of the troubles away". So far as is known these songs have never been written down.[15]

However, little was done to collect folk music until, unexpectedly, the Mississippi FMP dramatically changed course. In the summer of 1936 the State Board of Health ordered suspension of all classes with children under sixteen due to a few cases of poliomyelitis. Suddenly, teachers on the FMP payroll had no one to teach. By necessity the music project adapted, turning its idle hands to folk music collecting. Their first step was to inventory previous work done such as that available at the University of Mississippi Library. There they found Hudson's manuscripts and several theses by his graduate students, almost entirely consisting of song texts without music notation. An early but undated and unsigned report, "Research Work of the Federal Music Project," begins:

NEGRO SONGS

We do not need any spirituals, or any religious songs sung by quartets or trained groups. We are looking for:

(1) Old work and play "reels." The kind of game songs that children call "ring plays."

(2) The songs that the Negroes sing at work. One type we are especially anxious to get are those sung by groups of men working together. Examples: at cotton chopping, laying track on the railroad, or any other gang work.

(3) "Bad man" songs, "lonesome" songs, "hollers" that field hands use, or field calls of one to another.

(4) Any original or "jumped-up" songs. It should be emphasized that the songs do not have to be very long or serious - "little foolish songs," including lullabies, would be just fine.

(5) Tunes played on "quills," and quill songs.

(6) Chants. The following example was used by an old Negro "rouster" in a levee camp to wake up the "hands" each morning:

> "He didn' call one,
> He didn' call two,
> Cap'n called de boss
> An de whole damn crew."

(7) Vendor's Calls: fruit and vegetables; old clothes; shrimp, oysters, fish, etc.

WHITE

The kind of songs we are interested in locating are "sure 'nough old timey" songs; kind not heard over radio or on phonograph records, not learned from a book or notes; ones that are generally heard from older members of family-e.g. a grandfather, an uncle. We are not looking for 'good' singing, just for the old songs, or even pieces of them.

We want:

(1) Old love songs like "Barbara Allen," or "The Brown Girl," or "The House Carpenter."

(2) Songs, even newer ones, made up about something that really happened somewhere; an accident, a murder, or any local songs made up about some person or event.

(3) Old Play party songs: the kind that were sung in the old days by young folks at parties - like dances, only without instrumental music.

(4) Singing games that children play and sing - not those taught by teachers in school.

(5) Fiddle tunes: especially from players who tune the fiddle in different ways for different songs; also any of the "little old foolish songs" that are sometimes sung to, or with, fiddle tunes. We are not much interested in string bands.

(6) Old banjo tunes: songs that are sung and played on the old five-string banjo.

(7) Square dance calls: especially the kind that are called in rhyme like:

> "Horses to their traces,
> Ladies to their places."

(8) Vendor's Calls: fruit and vegetables; old clothes; shrimp, oysters, fish, etc.

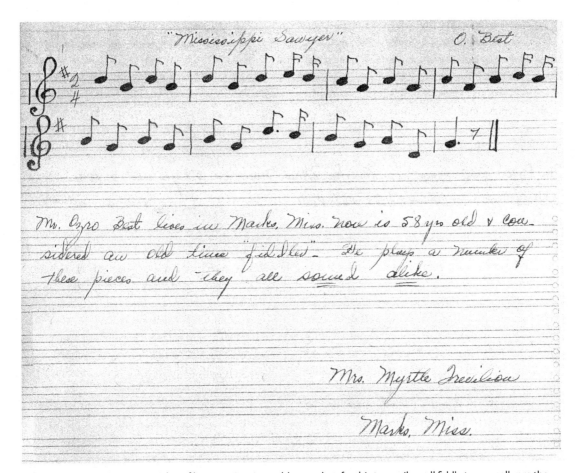

Judging by the rudimentary quality of her notation, it would seem that, for this transcriber, all fiddle tunes really are the same. Collected summer of 1936. Courtesy Mississippi Department of Archives and History.

Some months ago it became increasingly apparent that although extensive work had been done in collecting the texts of folk-songs and ballads, very little, comparatively, had been accomplished in recording the tunes and melodies. This is true, not only of Mississippi, but of other sections where any effort has been made to preserve the folk-music; the idea that "the text is the thing" had perhaps made collectors overlook the importance of saving the melody at the same time.[16]

Lists of folk songs previously found in Mississippi were created based on these books and theses. The lists were used by the field workers to prompt the interviewee and as a checklist of song melodies to be located.

In addition to the continuing search for ballads, there was an interest and directives to look for other kinds of folk music. There were two lists, one for white music to be collected and another for Negro music. In the white list were local event songs, play party songs, children's singing games, banjo tunes, square dance calls, and vendors' calls. And fiddle tunes, as specified in a FMP instructional handout sheet: "especially from players who tune the fiddle in different ways for different songs; also any of the 'little old foolish songs' that are sometimes sung to, or with fiddle tunes. We are not much interested in string bands."[17] The Negro list directed the search for "ring plays," work songs, "bad men" ballads, field hollers, "jumped-up" songs, lullabies, chants such as levee wake-up calls, and vendors' calls. The directive sheet begins, "we do not need spirituals, or any religious songs sung by quartets or trained groups." A later letter elucidates: "Our greatest concentration, however, will be on Negro music, and on saving all we can of the priceless form of folk-music. The attention of every worker has been called to the value of the Negro spiritual as distinguished from Negro religious songs which have been learned for the white man, and to the importance of retaining as far as possible the dialect and the notation."[18] There are a curious number of pop songs about Indians in the collection such as "Little Mohea," "Red Wing," and "Indian Naponee." There was a directive that it was of great interest to the project to document songs from the Indians of the state. However, no actual Indian songs were collected.

These music teachers turned field workers were novices and had not previously collected folk music, taken dictation of folk melodies, or studied folk music. Jerome Sage's letters and bulletins to them that summer encourage and prod the field workers to refer to the constantly updated lists of songs collected to avoid duplication and to search for music of real interest. Jerome Sage commented on the collecting process in early 1936: "Though not very many Old Fiddler's tunes have been submitted as yet, a few more are beginning to come in; with various Old Fiddler's contests to be held during this month, it is hoped that some generally, hitherto unpublished old tunes will be secured."[19] Appendix C contains a field worker's account of the Hazlehurst fiddle contest.

A. P. Hudson became aware of the fieldwork and approached the Mississippi office of the Federal Music Project in an attempt to improve his book by joining forces. In a letter to Nikolai Sokoloff, Jerome Sage wrote:

Dr. Palmer Hudson of the University of North Carolina, on learning that we had such a project in Mississippi, wrote urging that we collaborate with him in his new book which was at that time on the press, and the publication of which he was willing to hold up for our answer. I wrote him that all the material which we had collected had been collected

on Federal funds and for that reason it would not be possible for us to have any part in his book.[20]

By December 1936 the polio crisis had subsided, teaching was resumed, and the folk song collecting project was halted. Without Nikolai Sokoloff's support and funding it could not continue. Jerome Sage conveyed the news in a letter to a subordinate:

The research project is definitely canceled but I shall carry you as a supervisor on the teaching project as long as that project is in operation. Please do not feel that you have to hurry or that it is necessary to have anything ready to submit to Washington by January 1st. You are to work as leisurely as you care to work in order that you may do the job satisfactorily to yourself. Miss MacDonald is to come back to Oxford. I am also leaving Miss Wallace on the project and she is to continue her work of revising and editing under your directions.[21]

With the collecting over, and no publication in the works, the actual documents remained. But what to do with them? Jerome Sage wrote:

I have realized all along that the manuscripts were the possession of the Federal Government and we were in the process of indexing and filing them very carefully when your letter canceling the project was received. While the material is not in as good condition as I should like to have it, it is all carefully filed and is available at any time.... It is my opinion that we have some very valuable material and I hope that at some time we may be allowed to complete the monograph, which we had planned. My interest in the matter has really grown greatly since attending the meetings in Chicago, particularly the section on musicology.[22]

Sage and Eri Douglas, state director of the FWP, were reluctant to give up on the project, but there was little they could do to move it to publication. However, in 1939 a new field-recording project conceived in Washington raised their hopes of moving to publication with an even larger, more complete book on Mississippi folk song.

A New Deal for Folk Music

Record EVERYthing, Don't omit, don't concentrate on any single style. We know so little! Record everything!
—Charles Seeger[23]

Folklore efforts took a new direction during Roosevelt's administration. Working within government instead of universities, a new set of folklorists and administrators took an interest in collecting. Moreover, thoughts about what should be collected were changing, as author Bill Malone put it: "Significantly, they were no longer preserving the remnants of a dying or primitive culture, they were instead documenting cultures in transition."[24] Change was in the air. Capitalism had dramatically failed. Socialist and Communist political parties were attracting sizable followings. Workers were banding together in unions. Collective action was on the rise.

What had begun with individuals, starting with Francis Child and his groundbreaking ten-volume *The English and Scottish Ballads*, down through A. P. Hudson, continued within the New Deal through the efforts of a group of dedicated individuals working in concert, primarily John and Alan Lomax, Charles and Ruth Crawford Seeger, and B. A. Botkin. In a speech remembering Botkin, Alan Jabbour, a past head of the Archive of American Folk Song at the Library of Congress, describes this group as a folk music "directorate" that was able to utilize the WPA to further folk music collection, publication, and preservation. Their interests insured that their paths continually crossed in the 1930s.

Collecting and analyzing ballad texts was beginning to give way to scientific methods of survey and sampling. In the Mississippi Delta from 1941 through 1942, Fisk University and Alan Lomax conducted a comparative ethnological survey that set out to document adaptation and evolution within multiple forms of folk music in a single region, the Mississippi Delta. At the time, it was a new idea to look for folk song in the Delta. Jerome Sage, the head of the state's music project, cautioned Alan Lomax, "there are no folk songs and folklore typical of the Miss. Delta, since the region has been opened up and settled comparatively recently."[25] Lomax responded in disagreement: "It is a folklorists' illusion that folklore communities are pure, that the pure old tradition is the one most worth studying."[26]

In 1921 Ruth Crawford made her way to the American Conservatory of Music in Chicago to attain a music-teaching certificate. Teaching music was one of the few ways a female musician in the 1920s could respectably earn a living. Once at the conservatory, her one-year course of study expanded along with her interest in composing. It was here that Ruth Crawford was introduced to Carl Sandburg and for a short while was the piano teacher for his daughters. She grew close to the family, as a "sort of added informal unadopted daughter."[27] Sandburg turned to Crawford to create piano settings for four of the songs for the most successful folk music anthology of the 1920s, his *American Songbag* (1927). She continued to study in Chicago until 1929 when, at the urging of her friend and composer Henry Cowell, she began her study of advanced composition and dissonant harmony in New York with Charles Seeger. Her early Chicago compositions received critical acclaim, comparing her music most favorably to contemporary male composers. Her later work, from the early 1930s, established her reputation as a major American modern dissonant composer and the first major female one.

Charles Seeger studied music composition at Harvard in 1904 and read Chaucer under Professor Kittredge, who had assisted and succeeded Professor Francis Child. From 1921–33 Seeger taught at what later became the Julliard School of Music in New York, and lectured from 1933–35 at the New School of Social Research. There, as author Nolan Porterfield described, "he introduced the first courses of ethnomusicology, the study of music within its social and historical context."[28] Far more than composing, his main interests ran to advanced modern music theories, teaching, and politics. His relationship with Ruth Crawford began as her teacher in 1929, but by 1932 they had joined their considerable talents in marriage.

As American composers interested in developing a distinctive national style of music, the Seegers were drawn to the Composers Collective. Originally named the Pierre DeGeyter Club after the composer of the "Internationale," the Composers Collective was founded in 1931 in New York as a political organization under the direction of the Workers Music League of the American Communist Party. Seeger, along with other members Marc Blitzstein, Elie Siegmeister, and Henry Cowell, struggled to create a new music for the masses with the goal that, in the words of author Kenneth J. Bindas, "Proletarian" music had to be "politically correct, musically progressive, and provide a marching anthem for the people."[29]

However, the masses were not much interested in singing difficult, dissonant music. In 1935 the group began to accept vernacular music as valid, socially and politically. Alan Lomax brought Aunt Molly Jackson, an Appalachian protest folk singer, to a meeting. She and the composers found each other mutually incomprehensible. But as Jackson was leaving, Seeger told her, "You're on the right track and we're on the wrong track" in finding "the people's idiom."[30]

In New York, Charles and Ruth discovered George Pullen Jackson's book *White Spirituals in the Southern Uplands*, and particularly responded to the beauty of "Wondrous Love" and "Wayfaring Stranger." They met and became friendly with the painter Thomas Hart Benton and his wife, Rita. With the Bentons in their loft on 8th Street, the Seegers first played and sang folk songs. Charles's son from his first marriage, Pete Seeger, first heard "John Henry" played in the Bentons' loft. At the dedication of Benton's "America Today" murals at the New School in January 1931, Charles Seeger played "folk" guitar with Benton's "hillbilly" band. The program included many of the artist's favorites such as "Cindy," "Ida Red," and "My Horses Ain't Hungry," which were all new to Seeger.

After studying at Harvard and publishing *Cowboy Songs* in 1910, John Lomax had returned to Texas, where he taught, started the Texas Folklore Society, and raised a family. But in 1932, at sixty-four years of age, he was at a low point in his life. His beloved wife Bess had died. He found himself depressed, ill, unemployed, with two children Alan and Bess still in school. Urged by his oldest son John Jr. to revisit his early passion for folk song collecting and speaking, he rallied. On the strength of his previous book and his force of personality, he convinced Macmillan to agree to publish his proposed new book, *American Ballads and Folk Songs,* and to give him an advance on royalties. He proposed that it would be a collection of songs gathered from existing sources, buttressed by new Negro folksongs that he soon would collect. Next, he approached Herbert Putnam, the Librarian of Congress, and Carl Engel, the chief of the music division. He proposed a relationship to them in which he would collect field recordings for deposit in the Library of Congress. A few months later this matured into a small grant from the Library of Congress to fund travel expenses and use of recording equipment.

That summer, John Lomax with his son, Alan, who was on college break, toured Southern prisons recording blues, gospel, hollers, and worksongs under extraordinarily difficult circumstances. The radicalized younger Lomax drove and argued race, politics, and folk music with his conservative father throughout the trip. At the end of the summer, Herbert Putnam formalized and described John Lomax's relationship with the Library of Congress as "Honorary Conservator of our Archive of American Folksong, incidentally continuing, with our machine, at your own expense, to record and collect material in the field, and while in Washington, assisting in the response to inquiries involving the Archive itself."[31] Lomax received the title and status of working for the Library of Congress, $1 a month, and use of the Library of Congress's portable disc recorder, though he had to pay for his own blank discs. He was required to give the Library of Congress copies of his recordings but was able to retain ownership and use of the material. Though basically unpaid, his position with the Library of Congress burnished his reputation and enabled access to grants that funded his work.

During the 1930s, John and Alan Lomax deposited with the Archive of American Folk Song about ten thousand field recordings from their many expeditions. From those recordings and previously published songs, John and Alan assembled the book *American Ballads and Folk Songs,* and arranged for Kittredge to write the foreword. When the Lomaxes arrived to deliver the manuscript, they were surprised to find that Macmillan had invited Charles Seeger and Henry Cowell to the meeting in hopes that they would read the book and approve of it. The Lomaxes were suspicious and dubious over the presence of the ivory tower academics. However, Seeger and Cowell were enthusiastic about the book. Wary, Alan Lomax warmed to the Seegers over discussions of proletarian culture politics. Judith Tick quotes Lomax saying, "Charlie was the first person who gave me the feeling that there was a real connection between how people lived—social economics—and music."[32]

In 1935, with his prospects for work in New York poor and with a family to support, a lifeline for the Seegers appeared in the form of a job for Charles within the WPA's Resettlement Administration (RA) in the Special Skills Division. He had been recommended for the job by the painter Charles Pollock, whose brother Jackson was Thomas Hart Benton's student.

Poor farming methods and cycles of drought were serious problems for farmers even before the 1929 crash. There were massive areas of erosion. Land under cultivation was declining in nutrient value and prices were depressed. Many farmers lived at a bare subsistence level as sharecroppers, itinerant laborers, or harvest tramps. The RA was created to relieve farm and urban poverty. Its goals were to establish effective land-use programs, resettle destitute low income families, construct model communities in suburban areas, offer rural rehabilitation loans and grants to help farmers purchase land, and move rural populations to new farms and communities. The communities thus created from disparate groups of farmers were not harmonious.

Seeger's job was to develop and implement musical projects to pull people together, to "Encourage social integration"[33] using familiar music idioms, especially folk song. His plan was to introduce trained RA musicians to collect, and then teach their own folk music back to the farmers. He had difficulty finding the right musicians. In some cases, the RA musicians ignored Seeger's injunction to use familiar folk music and insisted on performing classical music. Only a very small number of RA musicians ultimately were fielded. Two of the most successful were Margaret Valiant, a conservatory trained Mississippian who was one of Ruth's close friends, and Sidney Robertson. Far from his earlier goal of trying to create music for the masses, along with his developing interest in folk music, Seeger had reformulated his position on the purpose of music: "The main question . . . should not be 'is it good music?' But 'what is the music good for?' And if it bids fair to weld the community into more resourceful and democratic action for a better life . . . then it must be conceded to be 'good for' that."[34]

Jesse Walter Fewkes had used an Edison cylinder recorder in 1890 to document Passamaquoddy Indians in Calais, Maine, thereby pioneering field recording. Excited by the results and the possibilities, he urged all collectors to use the new device. Ethnologists working with American Indian cultures, such as Franz Boaz of Columbia University, were quick to follow up, recording an estimated fifteen thousand cylinders. Europeans such as Percy Grainger and Béla Bartók also took up the challenge. John Lomax, Robert Winslow Gordon, and a few others made limited use of the cylinder recording equipment to document American folk music, but it was not until the early 1930s, when better and more portable disc recorders became available, that larger numbers of field recordings were made. Audio field recording transformed the collecting of folk music. No longer limited to music notation and description, the actual performance with all its nuance and context could be captured, uninterpreted or distorted by the collector.

Seeger planned to record folk music to bolster farmers' morale, train RA workers, and preserve the music. Seeger urged his staff to "collect everything" but to look for what was important to the folk; their preferences were as important as the music itself. Sidney Robertson did many of the recordings, Charles Seeger a few, and in all, RA workers recorded 159 Presto discs of various kinds of ethnic music. Seeger had folk song booklets made with the collected songs, published and distributed to foster community singing. As part of the job, Charles traveled extensively, experiencing live "folk," their living conditions, and their music for the first time. Ruth, at home with the children, was restless and very much wanted to see and hear for herself. In 1936 she got her chance. Charles, Pete, and Ruth Seeger, B. A. Botkin, and Sidney Robertson traveled together to Bascomb Lunsford's 1936 Mountain Dance and Folk Festival in Asheville, North Carolina. Pete was exposed to traditional banjo playing, in the person of Samantha Baumgarter, which made a lifelong impression. After getting a taste of field recording at the RA, Robertson energetically continued to record in association with the Library of Congress until 1940. Some of her work can be heard on the American Folklife Center website pages "California Gold: Northern California Folk Music from the 1930s."[35] In 1942, at the end of her field-recording career, she married Henry Cowell.

The RA ended in 1937 when the anti–New Deal Republicans in Congress succeeded in cutting its appropriations. The Seegers were unemployed again and scrambling to get by.

After five years of collecting, John Lomax was ready to produce the second volume of *American Ballads and Folk Songs*. Prompted by Harold Spivacke of the Archive of American Folk Song, he asked Charles Seeger to transcribe his field recordings to produce piano settings for his songbook. Charles declined but suggested his wife Ruth. Lomax was still sensitive over the reviews of his first book, *Cowboy Songs*, which had been criticized for its bad transcriptions. For his second

book, *Negro Folk Songs as Sung by Leadbelly*, he had hired George Herzog, a Hungarian musicologist working at Columbia University. Herzog had been trained by Erich von Hornbostel in Berlin to produce scientifically accurate transcriptions. It turned out that the transcriptions were too accurate. Alan Lomax summed it up, saying, "We sold 25 copies. Nobody could use the book in any way."[36] There had been more criticism by George Herzog, Herbert Halpert, and other academics about the inadequate Negro song transcriptions in the first volume of *American Ballads and Folk Songs*, prepared for him by a Washington music teacher, Mary Gresham. John Lomax defensively responded to Halpert's criticism, saying it "won't get him no folksongs."[37] In hiring Ruth Seeger, Lomax hoped to avoid mistakes in selection and musical notation. It was an inspired choice. Her rigorous work on the book made Ruth one of the foremost composer-transcribers of the twentieth century.

Transcription from a performance or recording is a delicate balancing act. Simplify too much and the song is lifeless; capture too much and it can be unreadable. Ruth took to the job with an intensity brought on by her recent conversion to folk music and her need to bring in money to support their family. Ultimately the financial rewards were small. She was extremely meticulous, wearing out the duplicate Library of Congress discs, playing them slowly for up to seventy-five times. Unable to settle for anything less than perfection, Ruth's scheduled one year for the transcriptions stretched into four. She transcribed 300 songs and tunes, 190 of which were used in the publication in 1941. One of them, fiddler William Stepp's "Bonaparte's Retreat," was selected and used by Aaron Copeland for his composition *Rodeo*. Ruth eventually transcribed some six thousand recordings in the Library of Congress archives.

After a long six months of no income, in June 1938 Charles was hired as deputy director for the Federal Music Project of the WPA. Director Nikolai Sokoloff assigned him the task of overseeing and developing projects in traditional music and recreational activities. He remained with the underfunded folk and social music division until the projects ended in 1941. Sokoloff and his staff were firmly in control and largely blocked Seeger's attempts to act on his more inclusive vision of music in America.

Benjamin A. Botkin had graduated from both Harvard and Columbia, taught English, edited, and studied anthropology before arriving in Washington in 1937. He had been granted a Julius Rosenwald Fellowship to do research at the Library of Congress in southern folk and regional literature. The next year he became Chief Editor of National Folklore at the FWP, after a controversy had ushered John Lomax from the position. Perhaps it was just envy, but the American Folklore Society, where John Lomax had twice been president, had turned on him. They passed a resolution distancing the society from the work Lomax had done at the FWP, upset that an academically trained folklorist had not done the work. The director, Henry Alsberg, resolved the controversy by hiring Botkin, whose credentials were exemplary. The Seeger and Botkin families became colleagues and friends, with many late-night conversations on politics and folklore's place in New Deal America. Ruth and Ben acted as sounding boards for each other as they developed their ideas on topics such as: does American have folk music of its own, how to educate Americans about folk music, debunking the academic misconceptions of "folk," how to use "recreational" programs to educate about folk music, and how should classical composers use folk music for fine-art music? Botkin is perhaps best remembered for his folklore anthologies, which he wrote after leaving governmental work, beginning in 1944 with the *Treasury of American Folklore.*

Robert Winslow Gordon contracted his obsession with folk music while studying with Wendall and Kittredge at Harvard. Though they did not meet at that time, he was a freshman in the same year when John Lomax attended. In much the same fashion as Lomax had begun collecting, but long after graduating from Harvard, Gordon wrote a folk music column for a men's magazine, *Adventure,* in which he solicited folk songs. He was teaching English in California, but in academic circles of the time his passion for collecting folk music, much less publishing in a men's magazine, was considered most disreputable. After a few years he was let go. He was a tinkerer, experimenting with photography, radio, and sound recording, and very much a loner. In 1927, with little to no funding, he managed four years of field recording in North Carolina. During his periodic research at the Library of Congress, Gordon had become known there as a folk music specialist. Gordon approached Carl Engel, chief of the music division with the idea to create a folk music archive at the Library of Congress. The Archive of American Folk Song was initiated in 1928 when Engels was able to raise funds from private sources for a one-year appointment of Robert Winslow Gordon as "Specialist and Consultant in the Field of Folk Song and Literature."[38]

Gordon was a very poor fit for the job. He had been hired to build a national repository of folk song, but he saw the job as a way to continue his collecting and was rarely in the Library of Congress. He did not communicate about his work or goals; no one knew what he was doing or often even where he was. He soon had no political allies. Only in the 1970s were his long-misplaced recordings discovered in the archive and made available. He had recorded close to a thousand cylinders and had collected nearly ten thousand song texts through his *Adventure* column. But by 1932, Gordon was finished at the Library of Congress.

From its inception the archive had relied on grants, but in 1937, for the first time, the federal government directly funded the archive. Alan Lomax was hired in 1938 as the first employee with the title of Assistant in Charge. John Lomax had been the archivist since 1932, but Alan carried out the day-to-day correspondence, meetings, and politics. At the time, John Lomax told Alan that he, Alan, "would soon be so firmly entrenched at the library that their critics couldn't touch him, not even 'the uppity Mr. Halpert.'"[39] A year later, the Library of Congress approached Carnegie Corporation of New York to fund a sound studio to press recordings for sale at cost to schools, colleges, students, and the public. The grant was made in 1940. Charles Seeger headed a catalog-ing project of four thousand recordings, which published the three-volume *Check-List of Record-ing Songs in the English Language in the Archive of American Folk Song to July 1940*. In 1941 Botkin became administrator and scholar at the AAFS as the Library of Congress Fellow in Folklore, then Assistant in Charge before serving as chief of the AAFS till 1944. In February 1943, AAFS began to issue compilations from the collection of field recordings, a project that eventually encompassed 71 long-playing records. Alan and John Lomax visited and made many field recordings in Mis-sissippi, but their focus was on African American sources and they made no recordings of Cauca-sian fiddlers in the state.

Herbert Halpert began a job in 1935 for the recreation division of WPA in NYC, collecting children's play rhymes and songs. He reflects on his introduction to field recording in an article for the *Journal of American Folklore*:

> In Greenwich Village one afternoon, I happened to meet one of my former English teachers at New York University, Mary Elizabeth Barnicle. She knew that I sang traditional songs, but I had not known that she was a folksong collector. She took me to her apartment to meet Alan Lomax, who was lis-tening to records that the two of them had recently collected in the south and West Indies. Although I had listened to many hillbilly records, and had learned and sung English folksongs, cowboy songs, and sea shanties, mostly from published collec-tions, I had never heard American folksongs as recorded in the field, and I found them enormously exciting. There was no chance that I could go on a recording trip with these two pioneering collec-tors—it was the Depression after all—but Professor Barnicle had read a newspaper story describing the Pineys of southern New Jersey and suggested that folksongs might be found there. She was quite right. During several years of visiting the area on weekends, I was able to collect a substantial num-ber of song texts.[40]

Ruth Benedict, then editor of the *Journal of Amer-ican Folklore*, read some of the material Halpert collected in New Jersey. She suggested and helped arrange that he study with George Herzog of Columbia on a part-time tuition scholarship. In 1936 Halpert transferred from the National Ser-vice Bureau to the Federal Theater Project as a folksong research worker and was soon appointed supervisor of the bureau's newly created Folk-song and Folklore Department. He worked as the acting director of the Music Department as well. Sponsored by Columbia University and the National Service Bureau, he went on folksong collecting trips to New Jersey in the summer and early fall of 1937. George Herzog allowed him to borrow a very bulky recording device that he used to record one hundred 12" discs on his first recording trip. In mid-1938 he was able to use a new Presto disc recorder and a camera on trips to New Jersey, the Ramapo Mountains, and the Catskills. Halpert became part of the Seegers' cir-cle and was particularly friendly with Ruth Seeger. As he recalled in an interview with Judith Tick: "I stayed at their house, she fed me, and she listened to me sing songs. She laughed at me when I said my version was the best. She knew the idiosyncra-sies of folksong collectors, knew their egos.... 'She knew that we thought our versions were the most artistically superior.'"[41]

The Joint Committee on Folk Arts and the 1939 Recording Trip

It is very unlikely that the records will be played anytime soon over the radio.
—Eri Douglas, State Director, FWP[42]

As B. A. Botkin described it, the Joint Committee on Folk Arts "has recently been set up in Wash-ington to integrate and coordinate all the folk-lore, folk music, folk drama and folk art and craft activities of the WPA, both within itself and with outside agencies. The original aim of the Joint Committee is to avoid needless duplication and overlapping to insure complete coverage of the field, but more than that it will provide new direc-tives and objectives in the training of personnel and the utilization of materials."[43]

Home of Mrs. Carrie Margaret Walker, Magee, Simpson County, May 27, 1939, where Herbert Halpert recorded the family of singers. Photo by Abbott Ferriss, 1939, courtesy Mississippi Department of Archives and History.

At the first meeting of the joint committee in December 1938, Botkin become chairman and Charles Seeger vice-chairman. Writing in an article about Ben Botkin, Alan Jabbour describes the joint committee:

> In the 1960s some student radicals used to denounce the "interlocking directorates" in American business. It is fair to say that the same sort of intricate networking occurred in the cultural sector during the WPA era in Washington. This was a kind of club of mostly men who shared many social and intellectual interests and often university ties, and who had in common a social vision that related powerfully to their New Deal mission. Many of them were relatively young, and the burgeoning of New Deal programs attracted them to Washington and placed them in positions of surprising authority in the Federal infrastructure.[44]

Other consultants who worked with the committee were Alan Lomax, Sidney Robertson, George Herzog, Ralph S. Boggs, Louise Pound, Reed Smith, and Harold Spivacke as Chief of the Music Division of the Library of Congress, who Ben Botkin described as "cooperating in every way consistent with the Library's policy and with in the limits of the Library's facilities," specifically through the Archive of American Folksong, which is "ready to receive, shelve, and make available recorded material" and to "aid in the actual recording by supplying discs and lending recording machinery."[45]

In February 1939 Charles Seeger inspected the 1936 Mississippi music notations and suggested to B. A. Botkin that some recordings should be made: "After some discussion, the committee decided to send a collector to record singers whose song texts had already been written down, primarily by workers on the Federal Writers Project in several southern states."[46] Spivacke offered to provide discs and preserve the records. Halpert was invited to undertake the fieldwork. In a 1992 essay Halpert described his qualifications

Eri Douglas, state director, FWP, and the "sound wagon." Photo by Abbott Ferriss, 1939, courtesy Mississippi Department of Archives and History.

in this manner: "The combination of my previous recording experience, my work with Herzog, and the convenient fact that my department had a recording machine made me eligible for the project. Also, as a very minor figure on the Federal Theatre Project, receiving a very modest salary, I could be spared for such a trip more easily than more important members of the committee."[47] The National Service Bureau was flattered that Halpert was asked and took care of transportation; they acquired, at no cost, an old army ambulance. WPA workers repaired and refurbished it with cabinets, storage batteries, and a converter to allow the Presto recorder to run on the batteries. They also equipped it with a narrow bed and cabinets for food, clothes, books, camera, and film. FWP Mississippi state director Eri Douglas called it the "sound wagon." "The best organized, most intensive, and probably most fruitful part of the trip was the month (8 May to 10 June) spent recording in Mississippi, where the Federal Music

Project had collaborated with the Federal Writers Project to supply informants."[48]

Through local contacts, FMP District Supervisor Sibyl McDonald arranged the itinerary in the northeast part of the state. The FMP's state director Jerome Sage and Jane Browne from the FWP did the rest of the state. A map of Halpert's trip appears in Appendix A. Just prior to Halpert's arrival in Mississippi, Miss Sage and Mrs. Brown interviewed fiddler Alvis C. Massengale and took down a list of his repertoire, which is contained in Appendix B. Massengale, who recorded commercially with the Newton County Hillbillies, recommended Leslie and Hendrix Freeny of Carthage, fiddling brothers who recorded 78s as Freeny's String Band, and W. D. Gilmer, a fiddler of the Leake County Revelers, Mississippi's most recorded string band. They later interviewed Charles Long of Quitman who recommended Mr. Kittrell in Meridian. They found W. A. Bledsoe while looking for Kittrell, his musical partner.

Herbert Halpert and the "sound wagon." Photo by Abbott Ferriss, 1939, courtesy Mississippi Department of Archives and History.

Bledsoe recommended Stephen B. Tucker. Long, Kittrell, Bledsoe, and Tucker were recorded by Halpert later that month.[49]

Inspired by Charles Seeger and Ben Botkin's changing conception of what folklore should be and noting the absence of documentation of the performers collected in 1936, arrangements were made to have the 1939 recordings augmented by careful documentation of the informants. In 1992 Halpert remembered the trip in an article for the *Journal of American Folklore*:

> For most of that period I was accompanied by Abbott L. Ferriss of the Mississippi Writers Project. As a consequence of his careful work, our field-work was admirably documented. He made nearly all the preliminary arrangements, took photographs, and interviewed all of the informants after they had been recorded, using in his questioning Botkin's version of the Herzog-Halpert questionnaire. We visited many of the singers whose texts

had been printed in Arthur Palmer Hudson's "Folksongs of Mississippi and their Background" and were able to record the songs and much information on their function. The 169 records made on that part of the expedition are a wonderful cross section of the varieties of local musical cultures, both Black and white, in the state.[50]

Those records, recorded at six sites, contained over three hundred performances; 115 were fiddle tunes. Most were solo fiddlers, though a few were accompanied by banjo or someone beating on the fiddler's strings with straws. One string band, the Canoys, was recorded. It seems that the instructions to field workers in 1936 were still in effect: "Types of Songs Desired, Item 5: Fiddle tunes: especially from players who tune the fiddle in different ways on different songs; also any of the 'little old foolish songs' that are sometimes sung to, or with fiddle tunes. We are not much interested in string bands."[51] Halpert had the foresight to record a pitch pipe playing the note A before each fiddler's performance, so that despite variations in recording speed and fiddle pitch, there is an objective reference on the recordings. Thanks to this, we can ascertain the key and tunings for the fiddle performances. In his *Journal of American Folklore* article Halpert described his expectations for the trip:

> When I returned to Washington I felt unhappy that I had not been able to make more recordings during the 14 weeks of the field trip. It therefore came as a pleasant surprise to learn that the members of the Joint Committee and Spivacke were delighted and impressed with what I had achieved. My frequent requests for new disks had been startling and unexpected. Only then did I realize their expectations for the Southern Recording Expedition had been considerably lower than mine![52]

Shortly after Halpert returned to New York the FTP was shut down, but its Folksong Department was sponsored by Columbia University and thus had the funding to survive a bit longer. Halpert used the recording truck and equipment on field trips to New Jersey and New York through the summer until the National Service Bureau was closed. In the fall, Botkin got the Writers Project to hire Halpert for a few months. Around this time, Halpert became interested in folktales and began to collect them as well. In 1940 he continued his education at Indiana University, studying under Stith Thompson, whose specialty was folktales. Halpert changed his dissertation topic to folk narratives and, after receiving his PHD, spent most of the rest of his career teaching and influencing his students to collect folklore.

Alan Lomax recorded in Mississippi but focused on black folklore there, and never recorded white fiddle music. So perhaps it is fortunate that he was not available or considered for the job at the time of Halpert's field trip in 1939. Lomax was then studying at Columbia University in New York with George Herzog. While there, he continued to work part-time for the Library of Congress recording New York City folklore. He became curious about what folk music

commercial recording companies had recorded, and discovered that seventy-six recording labels had recorded an enormous number of folk genres and performances. He created a discography and successfully solicited a large number of recordings for deposit at the Library of Congress. His interest foreshadows the 1960s enthusiasm for reissuing historic 78rpm folk recordings that passed the music on to new generations.

The End of the WPA Arts Programs

Pink slips and attacks from Congress kept us all in jitters.
—Dora Thea Hettwer, former executive secretary
for Henry B. Alsberg[53]

The New Deal activated opposition from the start. At every opportunity, the largely Republican opponents relentlessly forced budget cuts and attacked the WPA. The arts projects, although a very small part of the WPA, generated a mountain of bad press. In May 1938 Texas Republican Representative Martin Dies was appointed to lead the House Committee Investigating Un-American Activities. The committee was assembled to investigate American Nazi activities. Dies quickly abandoned investigations into right-wing sedition and shifted to communists, labor organizing, and attacks on the WPA. Dies exercised a special antipathy for the Federal One arts programs. His committee presaged the later McCarthy hearings in style and abuse of power and careless regard of facts. Dies, however, was very successful at staying in the newspapers, creating controversy, and galvanizing the opposition.

The WPA arts programs had become a political liability; there was a rising tide of charges of fraud, communist infiltration, scandal, corruption, and "boondoggling." Some of the charges were justified, but the attacks were out of proportion to the actual problems. By 1939 Roosevelt had distanced himself from arts programs. Top administrators had begun to leave the WPA in 1938 to take other administration posts. Henry Hopkins, for both personal and political reasons, had been inactive since 1937. The death of his wife and his battle with cancer kept him from defending the WPA. By 1938, when he became active again, much of his and the WPA's support was gone. Then in December, he left to become Secretary of Commerce. His replacement, Col. F. C. Harrington from the Army Corps of Engineers, was not sympathetic to the arts projects, and was unwilling to fight for them and perhaps jeopardize the rest of the WPA. Nikolai Sokoloff decided to resign in 1938, but stayed on till May 1939 for the transition of authority. Harrington removed Henry Alsberg in September. His successor, John Dimmock Newsom, stayed on long enough to see the American Guide book series through to completion. In the 1939–40 appropriations bill of June 21, the FTP and FAP were cut. By August the FWP and FMP had been transferred to state sponsorship and were off the federal payroll. Additionally, the appropriations bill required that no WPA worker could remain on the payroll for more than eighteen months. Wages were reduced and/or hours extended and a loyalty oath was required.

In 1939 world events overshadowed domestic issues: Germany invaded Czechoslovakia in March and Poland in September, marking the beginning of WWII; Roosevelt, proceeding cautiously due to political opposition, proposed boosting the military budget in 1940; Belgium fell; France fell. In December 1941, after the Pearl Harbor attack by Japan, the United States entered the war. The WPA turned its energies to supporting the military until June 30, 1943, when it closed.

The files of the 1936 FMP Mississippi fieldwork, and Abbott Ferriss's 1939 photographs, were returned to the state and now reside in the Mississippi Department of Archives and History in Jackson, Mississippi. The Halpert audio recordings and Ferriss's field notes from 1939 are housed in the Archive of American Folk Song in the Library of Congress in Washington.

The Music Lives On

This has been the story of two pivotal summers in Mississippi, a story that traces the early interest in folklore in Mississippi with A. P. Hudson's book *Folksongs of Mississippi and Their Backgrounds*. That book, for all its failings, informed the Mississippi FMP's improvised 1936 efforts to collect folk song—efforts to document fiddle tunes that otherwise would have been lost to us. The manuscripts of those tunes, in turn, caught the interest of Charles Seeger in Washington, sparking Halpert's trip in 1939, adding even more fiddle tunes. This living fiddle tradition had faded before its revival in the 1960s. But the manuscripts, the recordings, and the tunes themselves remain vital and now circulate far beyond the counties of their origin.

Notes

1. A. P. Hudson, *Folk Songs of Mississippi and Their Background* (Chapel Hill: University of North Carolina Press, 1936), v.

2. Letter (May 9, 1927) to Arthur Palmer Hudson, "Role of George Lyman Kittredge in American Folklore Studies, Some Notes on the Role of George Lyman Kittredge in American Folklore Studies," Esther K. Birdsall, *Journal of the Folklore Institute* vol. 10, no. 1/2, *Special Issue: American Folklore Historiography* (June–August 1973): 57–66; www.jstor.org/discover/10.2307/3813880?uid=3739832&uid=2&uid=4&uid=3739256&sid=21104780471763.

3. Alton C. Morris, *Folksongs of Florida* (Gainesville: University of Florida Press, 1950), xiii.

4. John Szwed, *Alan Lomax: The Man Who Recorded the World, a Biography* (New York: Viking, 2010), 140.

5. A. P. Hudson, "Notes by the Collector," *Folktunes from Mississippi* (New York: Da Capo, 1977), v. (Reprint of 1936 National Service Bureau publication No. 25, NYC.)

6. Daniel W. Patterson, *Sounds of the South* (Durham, NC: Duke University Press, 1991), 128.

7. Nancy Cassell McEntire, "Benjamin Botkin and Play-Party Scholarship in America" in Lawrence Rodgers and Jerrold Hirsch, eds., *America's Folklorist: B. A. Botkin and American Culture* (Norman: University of Oklahoma Press, 2010), 96.

8. Nick Taylor, *American Made: The Enduring Legacy of the WPA: When FDR Put the Nation to Work* (New York: Bantam, 2008), 172.

9. Ibid., 128.

10. Nikolai Sokoloff, "Short bulletin from FMP Washington, Press clips to 'Use at any time,'" Mississippi Department of Archives and History, Box 11074.

11. Kenneth J. Bindas, *All of This Music Belongs to the Nation: The WPA's Federal Music Project and American Society* (Knoxville: University of Tennessee Press, 1995), 13.

12. Ibid.

13. Bulletin from Jerome Sage, State Director of FMP, to state FMP workers, April 23, 1936, Mississippi Department of Archives and History, Box 11074.

14. Milton Meltzer, *Violins & Shovels: The WPA Arts Projects* (New York: Delacorte, 1976), 97.

15. Jerome Sage, "A Report of the Federal Music Project in Mississippi covering period from December 1, 1935 to April 1, 1936," Mississippi Department of Archives and History, Box 11074.

16. "Research Work of the Federal Music Project," Mississippi Department of Archives and History, Box AR 125.

17. "Types of Songs Desired" handout sheet, Mississippi Department of Archives and History, 439 Box 11077.

18. Mississippi Department of Archives and History, Box AR 126–127.

19. A letter, possibly from Jerome Sage, Mississippi Department of Archives and History, Box 11074.

20. Letter from Jerome Sage to Dr. Nikolai Sokoloff, January 4, 1937, Mississippi Department of Archives and History, Box 11074.

21. Letter from Jerome Sage to Mrs. Hugh E. Browne, September 10, 1936, Mississippi Department of Archives and History, Box 11074.

22. Letter from Jerome Sage to Dr. Nikolai Sokoloff, January 4, 1937, Mississippi Department of Archives and History, Box 11074.

23. Ann M. Pescatello, *Charles Seeger: A Life in American Music* (Pittsburgh: University of Pittsburgh Press, 1992), 141.

24. Bill C. Malone, *Music from the True Vine: Mike Seeger's Life and Musical Journey* (Chapel Hill: University of North Carolina Press, 2011) 24–25.

25. Hamilton, M., "The blues, the folk, and African-American history," *Transactions of the Royal Historical Society* 11 (2001): 27 (quoting Memo from Eri Douglass to Jerome Sage ["Subject: Data for Mr. Alan Lomax"], 29 October 1942, Folder 10 [Correspondence October 1942–January 1947], Fisk University Mississippi Delta Collection, AFC-LC).

26. Ibid. (Lomax field notes, July 1942 ALA-HC).

27. Judith Tick, *Ruth Crawford Seeger: A Composer's Search for American Music* (New York: Oxford University Press, 1997), 54.

28. Nolan Porterfield, *Last Cavalier: The Life and Times of John A. Lomax* (Champaign: University of Illinois Press, 1996), 390.

29. Bindas, 63.

30. Tick, 236.

31. Porterfield, 305.

32. Tick, 236.

33. Pescatello, 139.

34. Ibid., 142.

35. "California Gold: Northern California Folk Music from the 1930s," Library of Congress digital collection: memory.loc.gov/ammem/afccchtml/cowhome.html.

36. Tick, 246.

37. Porterfield, 415.

38. Ibid., 291.

39. Ibid., 415.

40. Herbert Halpert, "Coming into Folklore More Than Fifty Years Ago," *Journal of American Folklore* 105, no. 418 (Fall 1992): 443.

41. McEntire, 99.

42. Tom Rankin's liner notes for *Great Big Yam Potatoes: Anglo-American Fiddle Music from Mississippi* (LP, Jackson: Mississippi Department of Archives and History, 1985), quoting an Eri Douglas letter to Mrs. Charles Long in 1939 in answer to her question concerning the recordings made of her husband's fiddle music.

43. B. A. Botkin, "WPA and Folklore Research: Bread and Song," in Rodgers and Hirsch, *America's Folklorist*, 209; first published *Southern Folklore Quarterly* 3 (March 1939): 7–14.

44. Alan Jabbour, "Ben Botkin and the Archive of American Folk Song": www.alanjabbour.com/BenBotkinArchiveAmericanFolkSong.pdf.

45. Botkin, "WPA and Folklore Research: "Bread and Song," *America's Folklorist*, 210.

46. Halpert, "Coming into Folklore More Than Fifty Years Ago," 447.

47. Ibid., 448.

48. Ibid., 450.

49. Jerome Sage, "Notes trip May 1-3 Inclusive Miss Sage, Mrs. Browne," Mississippi Department of Archives and History 439 Box 10911.

50. Halpert, "Coming into Folklore More Than Fifty Years Ago," 450.

51. "Types of Songs Desired," Mississippi Department of Archives and History 439 Box 11077.

52. Halpert, "Coming into Folklore More Than Fifty Years Ago," 451.

53. Jerre Mangione, *The Dream and the Deal: The Federal Writers' Project, 1935–1943* (Syracuse: Syracuse University Press, 1996); see 1969 Dora Thea Hettwer interview, 95.

PART 2

The Music Transcriptions by Harry Bolick and Steve Austin

1

About the Notation

Transcriptions of 1936 manuscripts

My primary goal has been to remain faithful to the manuscripts collected in 1936 in Mississippi by the Federal Music Project. My secondary goal has been to ease the transition of these tunes back into circulation. In many cases, the original transcribers seem to have notated the tunes at the pitch level at which they were played, neglecting the fact that the particular fiddle was tuned uniformly higher or lower than the standard level. Therefore, I have transposed the tunes into the more usual fiddle keys. Any other changes are described in the comments for each tune.

Most importantly, I must emphasize that the music notations from 1936 included here can only be a crude outline of what the original source likely played. In some of these pieces, it may well not even be a good approximation. However, in the cases of tunes not known from any other source, these versions are valuable despite their incomplete nature. My presumption is that a knowledgeable player will be able to reconstruct a reasonable version of a given tune.

Posted on mississippifiddle.com are MP3 files of the playback from the 1936 manuscripts, to provide direct access to these tunes for those who do not read music. I look forward to hearing new

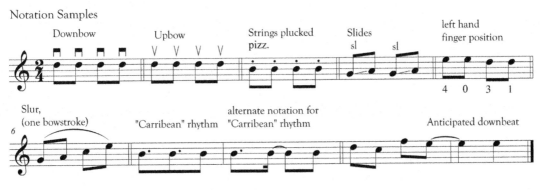

Figure 1

interpretations of these distinctive tunes. I have also recorded a number of these tunes in live string band settings. (See mississippifiddle.com for ordering information.)

We have used standard notation to indicate violin-specific information such as up and down bows, plucking of the strings (pizzicato), accents, and slurs (indicated by ties) (see examples in Fig. 1).

In the notes for each tune I list the collector (if known), the tuning—only if not the standard GDAE—the original performance pitch, and any comments by the collector or source.

Lyrics are taken from the field notes and the recordings.

—Harry Bolick
Sept 11, 2014

Transcriptions Based on 1939 Recordings

With the aim of capturing the authentic style of the individual performers on the source recordings, my preference was to avoid overly simplified transcriptions. However, the issue of readability versus complexity needed to be considered, and compromises have been made along the way. For example, in John Hatcher's "Tishomingo Blues" the rhythm is quite complex and the precise transcription challenging to read. A separate version of the tune is provided, with simplified rhythm. John Brown's "Cindy" is also transcribed in basic and detailed forms, to demonstrate Brown's use of double stopping and drones in the detailed version. This approach can then be applied to other tunes. For the most part, drones have been omitted in other transcriptions, with the assumption that the reader will be familiar with their use.

Most of the transcriptions fall between these extremes of simplicity and complexity. Alternate measures have at times been provided for variations, or at other times to offer simplified rhythmic notation.

On the available source recordings, surface noise and other artifacts obscure musical details,

and some of the recordings have skips, or are fragmented. When working from recordings, bow direction and fingering cannot be known with certainty. Therefore, these elements have been inferred, based on intensive listening and analysis during transcription, as well as familiarity with these tunes over years of listening to them and attempting to play them.

In addition, Halpert could not always be heard sounding the pitch pipe to check tunings. In these cases, tunings have been deduced by carefully listening to the tonality of the fiddle, and checking the order in which the tunes were recorded, as the fiddler would often play several tunes in a row in a certain tuning. This led me to conclude that "Poor Little Mary" by Enos Canoy was played in AEAC♯.

See Appendix D for information on recordings.

Terminology

In tunes with distinct high and low parts, the high part is called the fine and the low part the coarse. The fourth and third strings of the fiddle are called the "bass" and "counter," respectively. Thus, tuning to AEAE is "high bass and counter" tuning and to ADAE is "high bass" tuning.

Tunings and Scales

Tunings used are GDAE (standard tuning or "flat key"), ADAE (high bass), AEAE (high bass and counter), GDAD, DDAD ("Bonaparte's Retreat" tuning), and AEAC♯.

All tunes are transcribed as if played at A440, with string pitches as listed above for the various tunings. However, the individual fiddlers were often tuned higher or lower than A440.

John Brown played his tunes in GDGD or GDAD, Stephen Tucker tuned down a whole step for both standard and cross tunings, and Charles Long tuned down to either GDGD or GCGD for his tunes. W. E. Claunch was tuned higher than A440—probably inadvertently, as he says during the session that his fiddle is "keyed too high" to sing with. John Hatcher's and Enos Canoy's tunes are pitched higher than A440, which may be at least partially due to the recording and playback process.

When modal scales are used, it is typically in the key of A, either in standard or cross tunings. These tunes tend to use a minor seventh in the high octave, and a major seventh in the lower octave. The third usually tends toward major. However, the third and seventh notes are often indeterminate, falling somewhere between minor and major, and at times varying within the same tune (see Brown's "Dusty Miller" or Long's "Hard Road to Texas" for examples). We have chosen to write modal tunes in the key of A major, generally leaving the third as C♯ and using an accidental to indicate the flattened seventh. These tunes are labeled as "Modal" in the transcriptions.

Old-time Fiddle Style and Technique

Using a down bow for the start of a tune or phrase is the common practice with the fiddlers in this collection, and is assumed in the transcriptions unless otherwise indicated. Bowing patterns used include various combinations of saw strokes, long saw strokes, shuffles, and slurs. Using slurs to create syncopated phrasing is a characteristic feature of southern fiddling, and syncopated phrasing and/or tune structure are used by most of the fiddlers in this collection. Syncopation may be thought of as an alteration of rhythmic pattern, commonly a shift in the expected location of the downbeat, or placement of accents within a tune. This adds musical interest by breaking up what might otherwise be a monotonous or overly "square" structure.

The most common form of syncopation is anticipation of the beat at the beginning of a piece or phrase, often with a three-note slur (see Example 1). Three-note slurs are used to create syncopated patterns by dividing the usual duple series of four sixteenth notes into various groups of three, e.g., a 3-3-2 pattern (see Example 2) or 3-3-2 variation (see Example 3).

Example 1: Bear Creek's Up

Example 2

Example 3

These are used in various combinations within the body of a tune, including across bar lines (see Example 4). Two-note slurs are also common (see Example 5).

Example 4: Grey Eagle

Example 5: Raise Big Taters m. 7

An interesting syncopated bowing pattern found in Enos Canoy's playing is a variant of a 3-3-2 rhythmic pattern, consisting of two dotted eighth notes followed by a single eighth note (see Example 6). This is a common Sub-Saharan African rhythmic pattern, called Tresillo in Afrocaribbean music.

Example 6: 3-3-2 Canoy Variation

In measures 6-10 of "Poor Little Mary" Canoy uses a variant of this with dotted sixteenth notes (see Example 7). This was felt to be too challenging to read, so a simplified version is given with the dotted sixteenth pattern given as an alternate (see Example 8).

Example 7: Poor Little Mary m. 7

Example 8: Poor Little Mary m. 7

Odd numbers of beats or measures may be used as a form of syncopation in Mississippi fiddling. These have the effect of shifting the usual down beat of a phrase to the position of the off beat in the involved section of a tune. The underlying rhythmic pulse and melodic coherence of the tune is not disrupted, giving a seamless "non-square," or subtly polyrhythmic, feel to a tune. See Brown's "Sally Goodin" and "Wolves A' Howlin'" and Kittrell's "Cindy Jane," "Indian War Whoop," and "Little Boy Went A' Courtin'," for examples.

When an extra beat occurs in a tune, our usual practice was to insert a measure of 1/4 in the transcription, rather than lengthening the measure to 3/4 to encompass the extra beat. This preserves a duple rhythm, which was felt to be easier to read and to conceptualize rhythmically. As an alternative, the odd beats may be encompassed by using an odd number of measures within a tune (see the B part of Brown's "Dusty Miller").

John Hatcher's "Grub Springs" provides an example of creative use of bowing to generate syncopation. Here, the coarse part ends on a down bow, which is tied to the first beat of the fine part. The starting high A note in the fine part is on an up bow, and is shifted off of the down beat. Using

Example 9: Grub Springs m. 8

the up bow facilitates the string crossing from the A string to the E string (see Example 9).

The preference for syncopation in Mississippi fiddling suggests the assimilation of African rhythmic elements into Anglo fiddling tradition. This process was likely an ongoing one throughout the South from the early 1800s, but seems particularly well developed in Mississippi, as demonstrated in this collection.

Other bowing devices:

At fast tempos (Claunch, Hatcher, Bledsoe), certain notes in a series of sixteenth notes may be almost inaudible. The muffled or "ghost" note serves to change bow direction, but has no definite melodic value. The ghost note is indicated with an x as a note head (see Example 10). This is similar to a "retake" in classical violin bowing terminology.

Example 10: Going Up to Hamburg

Bow rocking, or a "pulsed" or divided up bow, is commonly used ending phrases. For bow rocking, the up bow crosses quickly to the adjacent string below the initial note, and then back to the same note. This facilitates starting the next phrase on the down bow. A variation of this in cross A is shown in Example 11. Here the initial note is an open A on the A string, and the second note is an A with the third finger on the D string. The pulsed up bow is produced with a slight increase

Key of G or D   Key of A - Tuned AEAE

Example 11

Example 12: Wolves A'Howlin'

in pressure in one up bow, which gives the sound of two separate notes (see Example 12).

Double Stops and Fingerings:
A common old-time fiddle device is using rhythmic bowing patterns with double stops, for example, shuffling and/or rocking the bow while holding a double stop. The double stop is maintained as much as possible throughout the passage and the fingers only lifted when needed to allow playing of the open notes (see Example 13; * indicates bow rocking).

Example 13: Raise Big Taters

This pattern is used most often in the keys of G or D, but a variant is also used in high bass and counter tuning. For the double stop, the third finger holds down the tonic note (A) on the third string with the second finger holding the third (C♯) on the adjacent second string. This tends to produce a slightly flattened third, which gives a distinctive sound. These in-between notes are essentially microtonal scale degrees which tend to be favored by old-time fiddlers of this era. In Example 14, the third finger of the left hand is held down wherever possible throughout the passage.

Example 14: Sally Goodin

Noting over unisons on the fifth scale degree are frequently used in the key of A or D (see Example 15). The fourth finger holds the note on the lower string with noting on the higher string.

Example 15: Cindy

Example 16: Rats in the Meal Barrel - GDAD

John Brown uses a similar pattern in GDAD tuning (see Example 16). The third finger of the left hand holds the D note on the A string wherever possible in the passage.

—Stephen T. Austin
September 11, 2014

2

Music Collected in 1936

MITTIE LEE ADAMS

Collector and likely the source: Mittie Lee Adams
Location: Coffeeville, Yalobusha Co.

All I Wants A Hogeye

Sal and I went fishin' one day   We went down on old Brunswick Bay

Sal caught a flounder   I caught a Shad   It mad old Sal tar - nat - tion mad.

She call'd me Whar - pus   I called her a whale   I wore Sal out with the old Shad's tail

Chorus

Row about a shore and a hog - eye   Row about a shore and a Hog - eye

Row about a____ shore and a hog - eye   All I want's Hog - eye

---

Comparable versions: All four of the tunes in the collection that mention "Hog Eye" have a few measures that sound related. In Stephen B. Tucker's 1939 "Hog Eye" version, the "B" part is related to the measures marked "Chorus" in Mittie Lee Adams's 1936 "All I Wants A Hogeye," Charlie Addison's 1936 "Hog Eye," and Birmah Grissom's 1939 "Hog-eye."

CHARLIE ADDISON

Collector and possibly the source: Charlie Addison, identified as African American in the FMP files
Location: Osyka, Pike Co.

Hogeye

Hog eye gal am a deb-bil of a gal, what a debbil All 'em 'e drinked a pint of but-ter milk

Chorus

answer by gosh it killed 'em   Roly Boly Smoly hog eye   Roly Boly Smoly hog eye

---

Comparable versions: All four of the tunes in the collection that mention "Hog Eye" have a few measures that sound related. In Stephen B. Tucker's 1939 "Hog Eye" version, the "B" part is related to the measures marked "Chorus" in Mittie Lee Adams's 1936 "All I Wants A Hogeye," Charlie Addison's 1936 "Hog Eye," and Birmah Grissom's 1939 "Hog-eye."

Liza Jane

I got a gal and you got none Little Liza Jane I took your gal just for fun,

Little Liz - a Jane   Oh little Liza, little Liza Jane, Oh little Liz - a, little Liz - a Jane,

---

Authors' comments: The A note in m7 could have been a C. The manuscript is unclear.

Comparable versions:
"Liza Jane" (E 21722/73), John & Emery McClung, 03/07/1927, NYC, Brunswick 573

Negro Reel

Laws - a - mercy, what have you done? You've married the old man instead of his son

His legs are all crook-ed and wrong put on They're all so sore at your old man Now you'-re mar-ried, you must obey, You

must prove true to all you say and as you have prom-ised So now you must go kiss him twice and say no more.

Old Mollie Hare

Old Moll-y Hare What you doing there, trotting cross the cotton patch as fast as you can tear

Ta da, ta da ta da da ta da ta da ta da da ta da ta da ta da da ta da ta da ta da da

The first three measures of this version are clearly related to the versions below.
Comparable versions:
"Largo's Fairy Dance," Gow, John and Andrew, *A Collection of Slow Airs, Strathspeys & Reels* (London: Wm. Campbell, ca. 1795) V, p. 19
Christy's Panorama Songster (New York: W. H. Murphy, ca. 1850s)
"Old Molly Hare," Fiddling Power & Family, 9/28/1927, Winston-Salem, NC, OKeh 45628
Other versions in this book by W. A. Bledsoe, Mrs. M. B. Brister, W. E. Claunch, J. A. Moorman, J. E. Shoemaker, and two versions by "Unknown"

Show Piece

Manuscript comments: A rural fiddler went to see a show, heard a band play, came back with the following tune in his head.
   He called it the "Show Piece."
Author's comments: The source transcription was in B♭, I believe, reflecting the fiddle was tuned low.

The Music Transcriptions

Want to Go to Meeting

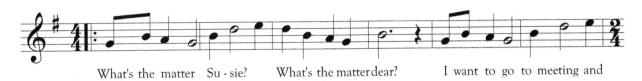

What's the matter Su-sie? What's the matter dear? I want to go to meeting and

Chorus

I have to stay here

Manuscript comments: "Incomplete."

Authors comments: note that m7 is missing two beats. This could be an error as the original manuscript simply omitted the two beats, or the tune could be as notated herein. The title of this version is usually paired with another melody. The "A" part of this version is related to the versions below.

Comparable versions:
"Cindy in the Meadows (81706-1), Samantha Bumgarner & Eva Davis, 4/22/1924, NYC, Columbia 167-D
"Cindy" (W 143867-), Riley Puckett & Clayton McMichen, 04/02/1927, Atlanta, GA, Columbia 15232-D
"Get Along Home, Miss Cindy" (BVE 41853-2), Pope's Arkansas Mountaineers, 02/06/1928, Memphis, TN, Victor 21577
Other versions in this book by John Brown ("Cindy"), W. E. Claunch ("Cindy"), Enos Canoy ("Where'd You Get Your Whiskey"), Mrs. R. C. Clifton ("Miss Cindy"), B. M. Guilette ("Liza Jane"), Frank Kittrell ("Cindy Jane"), Mrs. Joe McCoy ("Her Cheeks Are Like the Cherry"), Hardy Sharp ("Liza Jane"), Rev. J. E. Williams ("Cindy Waltz"), and Thaddeus Willingham ("Miss Cindy")

ALLEN ALSOP

Source: Allen Alsop
Collector: Mrs. Virginia R. Price
Location: Teoc, Carroll Co.

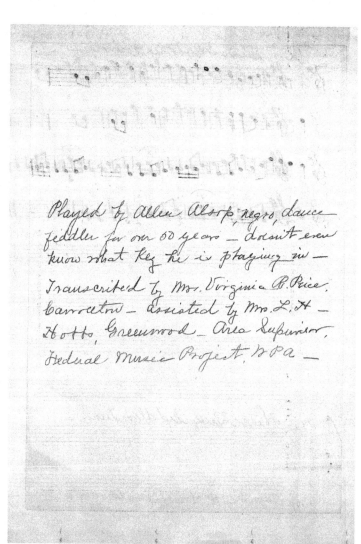

Federal Music Project manuscript. Courtesy Mississippi Department of Archives and History.

Manuscript comments: These are distinctive "Hill Billy Fiddle Tunes" handed down without benefit of script from father to son—This played by Allen Alsop, negro dance fiddler for the Teoc community for over 50 years—Transcribed by Mrs. Virginia R. Price Carrollton, Miss—Assisted by Mr. L. H. Hobbs Area Supervisor, Greenwood Federal Music Project WPA.

Authors' comments: The 1940 census lists Mr. Alsop, age 73, a Negro farm laborer, widowed and born 1867. The census for earlier years has a variety of birthdates for Mr. Alsop between 1861 and 1870.

The Music Transcriptions

Billy in the Lowground

Authors' comments: This version is unlike either of the usual melodies with this title.

Cotton-Eyed Joe

Hadn't been for Cotton Eyed Joe   I'd a' been married   seven years ago

Authors' comments: The original manuscript takes no notice of the missing beat in m4, so it is unclear if the tune was crooked or if this was a transcription error.

Comparable versions:

Ford, Ira, *Traditional Music of America* (New York: Dutton, 1940). 60

"Cotton-Eyed Joe" (M836-), Carter Brothers and Son, 11/22/1928, Memphis, TN, Vocalion 5349

"Cotton-Eyed Joe" (W146002-2), Gid Tanner & His Skillet Lickers, 04/10/1928, Atlanta, GA, Columbia 15283-D

"Cotton-Eyed Joe" (BVE 41852-2), Pope's Arkansas Mountaineers, 02/06/1928, Memphis, TN, Victor 21469

"Cotton-Eyed Joe," Rev J. E. Williams, in this book

Couldn't Hear Nobody Pray

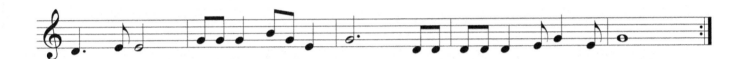

Way down yonder by myself, I couldn't hear
   nobody pray
Way down yonder by myself, I couldn't hear
   nobody pray,
I couldn't hear nobody pray

In the valley by myself, I couldn't hear nobody
   pray . . .

Cross that river by myself, I couldn't hear
   nobody pray . . .

Authors' comments: In the manuscript m9 the G was a dotted quarter; I reduced it to a quarter note to have the measure total
   four beats.

Comparable versions:
"I Couldn't Hear Nobody Pray," Work, J. W., *American Negro Songs* (New York: Bonanza Books, 1940), 72
"I Couldn't Hear Nobody Pray," Fisk University Jubilee Singers, 1909, Camden, NJ (www.loc.gov/item/jukebox.1798/)

Forked Deer

Authors' comments: This is not the usual tune for this title.

Going Away to Memphis, Dolly-O

Going away to Memphis, Dolly-O....Repeat ad lib

Authors' comments: In the original manuscript it is not clear where the ad-lib lyrics start.

Comparable versions:
Ford, Ira, *Traditional Music of America* (New York: Dutton, 1940), 35.
"Sail Away Lady" (W 141876-2-1), Uncle Bunt Stephens, 3/29/1926, NYC, Columbia 15071-D-
"Sail Away Ladies" (E 4936W), Uncle Dave Macon & His Fruit Jar Drinkers, 5/07/1927, NYC, Vocalion 5155
"Sail Away Ladies" (GE 14361-), Henry L. Bandy, 10/17/1928, Richmond, IN, Morning Star 45004

Old Rosin the Beau

Authors' comments: "On the minstrel stage it was one of the frequent songs of the character Mr. Corn Meal, a creation of the white blackface performer Jim 'Daddy' Rice, who based his version on that of a street singer he heard in New Orleans. As a dance tune it was cited as commonly played for Orange County, New York, country dances in the 1930s (as "Old Rosin the Bow")—Andy Kuntz (www.ibiblio.org/fiddlers/OLDNA_OLY.htm)

Comparable versions:
"Old Rosin the Bow," Ford, Ira, *Traditional Music of America* (New York: Dutton, 1940), lyrics 392

Possum Up a Gum Stump

Authors' comments: The last measure is as it was in the manuscript. However, I would suggest shortening the last note to allow
for the pickup notes upon repeats of the tune.

Comparable versions: Unrelated except by title to other versions.

Pretty Little Girl in the County

Authors' comments: This tunes appears to be a fragment of the versions listed below.

Comparable versions:
"Dandy Jim of Caroline," Thomas "Daddy" Rice of the Virginia Minstrels, A. Fiot, Philadelphia, 1844 (www.loc.gov/item/
   sm1844.391720/)
"Prettiest Little Girl in the County" (W 146004-3), Skillet Lickers, 04/10/1928 Atlanta, GA, Columbia 15315-D
"Little More Sugar in the Coffee" (W 404626-B), Fiddlin' John Carson & His Virginia Reelers, 12/09/1930, Atlanta, GA, OKeh 45542
"Purtiest Little Girl in the County," W. A. Bledsoe, 1939 in this book.

Running Water

Manuscript comments: "Dance Fiddler, Played by Allen Alsop, colored man."

Authors' comments: "Running Water" is unique in Mr. Alsop's repertoire. It is in 6/8 time, has three distinct parts, and is melodically ornate with technically demanding flourishes in the last part. Judging by the rest of his repertoire, I suspect it might well have exceeded his abilities. However Mrs. Virginia R. Price's handwritten notes on the back of the manuscript read "Dance Fiddler. Played by Allen Alsop, colored man. Transcribed by Mrs. Virginal R. Price, Carrolton Miss." The notation is my best guess as to the original intent. In m15 I changed the eighth note to a dotted eighth note to compensate for the missing sixteenth beat in the original.

Scrub Waltz

The Music Transcriptions

Soapsuds Over the Fence

Authors' comments: This tune shares only some of the title with Stephen B. Tucker's "Throw the Soap Suds in the Corner of the Fence," in this book. Every version I have heard with something like this title has been different.

Sugar in the Gourd

Authors' comments: This is not the usual tune for this title.

Sweet Milk and Peaches

Authors' comments: This version has only a faint resemblance to the Narmour and Smith version, but being only separated by a few miles and a few years is cause to wonder if Willie T. Narmour was influenced by this version.

Comparable versions:
"Sweet Milk and Peaches" (W 402995-B). W. T. Narmour & S. W. Smith 09/25/1929, NYC, OKeh 45424

Taters in the Sandy Land

DR. ASHLEY

Source: Dr. Ashley
Collector: Maggie Belle Robertson
Location: Hazlehurst, Copiah Co.

Muddy Road to Texas

Authors' comments: In the original manuscript m4 is not marked as a 1/8 time. Perhaps m4 and m5 were intended to be one measure with the dotted eighth reduced to a sixteenth, though that sounds less likely to me.

CLEVE BASS

Source: Cleve Bass
Collector: Mrs. I. A. Stewart
Location: Hinds Co.

Flop Eared Mule

Authors' comments: If all the quarter notes became eighth notes this tune would have eight measure phrases and more closely
resemble other versions.

Comparable versions:
"Karo" (W 143004-), Uncle Jimmy Thompson, 11/01/1926 Atlanta, GA, Vocalion 15368
"The Long Eared Mule" (S 73378), Emmett Lundy & Ernest Stoneman, 05/27/1925, NYC, OKeh 40405
"Old Virginia Reel, Pt. 2" (W 81644-A), Fiddlin' John Powers & Family, 09/28/1927, Winston-Salem, NC, OKeh 45154
Other versions in this book by Mrs. Maud Freeman ("G & C Schottiche"), John Hatcher ("Long Eared Mule or Baldin"), and
J. E. Shoemaker ("Gulfport").

Walking in My Sleep

Comparable versions:
"Walking in My Sleep," Haun, Mildred, "Cooke County Ballads and Songs" (M.A. thesis, Vanderbilt University, Nashville, TN, 1937, 237–38 (learned before 1900)
"Walking in My Sleep" (BS 07122-1), Arthur Smith Trio, 02/17/1937, Charlotte, NC, Brunswick B7043
"Walking in My Sleep" (MEM 51-), Roy Acuff & His Smoky Mountain Boys, 10/1939, Memphis, TN, Vocalion 05093
Other version in this book by Alvis Massengale ("Sebastapol").

ELLA MAE BERRY

Source: Ella Mae Berry

Collector: Ava White

Location: Clover Valley Community (near Bovina), Warren Co.

I'm Gwine Keep My Husband Workin' If I Can

If I can, can, can, If I can, can, can
I'm gwine a keep my hus-band work-in if I can
He's gonna buy me a barrel of flour ahm gwine
    cook it every hour,
Ahm' gwine keep my hus-band workin' if I can

If I can, can, can, If I can, can, can
I'm gwine a keep my hus-band work-in if I can
He's gonna buy me a barrel of meat ahm keep me
    off the street,
Ahm' gwina keep my hus-band workin' if I can

MR. JIM HENRY BOLEY

Source: Mr. Jim Henry Boley
Collector: Mrs. George Stricklin
Location: Paden, Tishomingo Co.

Loving Nancy

On yon-der's high mountain, There was a fine place Where small birds were singing

their notes to in - crease, The charm of loving Nan - cy, and her ways so com -

plete, I'll re - sign all better pass time, to be with Nan - cy

Manuscript comments: "Mr. Boley is a man of sixty years or more and has a reputation of being one of the best fiddlers in Tishomingo County. He states that so far as he knows this tune has never been written. He learned it by hearing his mother sing it when he was a child. He states that she sang it most beautifully and her voice was very clear and sweet on the little embellishment, which is sung on the last syllable of the word 'complete'. He also states that there were other verses to this number, but he does not recall them."

Authors' comments: The 1940 census has Mr. Boley listed as a White farmer working with the WPA, his birthdate as 1879, living with his wife, brother, and nephew.

MRS. W. J. BONDS

Source: Mrs. W. J. Bonds

Collector: Mae Belle Williams

Location: Iuka, Tishomingo Co.

Good Bye Liza Jane

Buzzard and Hawk went off to law, Good Bye   and   a goodbye Hawk come back with a   broken jaw

Goodbye Liza   Jane Goin' away to leave you   Good Bye and goodbye Goin' away to leave you   Good Bye Liza   Jane

Rabbit in the garden sittin' by a stump
Good Bye and a good bye
Hopped and skipped till he couldn't make a jump

Goodbye Liza Jane
Goin' away to leave you
Good Bye and a good bye
Goin' away to leave you
Good Bye Liza Jane

Manuscript comments: Sung by Mrs. W. J. Bonds as her mother sang it more than 50 years ago.

Comparable versions:

In this book this version is closest to the melody in J. E. Tartt's "Go Long Liza," and is only loosely related to the melodies from Enos Canoy's "Where'd You Get Your Whiskey," Horace Kinard's "Liza Jane," Everett Mitchell's "Liza Jane," and Thaddeus Willingham's "Liza Jane."

ETHEL BOWEN

Source: Unknown

Collector: Mrs. Ethel Bowen

Location: Marshall Co.

Carve Dat Possum

Transposed from original key of F

Authors' comments: The harmony is directly from the manuscript. The double stops that would be required in order to play that harmony lead me to suspect that the transcriber was not a fiddler. Note that at the key change the tune is "Golden Slippers." At m44, the 1/4 measure was not so indicated in the manuscript but simply as a measure totaling only one beat.

Comparable versions:

"Carve that Possum," Sam Lucas, 1875, John F. Perry, Boston

"Carve that Possum," Harry C. Browne, 04/06/1917, Columbia 2590

"Carve that Possum 1,2" (E 4931/32), Uncle Dave Macon & His Fruit Jar Drinkers, 05/27/1927, NYC, Vocalion 5151

DALTON BRANTLEY

It is unclear whether Brantley is source, collector or both.
Location: Wyatte, Tate Co.

Crap Game

If I win let me win, oh my darling. If I lose let me lose not your

love

Source: "Fiddlers in Tate County" via the playing of Dalton Brantley
Collector: Mrs. Mary G. Jackson
Location: Wyatte, Tate Co.

Soldier's Joy

Comments: Perhaps the most widely known fiddle tune.

Comparable versions:
Aird, James, *A Selection of Scotch, English, Irish and Foreign Airs*, vol 1, no. 109 (1778)
"Soldier's Joy" (9189-A), Fiddlin' John Carson & His Virginia Reelers, 06/30/1925, Atlanta, GA, OKeh 45011
"Soldier's Joy" (GE 12747), Taylor's Kentucky Boys, 06/27, Richmond, IN, Silvertone 5060
"Soldier's Joy" (E29273), Kessinger Brothers, 02/05/1929, NYC, Brunswick 341
See other versions in this book by W. A. Bledsoe ("Farewell Mary Ann"), W. E. Claunch, Charlie Edmondson, John Hatcher,
W. E. Ray, Stephen B. Tucker, and Rev. J. E. Williams ("Rickets Hornpipe")

MRS. M. B. BRISTER

Source: Unknown
Collector: Mrs. M. B. Brister assisted by John Hurst
Location: Shaw, Bolivar Co.

Old Hen Cackled on the Pot

The old hen cackled and she cackled in the lot The old hen cackled and

the rooster laid the egg The next time she cackled she cackled in the pot

---

Authors' comments: The source transcription was in E♭, likely reflecting the fiddle was tuned high. This tune appears to be
incomplete. In the manuscript, even though the time signature was indicated as 2/4, it had bar lines as if it was in 1/4.
Curious.

Comparable versions:
"The Old Hen Cackled and the Rooster is Going to Crow" (8375-A-B), John Carson, 06/14/1923, Atlanta, GA, OKeh 4890
"Hen Cackle" (81630-2), Gid Tanner & Riley Puckett, 03/08/1924, NYC, Columbia 110-D
"Cackling Hen" (9307-A), J. D. Harris, 1925, Asheville, N.C., OKeh 45024
Other versions of "Old Hen Cackled" in this book: John Brown, W. M. Collom ("Rabbit in a Ditch"), Jim Gooch, and Dr. F. H.
Smith.

Old Mollie Hare

Old Mollie Hare   what you doing there   Running down   the cotton row   as fast

as I can   tear   Won't pull cotton won't pull hay won't do   nothing the white folks   say

Old Mollie Hare what you doing there
Sitting on the cotton row combing out your hair
Won't pull cotton won't pull hay won't do noth-
    ing the white folks say

Authors' comments: The source transcription was in E♭, I believe reflecting that the fiddle was tuned high. The original tran-
    scriber had the time signature as 2/4 but most measures counted only to 1/4. However some measures contained a half note. I
    have shown those notes here by tying two quarter notes. The "A" part of this version is clearly related to the versions below.

Comparable versions:
"Largo's Fairy Dance," Gow, John and Andrew, *A Collection of Slow Airs, Strathspeys & Reels,* vol. V (London: Wm. Campbell, ca.
    1795), 19
Christy's Panorama Songster (New York: W.H. Murphy, ca. 1850s)
"Old Molly Hare," Fiddling Power & Family, 9/28/1927, Winston-Salem, NC, OKeh 45628
Other versions in this book by W. A. Bledsoe, W. E. Claunch, J. A. Moorman, J. E. Shoemaker, and two versions by "Unknown"

Run Nigger, Run

Run nigger run, the patroll catch you Run nigger run, it's almost day dat nigger run, dat nigger flew

that nigger lost his Sunday shoe Run nigger run, the patroll catch you Run nigger run, it's almost day

---

Authors' comments: The manuscript had the time signature as 2/4 but the measures counted only to 1/4.

Comparable versions:
"Run Nigger, Run," Allen, William Francis, *Slave Songs of the United States* (New York: A. Simpson, 1867), #110, 89
"Run Nigger, Run" (8709-A), Fiddling John Carson, 08/27/1924, Atlanta, GA, OKeh 40230
"Run Nigger, Run" (667/668), Uncle Dave Macon, 04/13/1925, NYC, Vocalion 15032
"Run Boy, Run" (BVE 56361-2), Eck Robertson & Dr. J. B. Cranfill, 10/10/1929, Dallas, TX, Victor V40205
Other versions of "Run Nigger, Run" in this book by W. E. Claunch, Mr. John McCartie, Jr., Stephen B. Tucker, Mrs. A. Tynes, Mrs. Louise Walker Wallace, and Thaddeus Willingham.

C. BRONTON

Source: C. Bronton, hummed by Mrs. Robert May
Collector: Mrs. Louise Wallace
Location: Independence, Tate Co.

Jewel Waltz

Manuscript comments: "I wasn't sure that original compositions would be wanted but this was composed by Mrs. May's father and she asked that I send it in."

Tuning: The source transcription was in E♭. I have moved it to a more usual fiddle key.

Authors' comments: The 1940 census lists Robert May, age 27, as a white farmer, living with his wife and a daughter.

JOHN ALEXANDER BROWN

Source: John Alexander Brown
Mr. Brown is the only fiddler who was collected in 1936 and in 1939.
The field notes describing him along with the rest of his tunes are in the 1939 section.
Collectors: Miss Mae Belle Williams, and Mrs. Geo. W. Strickin
Location: Iuka, Tishomingo Co.

Black Eyed Susan

Rain come and wet me, sun come and dry me Stand back pretty girls don't come nigh me

She's so sweet that I could eat her She's my pretty little black eyed creature

Collector: Miss Mae Belle Williams

Manuscript comments: "Mr. John Brown is more than 60 years of age, He learned this and many other tunes from his father, who came from Tennessee before the Civil War and settled on Bear Creek about six miles from Iuka."

Comparable versions:
"Black Eyed Susie" (81635-1), Gid Tanner and Riley Puckett, 03/08/1924, NYC, Columbia 119-D
"Black Eyed Susie" (GE 13040), Fiddlin' Doc Roberts, 09/1927, Richmond, IN, Gennett 6257
"Black Eyed Susie" (BVE 39747), J. P. Nestor, 08/01/1927, Bristol, TN, Victor 21070
Other versions of "Black Eyed Susan" in this book by John Brown, W. E. Claunch ("Black Eyed Susie"), John Hatcher, Charles Long ("Big Eyed Rabbit"), J. A. Moorman, and Thaddeus Willingham ("Black Eyed Susie").

John Butter and the Fat

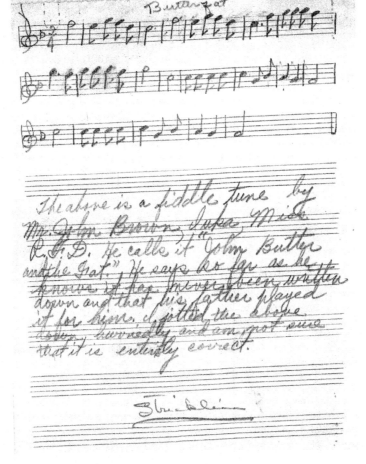

Manuscript notation for "John Butter and the Fat." Courtesy Mississippi
Department of Archives and History.

Collector: Mrs. Geo. W. Strickin

Manuscript comments: "The above is a fiddle tune by Mr. John Brown of Iuka, Miss. RFD. He calls it 'John Butter and the Fat'.
   He says so far as he knows it has never been written down and that his father played it for him. I jotted the above down
   hurriedly and am not sure that it is entirely correct."

Authors' comments: The source transcription was in F, reflecting that the fiddle was tuned low.

Molly Put the Kettle On

Molly put the kettle on, we'll all have tea   Molly put the kettle on, we'll all have tea

Molly put the kettle on, we'll all have tea   Molly put the sugar in and that'll suit me

Collector: Miss Mae Belle Williams

Tuning: The source transcription was in A♭, reflecting the fiddle was tuned low. However, the tuning was given as AEAE.

Authors' comments: The first eight measures are all that we have from John Brown for this tune. However, I was quite intrigued by them and added the last four measures to make it more enjoyable to play. The first two of those measures are based on Rev. J. E. Williams's "Polly Put the Kettle On"; the latter two are a repeat of John Brown's measures seven and eight. This is the only tune in this collection where I have added to or altered the music.

Comparable versions:

"Molly Put the Kettle On," White, Charles, *White's New Illustrated Melodeon Song Book* (New York: H. Lond & Brother, 1851), 29

"Molly Put the Kettle On" (W 147631-) Leake County Revelers, 12/13/1928, New Orleans, LA, Columbia 15380

"Molly Put the Kettle On" (W 151918-1), Gid Tanner & His Skillet Lickers, 10/24/1931, Atlanta, GA, Columbia 15746-D

Other versions in this book by Mr. T. W. Cooper ("Mollie Bring the Kettle") and J. E. Shoemaker ("Ladies Fancy").

Old Hen Cackled

Authors' comments: The source transcription was in F♯, reflecting the fiddle was tuned low. The tune appears to be incomplete.

Comparable versions:
"The Old Hen Cackled and the Rooster is Going to Crow" (8375-A-B), John Carson, 06/14/1923, Atlanta, GA, OKeh 4890
"Hen Cackle" (81630-2), Gid Tanner & Riley Puckett, 03/08/1924, NYC, Columbia 110-D
"Cackling Hen" (9307-A), J. D. Harris, 1925, Asheville, NC, OKeh 45024
Other versions of "Old Hen Cackled" in this book: Mrs. M. B. Brister ("Old Hen Cackled on the Pot"), W. M. Collom ("Rabbit in a Ditch"), Jim Gooch, and Dr. F. H. Smith.

Old Joe Clark

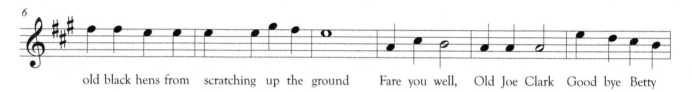

If I had ten thou-sand rails, I'd fence my farm around,   To keep the widow's

old black hens from   scratching up the ground   Fare you well,   Old Joe Clark   Good bye Betty

Brown,   Fare you well,   Old Joe Clark,   I'm bound to leave this town

Collector: Miss Mae Belle Williams

Tuning: AEAE

Authors' comments: The usual versions of this tune are mixolydian. Note the G♯ in this version.

Comparable versions:

Sharp, Cecil J., & Maud Karples, *English Folk Songs from the Southern Appalachians,* vol. 2 (Oxford: Oxford University Press, 1932), 259

"Fare Thee Well, Old Joe Clark" (S 72-016-B), Fiddlin' John Carson, 11/071923, NYC, OKeh 40038

"Old Joe Clark" (B 30582-1), Fiddlin' Powers & Family, 08/18/1924, Camden, NJ, Victor 19434

"Old Joe Clark" (S 73117-A), The Hillbillies, 01/15/1925, NYC, Victor 19434

Other version in this book by Thaddeus Willingham.

WILLIE CAMPBELL

Source: Willie Campbell
Collector: Anna Wallace
Location: Lafayette Co.

Chicken Reel Waltz

Manuscript comments: "as played in fiddle contest."
Authors' comments: This is an unusual tune for this title and a bit odd that a tune in waltz time is called a reel.

BABE CASEY

Source: Babe Casey
Collector: Mr. Dalton Brantley
Location: Wyatte, Tate Co.

Grasshopper on Sweet Tater Vine

Grasshopper sitting on Sweet Tater vine, sweet tater vine, sweet tater vine Grasshopper sitting on

sweet tater vine so early in the morning Along came a turkey and nabbed him by the neck, by the neck.

Along came a turkey and nabbed him by the neck, by the neck, Along came a turkey and nabbed him so early in the morning

Authors' comments: Mr. Brantley learned the tune from Mr. Casey and played it for Mrs. Mary T. Jackson, who I assume transcribed it. Not all of the FMP music teachers turned collectors could transcribe. In those cases they learned the tune from the source and then in turn played it for a project worker who could transcribe.

Comparable versions:

"Midnight Serenade," Knauff, George P., *Virginia Reels*, vol. 1, no. 4 (Baltimore, c. 1839)

"Round Town Gals" (GEX 498-A), Ernest V. Stoneman & His Grayson County Boys, 02/02/1927, NYC, Gennett 6052

"Buffalo Gals" (8514-1-2), Pickard Family, 01/31/1929, NYC, Banner 6371

Versions of "Buffalo Gals" in this book by R. H. Ellis, John Hatcher ("Buffalo Girl"), A. J. Howell ("Buffalo Girl"), Edward Kittrell, and Ben Wall.

J. O. CASEY

Source: The Holland Brothers via J. O. Casey
Collector: Mrs. Ida Burke and Mr. Brantley
Location: Ingram's Mill, Desoto Co.

Holland Waltz

Manuscript comments: "This is supposed to have been composed by the Holland Brothers, natives of Desoto Co. living near Ingrams Mill. Used quite a bit at one time for olden dances. A cousin of the Hollands, J. O. Casey of Wyatte, Miss gave us the melody, learned by Mrs. Burke and Mr. Brantley of Wyatte and Raymond Williams of Senatobia gave assistance to them in writing it down."

Authors' comments: In the comparable versions below, only the first strains of the melodies are similar.

Comparable versions:
"A Kiss Waltz" (W-142644-1), The North Carolina Ramblers, 9/18/1926, NYC
"Kiss Waltz," Emmett Lundy, Library of Congress field recordings, Alan Lomax, Galax, VA, 1941, AFS 04939 A06
"Kiss Waltz," Charlie Edmundson in this book

MR. R. C. CLIFTON

Source: Mr. R. C. Clifton
Collector: Mrs. H. H. Weedy
Location: McLain, Greene Co.

Hardy Smith

Manuscript comments: "Repeated several times with much decoration"

Authors' comments: The source transcription was in E♭, reflecting the fiddle was tuned high. The unlikely double stop in the last measure and the absence of the note G or G♯ suggests that the fiddle was tuned AEAE.

Miss Cindy

Comparable versions:
"Cindy in the Meadows" (81706-1), Samantha Bumgarner & Eva Davis, 4/22/1924, NYC, Columbia 167-D
"Cindy" (W 143867-), Riley Puckett & Clayton McMichen, 04/02/1927, Atlanta, GA, Columbia 15232-D
"Get Along Home, Miss Cindy" (BVE 41853-2), Pope's Arkansas Mountaineers, 02/06/1928, Memphis, TN, Victor 21577
Other versions in this book by Charlie Addison ("Want to Go to Meeting"), John Brown ("Cindy"), W. E. Claunch ("Cindy"), Enos Canoy ("Where'd You Get Your Whiskey"), B. M. Guilette ("Liza Jane"), Frank Kittrell ("Cindy Jane"), Mrs. Joe McCoy ("Her Cheeks Are Like the Cherry"), Hardy Sharp ("Liza Jane"), Rev. J. E. Williams ("Cindy Waltz"), and Thaddeus Willingham ("Miss Cindy").

ALICE COLE

Source: Alice Cole
Collector: Barbara Harrison
Location: Clarksdale, Coahoma Co.

First Time I Saw Liza

The first time I saw Liz - a She was in the rain Next time I saw

Liza, she was wearing a golden chain With my horse and buggy Drove all round this town It

almost broke my Liza's heart to see me turn around Hoof a long Liza, poor gal.

Hoof a long Liza Jane Hoof a long Liza, my Lord, she died on the train

Manuscript comments: "a play song, by Alice Cole a native of Berlin, Canada, who came from there to Mississippi"
Authors' comments: The 1940 census has an Alice Cole listed as Negro, age 48, widowed, with five granddaughters and a grandson, working as a laundry maid.

Comparable versions:
"Lil Liza Jane," Harry C. Browne, 07/02/1918, Columbia A2622

W. M. COLLUM

Source: W. M. Collum, 60 yrs. old
Collector: Mrs. E. M. Purcell
Location: Tippo, Tallahatchie Co.

Indian Eat the Woodchuck

Indian eat the wood chuck, All but the head, Parson didn't eat that was

cause he had no bread

Comparable versions:
"Indian Eat a Woodpecker" by Stephen B. Tucker in this book has a similar title but not a similar melody.

Rabbit in a Ditch

Manuscript comments: "All tunes given by Mr. Collum were learned by him when a boy from an old fiddler living in the neighborhood"

Comparable versions:
"The Old Hen Cackled and the Rooster is Going to Crow" (8375-A-B), John Carson, 06/14/1923, Atlanta, GA, OKeh 4890
"Hen Cackle" (81630-2), Gid Tanner & Riley Puckett, 03/08/1924, NYC, Columbia 110-D
"Cackling Hen" (9307-A), J. D. Harris, 1925, Asheville, NC, OKeh 45024
Other versions of "Old Hen Cackled: in this book: Mrs. M. B. Brister ("Old Hen Cackled on the Pot"), John Brown, Jim Gooch, and Dr. F. H. Smith.

JOSEPHINE COMPTON

Source: Josephine Compton
Collector: L. S. Virgil
Location: Gulfport, Harrison Co.

Go Long Liza

Go Long Liz-a tell your name   Run Liz-a Jane   You had no right steal dat cane   Run Liz-a Jane

Master go give O Liz-a a taste   so she got to work at last Run Liz-a Jane   Run Long Liz-a tell your name Run Liz-a Jane

Authors' comments: The WPA lists of informants indicate that Ms. Compton was African American.

MR. T. W. COOPER

Source: Mr. T. W. Cooper
Collector: Mrs. Evelyn Nation
Location: Purvis, Lamar Co.

Irish Washerwoman

Authors' comments: The first measure in "B" part is duplicated, making tune crooked, which might be a transcription error. A T. W. Cooper is listed in the 1940 census as a sixty-year-old white head of household with wife and two lodgers. His occupation was listed as deputy sheriff.

Comparable versions:

Gow, Neil, *A Third Collection of Strathspey Reels &c for the Piano-forte, Violin and Violoncello* (1792), 31 imslp.org/wiki/A_Third_Collection_of_Strathspey_Reels,_etc._(Gow,_Niel)

"Medley of Jigs: Irish Washerwoman" (BVE 34528-4), Mellie Dunham, 02/03/1926, Camden, NJ, Victor 20537

"Irish Washerwoman" (GE 13836), Doc Roberts & Asa Martin (as Jim Burke), 05/14/1928, Richmond, IN, Silvertone 8176

Other versions of "Irish Washerwoman" in this book by Billie Mansfield/Chris Martin and unknown ("Virginia Reel").

Mollie Bring the Kettle

Comparable versions:

"Molly Put the Kettle On," White, Charles, *White's New Illustrated Melodian Song Book* (New York: H. Lond & Brother, 1851), 29

"Molly Put the Kettle On" (W 147631-), Leake County Revelers, 12/13/1928, New Orleans, LA, Columbia 15380

"Molly Put the Kettle On" (W 151918-1), Gid Tanner & His Skillet Lickers, 10/24/1931, Atlanta, GA, Columbia 15746-D

Other versions in this book by John Brown ("Molly Put the Kettle On") and J. E. Shoemaker ("Ladies Fancy")

Untitled (Devil's Dream)

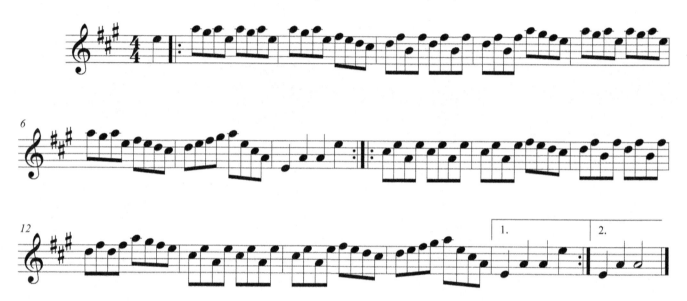

Tuning: GDAD

Authors' comments: This is the widely known tune "Devil's Dream."

Comparable versions:
Howe, Elias, *Howe's School for the Violin* (Boston: Oliver Ditson, 1851), 29
"Devil's Dream" (AL 213), Kessinger Bros., 02/10/1928. Ashland, KY, Brunswick 256
"Devil's Dream" (65713-A), Clayton McMichen, 06/01/1931, NYC, Decca 2649
Other versions of "Devil's Dream" in this book by W. E. Claunch and Stephen B. Tucker.

MRS. RUBY COSTELLO

Collector: Leslie Turner
Location: Leakesville, Greene Co.

I Want to Go to Meeting

Want to go to meetin' and I got no shoes carry
    me back to mammy Oh!
Want to go to meetin' and I got no shoes carry
    me back to mammy Oh!
Mam-my's Chim-ney Cor-ner big e-nough to
    hold me
Want to go to meetin' and I got no shoes carry
    me back to mammy Oh!

Second verse: "got no clothes" instead of "shoes"

Third verse: "got no hat"

Comparable versions:

Belden, H. M., and Arthur Palmer Hudson, *Frank C. Brown Collection of North Carolina Folklore, Vol. 3: Folk Songs* (Durham, NC: Duke University Press, 1952), 510, 565

"Been to the East Been to the West" (W 146208-2), Leake Co. Revelers, 04/27/1928, New Orleans, LA, Columbia 15318-D

"Share 'Em" (W 402127-A), Scottsdale String Band, 08/10/1928, Atlanta, GA, OKeh 45256

"Shear the Sheep Bobbie" (W 147647-1), Gatwood Square Dance Band, 12/15/1928, New Orleans, LA, Columbia 15363

"Take Me Back to Tulsa" (Dal 1180-1), Bob Wills & His Texas Playboys, 02/25/1941, Dallas, TX, OKeh 06101

Other versions in this book by Enos Canoy ("Possum and Coon"), W. E. Claunch ("Chicken Pie" and "Miss Sally at the Party"), John Hatcher ("Old Miss Sally"), Charles Long ("Jones County" and "Steamboat"), and Hardy Sharp ("Great Big Yam Potatoes").

C. M. COURSAN

Source: C. M. Coursan
Collector: W. A. Harrison
Location: Ashland, Benton Co.

Big Tom Bailey

Big Tom Bailey, Big Tom Bailey. He had'a wife and two little babies

One named Pick and the other one Davy. One eats grease and the other one gravy. Ho! Ho! Big Tom

Bailey. Ho! Ho! Big Tom Bailey. Ho! Ho! Big Tom Bail ey.

Manuscript comments: "This is an old fiddle tune in this county. This tune was played at all the dances. Every Fiddler know how to play this."

Comparable versions:
"Old Dan Tucker," Dan Emmett, *Aldophous Morning Glory Songster*, 1843, 14
"Old Dan Tucker" (669/70), Uncle Dave Macon, 04/13/1925, NYC, Vocalion 15033
"Old Dan Tucker" (S 73-039-A), Fiddlin' John Carson, 12/18/1924, NYC, OKeh 40263
Other version of "Old Dan Tucker" in this book by Thaddeus Willingham.

NARVELL COVINGTON

Source: Narvell Covington
Collector: Paul Boensch
Location: Meridian, Lauderdale Co.

Going from the Cottonfield

I'm going from the cotton field, I'm going from the cane. I'm

going from a little log hut that stands down in the lane. The boat am on the river that's

going to take me off, for I am going to join the regiment thats starting for the north

But Dinah she don't want to go
She says we're getting' old
Oh she afraid we'll freeze to death
The country am so cold
But the boat am on the river that
Goin to take me off
And I'm gonna join the regiment
That's starting from the north

Authors' comments: The source transcription was in A♭, I suspect reflecting that the fiddle was tuned low or that the tune was transcribed from a singer.

Comparable versions:
"Gonna Leave Old Arkansas" (151925-1), A. E. Ward's Plowboys, 10/25/1931, Columbia 15734-D

SINCLAIR CROCKER

Source: Sinclair Crocker
Collector: Miss Mittie Lea Adams
Location: Coffeesville, Yalobusha Co.

Fiddler's Reel (Mrs. McCloud's)

Comparable versions:

"Mrs. Mclouds Reel," O'Neil, Francis, *The Dance Music of Ireland* (Chicago: Lyon and Healey, 1907), no. 1418, 263

"Hop Out Ladies" (S 72-348-A), Henry Whitter, 2/1924, NYC, OKeh 40064

"Hop Light Lady" (9186-A), Fiddlin' John Carson & His Virginia Reelers, 06/30/1925, Atlanta, GA, OKeh 45011

"Hop High Ladies, The Cakes All Dough" (E 4933/34W), Uncle Dave Macon & His Fruit Jar Drinkers, 05/07/1927, NYC, Vocalion 5154

"McCloud's Reel" (E 30191), Kessinger Brothers, 06/25/1929, NYC, Brunswick 580

Other version in this book by Rev. J. E. Williams ("Scotch Hornpipe").

Mississippi Sawyer

Manuscript comments: "Played on the violin by Sinclair Crocker, Coffeeville.
This tune has been popular in this County among the old fiddlers for two centuries."

Comparable versions:

"Love from the Heart," George P. Knauff, *Virginia Reels*, vol. 4, no. 4 (Baltimore, 1839)

"Mississippi Sawyer" (W 148200-1), Gid Tanner and His Skillet Lickers, 04/08/1929, Atlanta, GA, Columbia 15420-D

"Mississippi Sawyer" (E 29271-), Kessinger Brothers, 02/05/1929, NYC, Brunswick 309

"Old Time Corn Shuckin' pt 1" (BVE 39270-2), Ernest Stoneman & the Blue Ridge Corn Shuckers, 07/27/1927, Bristol, TN, Victor 20835

Other versions of "Mississippi Sawyer" in this book by W. E. Claunch, Hardy Sharp, J. E. Shoemaker, Stephen B. Tucker, Rev. J. H. Wheeler, and Rev. J. E. Williams.

Old Zip Coon

Oh I went to Sandy Hollar 'tother afternoon and the first man I chanced to meet was Old Zip Coon.

He's a nimble feller and a very learned scholar for he plays a tune upon his banjo "Cooney in de Holler"

Chorus

Possum up a gum tree, Cooney on a stump Throw a stick a whizzin' Watch old Cooney jump

Ebry time de wild goose beckons to de swallar you can hear old Zip a play-in "Cooney in de Holler"

Oh, it's blue skin Lucy who has fall in
Love with me when I went 'tother
Afternoon to take some tea, Now what
do you think my blue skinned Lucy had
for supper? Why some chicken feet and
Possum heel with out a bit o' butter

Many things to talk about but don't know
which come first, Old Zip Coon drank some
liquor for to quench his thirst then he pick
de banjo strings until they shot and shiver
and he played de music faster till your
bones they start to quiver

Authors' comments: A widely known minstrel song from the 1800s purported to come from the lower section of Vicksburg known as Natchez Under-the-Hill, where a rough crowd danced, drank, and amused themselves.

Comparable versions:

"Zip Coon," Thos. Birch, NY, 1834 (www.loc.gov/item/sm1834.360780/)

"Natchez on the Hill," Knauff, George, *Virginia Reels*, vol. 1 (Baltimore: George Willig, Jr., 1839) (dc.lib.unc.edu/cdm/ref/collection/sheetmusic/id/9230)

"Turkey in the Straw" (B 26663-2), Henry Gilliland & A. C. "Eck" Robertson, 06/30/1922, NYC, Gennett 4974

"Turkey in the Straw" (1790-1), Dr. D. Dix Hollis, 06/1924, NYC, Paramount 33153

Other versions of "Old Zip Coon" in this book by Berlon Flynt and Mrs. Della Patterson ("Turkey in the Straw").

MRS. WILLIE DAVIS

Source: Unknown
Collector: Mrs. Willie Davis
Location: Forrest Co.

Go Long Liza

You go up the new cut road   I'll go down the lane   throw my hat in   a hollow stump

Out jumped Li-za   Jane   Go Long Li-za,   sweet little gal   Go Long Li-za,   Jane

Go Long Li-za,   sweet   little   gal   Ain't   that a   scandal and a   shame

Comparable versions:
Other versions of "Go Long Liza" in this book by Josephine Compton and Mr. G. E. Tartt.

CHARLIE EDMUNDSON

In a letter to the state director of the Federal Music Project dated August 13, 1936, field worker Mary Armstrong said: "I am enclosing a number of old fiddler's runes that I secured from Mr. Charlie Edmundson who lives on Route 1, Hattiesburg. He learned them years ago from an old fiddler by the name of Tom Dossett who lived in Forrest County all of his life."

Collector: Lois Armstrong

Location: Hattiesburg, Forrest Co.

Dutch Waltz

Comparable versions:

"Lauterbach Waltz," Boettger, Theo. G. (Philadelphia: G. Andre & Co., 1870) (www.loc.gov/item/sm1870.05557/)

Ford, Ira, *Traditional Music of America* (New York: Dutton, 1940), 139

"Lauterbach Waltz" (E 34422-A), Kessinger Brothers, 09/15/1930, NYC, Brunswick 567

"Where Has my Little Dog Gone" (C 2434-), Hoosier Hot Shots, 02/02/1939, Chicago, IL, Vocalion 04688

Other versions in this book by Richard Scovel ("Little Dog"), Billie Mansfield ("The Goose Girl"), and Rev. J. E. Williams ("Polly Put the Kettle On").

Eighth of January March

Authors' comments: According to Andy Kuntz at the Traditional Tune Archive [tunearch.org/wiki/Annotation:Eighth_of_Janu ary_(1)], the tune was originally titled "Jackson's Victory" after Andrew Jackson's defeat of the British at New Orleans on January 8, 1815. With the later decline in his reputation, the tune was renamed "The Eighth of January."

Comparable versions of "Eighth of January":
Ford, Ira, *Traditional Music of America* (New York: Dutton, 1940), 63
Arkansas Barefoot Boys (W 400229-B), 02/11/1928, Memphis, TN, OKeh 45217
Fox Chasers (W 5404166-A), 06/11/1930, San Antonio, TX, OKeh 45496
Ted Gossett's Band (GN 17041), 09/16/1930, Richmond, IN, Champion 16160
Other versions of "Eighth of January" in this book by Enos Canoy, W. E. Claunch, John Hatcher, Hardy Sharp, and J. A. Moorman.

Evening Star Waltz

Comparable versions: Seems to have derived from piano sheet music from the mid-1800s, but there is great variation in the versions below.

Lanner, Joseph with arranger Scherpf, John C., sheet music (New York: William Vanderbeek, 1849) (www.loc.gov/item/sm1849.110280/)

Emmett Lundy, Grayson Co., VA, Library of Congress field recording, Virginia, 1941 AFS 4940 B3

"Evening Star Waltz" (GE 12782), Da Costa Woltz's Southern Broadcasters, 05/1927, Richmond, IN, Gennett 6240

Jenny Lind Polka

Authors' comments: This was composed in 1846 as "Jenny Lind's Lieblings-Polka," attributed to the composer Anton Wallerstein and named for the famous operatic soprano Johanna Maria "Jenny" Lind (1820–1887)

Comparable versions:
Robert Kelley, "Jenny Lind polka and waltz" (New York: William Hall and Son, 1848) (www.loc.gov/item/sm1848.081390/)
"Jenny Lind Polka" (S 72-684-A), Henry Whitter's Virginia Breakdowners, 07/22/1924, NYC, OKeh 40211
"Heel and Toe Polka" (BVE 34004-2), Henry Fords Old Time Dance Orchestra, 12/02/1926, Dearborn, MI, Victor 19909
"Dance With a Girl With a Hole in Her Stocking" (GE 12799-A), Doc Roberts & Asa Martin, 05/15/1928, Richmond, IN, Gennett 6495
"Heel and Toe Polka" (W 400235-B), W. T. Narmour & S. W. Smith, 02/14/1929, Memphis, TN, OKeh 45276

Kiss Waltz

Authors' comments: m25, I suspect that should be a C natural.

Comparable versions:
"Kiss Waltz" (81733-2), North Carolina Ramblers, 09/18/1926, NYC, County 3508 CD
"Kiss Waltz" (AFS 04939 A06), Emmett Lundy, Grayson Co., VA, Library of Congress field recording, 1941

Rochester Schottische

Authors' comments: Vivian Williams writes: "'Rochester Schottische' was written in 1852 by William Rulison, who went to California for the Gold Rush, actually made some money (unlike most!), returned to his hometown of Rochester, NY, and opened up a music store." (www.voyagerrecords.com/LN371.htm)

Comparable versions:
"Rochester Schottische," Howe, Elias, *Musician's Omnibus* (Boston: Elias Howe, 1863–82), 56
"Rochester Schottische," Ford, Ira, *Traditional Music of America* (New York: Dutton, 1940), 60
"Patrick County Blues" (W 403123-A), John W. Spangler & Dave Pearson, Old Virginia Fiddlers, 10/14/1929, Richmond, IN, OKeh 45387
Other versions of "Rochester Schottische" in this book by Mrs. E. M. Purcell and Mrs. Ben Walker ("Schattiche #2").

Shoofly

Comparable versions:

"Shew! Fly, don't bother me," words by Billy Reeves & music by Frank Campbell (Boston: White, Smith & Perry, 1869) (memory.
   loc.gov/cgi-bin/query/r?ammem/AMALL:@field(NUMBER+@band(rpbaasm+0194)))

"Shoo Fly" (E 34478-A), Kessinger Brothers, 09/18/1930, NYC, Brunswick 554

"Shoo Fly" (C 1345-1), Crockett's Kentucky Mountaineers, 08/1931, NYC, Crown 3159

"Sho' Fly, Don't Bother Me" (E 3740/41 W), Uncle Dave Macon, 09/09/1926, NYC, Vocalion 15448

The Music Transcriptions

Sleepy Waltz

Soldier's Joy

Comparable versions:

Aird, James, *A Selection of Scotch, English, Irish and Foreign Airs*, vol. 1, no. 109 (1778)

"Soldier's Joy" (9189-A), Fiddlin' John Carson & His Virginia Reelers, 06/30/1925, Atlanta, GA, OKeh 45011

"Soldier's Joy" (GE 12747), Taylor's Kentucky Boys, 06/27, Richmond, IN, Silvertone 5060

"Soldier's Joy" (E29273), Kessinger Brothers, 02/05/1929, NYC, Brunswick 341

See other versions in this book by W. A. Bledsoe ("Farewell Mary Ann"), Dalton Brantley, W. E. Claunch, Charlie Edmondson, John Hatcher, W. E. Ray, Stephen B. Tucker, and Rev. J. E. Williams ("Rickets Hornpipe").

R. H. ELLIS

Source: R. H. Ellis
Collector: Mrs. Ida Burke
Location: Wyatte, Tate Co.

Buffalo Gals

Chorus

As I was walking down the street, down the street
a pretty girl I chanced to meet Under the silver moon
Oh she was chewing gum, chewing gum, chewing gum
Oh how she chawed that chewing gum with her two front teeth

Chorus:
Buffalo Gals won't you come out tonight, come out tonight, come out tonight

Buffalo Gals won't you come out tonight, come out tonight, come out tonight and dance by the light of the moon.

I asked if she would stop and talk, stop and talk, stop and talk
Her feet covered the whole sidewalk, whole sidewalk, whole sidewalk
She looked good to me. I asked her to be my wife, be my wife
Then I would be happy all my life

Comparable versions:
"Midnight Serenade," Knauff, George P., *Virginia Reels*, vol. 1, no. 4 (Baltimore, ca. 1839)
"Round Town Gals" (GEX 498-A), Ernest V. Stoneman & His Grayson County Boys, 02/02/1927, NYC, Gennett 6052
"Buffalo Gals" (8514-1-2), Pickard Family, 01/31/1929, NYC, Banner 6371
Versions of "Buffalo Gals" in this book by Babe Casey ("Grasshopper on a Sweet Tater Vine"), John Hatcher ("Buffalo Girl"), A. J. Howell ("Buffalo Girl"), Edward Kittrell, and Ben Wall.

MR. P. F. EZELL

Source: Mr. P. F. Ezell

Collector: Mrs. Flora Ashcroft

Location: Greenwood, Leflore Co.

Eighth of January Waltz

BERLON FLYNT

Source: Unknown
Collector: Berlon Flynt
Location: Collins, Covington Co.

Old Zip Coon

Authors' comments: The source transcription was in F, I suspect reflecting that the fiddle was tuned low. This is a widely known minstrel song from the 1800s purported to come from the lower section of Vicksburg known as Natchez Under-the-Hill, where a rough crowd danced, drank, and amused themselves.

Comparable versions:
"Zip Coon," Thos. Birch, New York, 1834 (www.loc.gov/item/sm1834.360780/)
"Natchez on the Hill," Knauff, George, *Virginia Reels*, vol. 1 (Baltimore: George Willig, Jr., 1839) (dc.lib.unc.edu/cdm/ref/collection/sheetmusic/id/9230)
"Turkey in the Straw" (B 26663-2), Henry Gilliland & A. C. "Eck" Robertson, 06/30/1922, NYC, Gennett 4974
"Turkey in the Straw" (1790-1), Dr. D. Dix Hollis, 06/1924, NYC, Paramount 33153
Other versions of "Old Zip Coon" in this book by Sinclair Crocker and Mrs. Della Patterson ("Turkey in the Straw")

J. C. FOSTER

Source: J. C. Foster

Collector: Mrs. Mary Foster Harper

Location: Edinburg, Leake Co.

A Hungry Confederate Soldier

The streets are all lone-ly and drear love, and all be-cause you are not here

love. If you were you would shed a sad tear love and o-pen your cup-board to me

My feet are all wet with dew, love
There's nothing so good as a hot stew, love
Oh, get up and do make some, pray do, love
And open your cupboard to me

Get out of that soft feather bed, love
And make me a pone of cornbread, love
I'm suffering now to be fed love
Do open your cupboard to me.

Authors' comments: Only the first verse was collected in the 1936 manuscript, but the instructions to the field workers specified that they should re-interview Hudson's subject and retrieve the melodies. The second and third verses are from Hudson's book *Folksongs of Mississippi and Their Background*.

Comparable versions:

Hudson, A. P., *Folksongs of Mississippi and Their Background* (Chapel Hill: University of North Carolina Press, 1936), 255

MRS. MAUD FREEMAN

Source: Mrs. Maud Freeman
Collector: Ida Burke
Location: Wyatte, Tate Co.

G & C Schottiche

Authors' comments: The 1940 census lists a Maud Freeman as white, born 1886, and married to Ira Freeman, a retail store merchant.

Comparable versions:
"Karo" (W 143004-), Uncle Jimmy Thompson, 11/01/1926, Atlanta, GA, Vocalion 15368
"The Long Eared Mule" (S 73378), Emmett Lundy & Ernest Stoneman, 05/27/1925, NYC, OKeh 40405
"Old Virginia Reel, Pt. 2" (W 81644-A), Fiddlin' John Powers & Family, 09/28/1927, Winston-Salem, NC, OKeh 45154
Other versions in this book by Cleve Bass ("Flop Eared Mule"), John Hatcher ("Long Eared Mule or Baldin"), and J. E. Shoemaker ("Gulfport").

CHARLEY GOFF

Source: Charley Goff
Collector: Mrs. Jessie Lane
Location: Lucedale, George Co.

Big Bill's in Jail, Boys

Authors' comments: The 1940 census lists a Mr. Goff as born 1889, white, head of household, married with six children. His occupation was listed as mail messenger for the Post Office.

Comparable versions:
"Roll on the Ground" (B-377/2), Billy Golden, 09/01/1903, Philadelphia, Victor 616 (www.loc.gov/jukebox/recordings/detail/id/253/)
"Big Ball in Town" (W 145049-1), Gid Tanner & His Skillet Lickers, 10/31/1927, Atlanta, GA, Columbia 15204
"Big Ball Uptown" (BVE 47022-1-2), Taylor Griggs Louisiana Melody Makers, 09/13/1928, Memphis, TN, Victor 21768
Other versions in this book by Thaddeus Willingham ("Roll on the Ground").

Whistling Rufus

Authors' comments: This is a very condensed version of the original late 1800s sheet music.

Comparable versions:

"Whistling Rufus," words by Kerry Mills (New York: F.A. Mills Music, 1899) (clio.lib.olemiss.edu/cdm/ref/collection/sharris/
    id/1663)

"Rufus Blossom" (E 5026/27W). Sam & Kirk McGee w/Maizi Todd, 05/11/1927, NYC, Vocalion 5170

"Whistling Rufus" (E 30193-), Kessinger Brothers, 06/25/1929, NYC, Brunswick 521

"Whistling Rufus" (W 151921), Gid Tanner & His Skillet Lickers, 10/24/1930, Atlanta, GA, Columbia 15730-D

Other version in this book by Mrs. J. C. King.

JIM GOOCH

Source: Jim Gooch

Collector: Mrs. Jeff Purcell

Location: Macel, Tallahatchie Co.

Old Hen Cackled

Authors' comments: The source transcription was in F, I suspect reflecting that the fiddle was tuned low. The source is described as Afro-American in the manuscript.

Comparable versions:

"The Old Hen Cackled and the Rooster is Going to Crow" (8375-A-B), John Carson, 06/14/1923, Atlanta, GA, OKeh 4890

"Hen Cackle" (81630-2), Gid Tanner & Riley Puckett, 03/08/1924, NYC, Columbia 110-D

"Cackling Hen" (9307-A), J. D. Harris, 1925, Asheville, NC, OKeh 45024

Other versions of "Old Hen Cackled" in this book by Mrs. M. B. Brister ("Old Hen Cackled on the Pot"), John Brown, W. M. Collom ("Rabbit in a Ditch"), and Dr. F. H. Smith.

B. M. GUILETTE

Source: Unknown
Collector: B. M. Guilette
Location: Mississippi

Liza Jane

Chorus

Comparable versions:

"Cindy in the Meadows" (81706-1), Samantha Bumgarner & Eva Davis, 4/22/1924, NYC, Columbia 167-D

"Cindy" (W 143867-), Riley Puckett & Clayton McMichen, 04/02/1927, Atlanta, GA, Columbia 15232-D

"Get Along Home, Miss Cindy" (BVE 41853-2), Pope's Arkansas Mountaineers, 02/06/1928, Memphis, TN, Victor 21577

Other versions in this book by Charlie Addison ("Want to Go to Meeting"), John Brown ("Cindy"), W. E. Claunch ("Cindy"), Enos Canoy ("Where'd You Get Your Whiskey"), Mrs. R. C. Clifton ("Miss Cindy"), Frank Kittrell ("Cindy Jane"), Mrs. Joe McCoy ("Her Cheeks Are Like the Cherry"), Hardy Sharp ("Liza Jane"), Rev. J. E. Williams ("Cindy Waltz"), and Thaddeus Willingham ("Miss Cindy")

Spanish Waltz

5 Chorus

Authors' comments: The source transcription was in D♭, I suspect reflecting that the fiddle was tuned low. The "A" part bears some resemblance to the "A" part of Narmour & Smith's "Avalon Quickstep" (404082-A), 6/7/1930, San Antonio, TX, OKeh 45469.

MRS. R. L. HALBERG

Source: Mrs. R. L. Halberg
Collector: Herbert Halpert
Location: Vicksburg, Warren Co.

Whoa Mule

I'm go-in' down to the par-sons Now Li-za you keep cool, 'ain't got time to

kiss you now, I'm bu-sy with this mule Whoa! Ah tell you, Whoa' ah

say Keep yo seat Miss Li-za Jane and hold on to dat sleigh

Manuscript comments: Remembered from childhood by Mrs. Halberg and her cousin Mr. Watts whose father (Richard Fenni-more) used to sing to them.

Authors' comments: The 1940 census lists a Mr. Robert L. Halberg as age 47, a white salesman in a retail hardware store, living with wife and two children.

Comparable versions:
"Whoa Mule" (1487/8/9), Bill Chitwood and Bud Landress, 11/21/1924, NYC, Brunswick 2811
"Whoa, Mule" (S 73120-A), The Hillbillies, 01/15/1925, NYC, OKeh 40376
"Hold on to the Sleigh" (E 3720/21), Uncle Dave Macon, 09/09/1926, NYC, Brunswick 114
Other versions in this book by J. W. McDonough ("My Old Coon Dog") and Thaddeus Willingham ("Humpbacked Mule").

MRS. J. M. T. HAMILTON

Source: Mrs. J. M. T. Hamilton and W. R. Flanagan
Collector: Bessie Mae Tartt and Mrs. Lois Armstrong
Location: Meridian, Lauderdale Co.

The Yankees Are Coming

Manuscript comments: It is the same tune as "The Campbells Are Coming," which tune I have copied from an old book.

Authors' comments: As it was copied from a book, the double stops most likely represent a piano harmony, not fiddle double stops. As fiddle double stops, they would be quite demanding to execute, but simple on piano.

Comparable versions:

"Campbells are coming, O ho," Robert Bremner, *Scots Reels* (1757), 83 (imslp.org/wiki/A_Collection_of_Scots_Reels_or_ Country_Dances_(Bremner,_Robert)

"Medley of Reels: Campbells Are Coming" (BVE 34528-4), Mellie Dunham & His Orch., 02/03/1926, Camden, NJ, Victor 20537

MRS. WILLIAM W. HARRISON

Source: Mrs. William W. Harrison
Collector: Mrs. Flora Ashcraft
Location: Greenwood, Leflore Co.

Buckeyed Rabbit

The coon clam up de simmon tree the possoms on on de ground De

possom say to Mr Coon Can't you fling me some simmons down?

Refrain:

Buckeyed Rabbit who who Buckeyed rabbit who Buckeyed rabbit who who buckeyed rabbit who

MRS. J. A. HICKMAN

Mrs. J. A. Hickman
Collector: Modena Hickman
Location: Copiah Co.

To Merileo

Had an old hat that had no brim,   looked like a crow's nest hanging on a limb.

To Me-ri-leo! To Me-ri-leo! You won't go home you're here in the   way, So choose you out a

part - ner,   who'll help   pay your way,   To   Me-ri - leo!   To   Me-ri - leo!

Had an old coat that had no tail,
looked like a sheep skin hanging on a nail.
To Me-ri-leo! To Me-ri-leo!

Had an old shoe that had no heel,
looked like a stump in the middle of a field.
To Me-ri-leo! To Me-ri-leo!

Had an old cap that had no peak,
looked like a terrapin fording on a creek.
To Me-ri-leo! To Me-ri-leo!

Manuscript comments: "This old fiddling tune was very popular seventy-five years ago. Mr. Hickman beat straws to the tune many times when he was a young man 40 years ago and it continued to be popular for a good many years later. Used in eastern section of Copiah County. Melody written by Modena Hickman."

The Music Transcriptions

DAVE HOLLAND

Source: Dave Holland
Collector: Mrs. Mary T. Jackson
Location: Ingram's Mill, Desoto Co.

Plowman's Drag

LEE HOLT

Source: Lee Holt via Eddie Scovel
Collector: Miss Elizabeth Gordon
Location: Pascagoula, Jackson Co.

Grand Bay Schottische

Manuscript comments: "As far as I have been able to discover, this piece has never been published. Grand Bay is in Alabama, about 18 miles east of Pascagoula. Mr. Eddie Scovel, the man who played this on the guitar for me, learned it there from 'old blind Lee Fort.' Mr. Fort died about three years ago. He was blind from smallpox. This piece is generally ascribed to him. He was a violinist who played for dances for miles around."

Authors' comments: This piece ends on the "A" part with the last note dropped to C as shown in the last measure.

FLORENCE HOSKINS

Florence Hoskins
Collector: Mrs. B. H. Brown
Location: Leflore Co.

The Jay Bird

A Jay Bird sit-ing on top of a saw pit Sally ma - ri no, ho! Watching of a

blue bird courtin of a tom tit, Sally ma - ri no, ho! The jay bird laughed at a sight so cur-i-ous

Sally ma - ri no, ho! This made the blue bird migh-ty fu-ri-ous Sally ma - ri no, ho!

The bluebird whipped the jaybird's wife
Sally ma-ri no, ho!
This well nigh too that jay bird's life
Sally ma-ri no, ho!

The jaybird flew to Arkansas
Sally ma-ri no, ho!
But still that bluebird stuck in his craw
Sally ma-ri no, ho!

The jaybird died of the melancholy
Sally ma-ri no, ho!
Because he had committed such a folly
Sally ma-ri no, ho!

But to his son he made this request
Sally ma-ri no, ho!
Never to spoil the bluebird's nest

Authors' comments: The source transcription, from a singer, was in B♭.

A. J. HOWELL

A. J. Howell
Collector: Mr. G. B. Langston
Location: Dublin Coahoma Co.

Buffalo Girl

Authors' comments: The 1940 census lists an Arnold Howell, born 1910, as a single white male working as a clerk.

Comparable versions:
"Midnight Serenade," Knauff, George P., *Virginia Reels*, vol. 1, no. 4 (Baltimore, ca. 1839)
"Round Town Gals" (GEX 498-A), Ernest V. Stoneman & His Grayson County Boys, 02/02/1927, NYC, Gennett 6052
"Buffalo Gals" (8514-1-2), Pickard Family, 01/31/1929, NYC, Banner 6371
Versions of "Buffalo Gals" in this book by Babe Casey ("Grasshopper On a Sweet Tater Vine"), R. H. Ellis, John Hatcher ("Buffalo Girl"), Edward Kittrell, and Ben Wall.

Lazy Kate

Authors' comments: This version is unrelated to other versions, except by title.

R. N. HUDSPETH

Source: R. N. Hudspeth
Collector: Mary T. Boone
Location: Ashland, Benton Co.

Georgia Camp Meeting

Authors' comments: Along with this tune, Kerry Mills also wrote "Redwing" and "Whistling Rufus," represented in this book by
   Richard Scovel and Mrs. J. C. King, respectively.

Comparable versions:

"At a Georgia Camp Meeting," Kerry Mills words and music, 1897 imslp.org/wiki/At_a_Georgia_Campmeeting_(Mills,_Kerry)
"Georgia Camp Meeting" (W 148319-2), Leake County Revelers, 04/16/1929, Atlanta, GA, Columbia 15409-D
"Choctaw County Rag" (BVE 62532-2), Ray Brothers, 05/28/1930, Memphis, TN, Victor V40313
"Peaches Down in Georgia" (BVE 56616-2), Georgia Yellow Hammers, 11/27/1929, Atlanta, GA, Victor 23683

MR. JENNINGS

Source: Mr. Jennings
Collector: Juliette Baab
Location: Vicksburg, Warren Co.

Seaside Polka

Manuscript comments: "Old fiddlers tune, taught me about 8 years ago by a Mr. Jennings, a banker, now deceased."

Comparable versions:
Mellie Dunham's 50 Fiddlin' Dance Tunes (New York: Carl Fischer, 1926) #44, 20
"Women Wear No Clothes at All" (400290-A), Bob Larkin & His Music Makers, 02/22/1928, Memphis, TN, OKeh 45349

J. H. JOHNSON

Source: J. H. Johnson
Collector: Mrs. D. Joiner
Location: Greenwood, Leflore Co.

Possum Up a Simmon Tree

Oh my darling I'm bound for Texas It nearly kills me Oh Lord have mercy.

Possum up de simmon tree, can't get im down   Possum up de simmon tree, holler for the hound

Possum up de simmon tree, cain't get im down   Swinging them pretty gals all around

---

Comparable versions:
"Roll them Simelons," A. P. Hudson, *Folk Tunes from Mississippi* (National Service Bureau pamphlet, NYC, 1937)
Other version in this book by W. S. Robertson ("Roll them Simelons").

REV. R. R. KEITHLEY

Source: Rev. R. R. Keithley

Collector: Mrs. Pearl H. Steele

Location: Shuqualak, Noxubee Co.

Gee Whiz

MRS. J. C. KING

Source: Mrs. J. C. King
Collector: Mrs. Evelyn Nation
Location: Purvis, Lamar Co.

Whistlin' Rufus

Way down South where the shy ole pos-sum climbed up a sy-ca-more tree   There   lives a coon called

Ruf-us Blos-som, Black as a nig-ger could be.   Ruf-us had a head like a big sledge ham-mer mouth like a ter-ri-ble

scar   But no one could touch him, Old Al-a-ba-ma, when he played on his big gui - tar   Don't make no

blun - der, you could not lose him a per-fect won - der you had to   choose

a great mu - sic - ian   with a high po - sit - ion Whist-ling   Rufus the one man band

---

Manuscript comments: "These songs were sung for my by Mrs. J.C. King of Purvis Miss.
She learned them as a child listening to the turpentine Negroes sing them at their work boxing the trees."

Comparable versions:
"Whistling Rufus," words by Kerry Mills, (New York: F.A. Mills Music, 1899) (clio.lib.olemiss.edu/cdm/ref/collection/sharris/id/1663)
"Rufus Blossom" (E 5026/27W), Sam & Kirk McGee w/Maizi Todd, 05/11/1927, NYC, Vocalion 5170
"Whistling Rufus" (E 30193-), Kessinger Brothers, 06/25/1929, NYC, Brunswick 521
"Whistling Rufus" (W 151921), Gid Tanner & His Skillet Lickers, 10/24/1930, Atlanta, GA, Columbia 15730-D
Other version in this book by Charley Goff.

EDWARD KITTRELL

Source: Mrs. Kittrell and Edward Kittrell, 15 yrs. old
Collector: Mrs. Flora Ashcraft
Location: Greenwood, Leflore Co.

Buffalo Gals

As I was walking down the street, Down the street, Down the street
A pretty girl I chanced to meet, under the silvery moon

Buffalo Gals won't you come out tonight, come out tonight come out tonight
Buffalo Gals won't you come out tonight, and dance by the light of the moon

Comparable versions:
"Midnight Serenade," Knauff, George P., *Virginia Reels*, vol. 1, no. 4 (Baltimore, ca. 1839)
"Round Town Gals" (GEX 498-A), Ernest V. Stoneman & His Grayson County Boys, 02/02/1927, NYC, Gennett 6052
"Buffalo Gals" (8514-1-2), Pickard Family, 01/31/1929, NYC, Banner 6371
Versions of "Buffalo Gals" in this book by Babe Casey ("Grasshopper On a Sweet Tater Vine"), R. H. Ellis, John Hatcher ("Buffalo Girl"), A. J. Howell ("Buffalo Girl"), and Ben Wall.

Good Night Waltz

Comparable versions:
Leake Co Revelers (W 143970-1), 04/13/1927, New Orleans, LA, Columbia 15189-D
Kessinger Brothers (AL 219), 02/11/1928, Ashland, KY, Brunswick 220
Other version in this book by Alvis Massengale.

ELMER LADNER

Source: Elmer Ladner

Collector: Mrs. Evelyn Nation

Location: Purvis, Lamar Co.

Paddy's Welcome

Authors' comments: The 1940 census lists a Mr. E. A. Ladner as a 54 yr. old white male married to Laura E. Ladner, working as a farmer.

Untitled Jig

Manuscript comments: "This tune sounds like an Irish melody and it probably is since many of the people here are Scotch-Irish."

Comparable versions:
Elias Howe, *The Complete Preceptor for the Accordeon* (Boston: Elias Howe, 1843), 38 (imslp.org/wiki/The_Complete_Preceptor_for_the_Accordeon_(Howe,_Elias)
"St. Patrick's Day - Medley Jigs" (7013), Joseph Samuels, 11/07/1919, NYC, Edison 50870
(archive.org/details/JosephSamuels-St.PatricksDayMedley1920)

JERRY LARCO

Source: Jerry Larco
Collector: Unknown
Location: Mississippi

Merry Widow Waltz

Manuscript comments: "This party is very interested in music and has ambitions to learn if an opportunity was given—had never before been accompanied. Fiddled by Jerry Larco, Lakeshore school house accompanied by Marie P. Weber."

Authors' comments: Larco only plays the first strain of the full composition. The Leake County Revelers made a 78rpm recording of an unrelated melody with the same title.

Comparable versions:
Victor Dance Orchestra, 07/15/1907, From the operetta *The Merry Widow* by Franz Lehár, Victor 16577 www.loc.gov/jukebox/recordings/detail/id/1303/

ANNIE LEE

Source: Annie Lee
Collector: Mrs. I. A. Stewart
Location: Hinds Co.

Raggedy Ann

Comparable versions:

Ford, Ira, *Traditional Music of America* (New York: Dutton, 1940), 44

"Ragtime Annie" (B 26667-2), A. C. "Eck" Robertson, 07/01/1922, NYC, Victor 19149

"Ragtime Annie" (W 142642-1), North Carolina Ramblers, 09/18/1926, NYC, Columbia 1512-D

"Ragtime Annie" (SA 211-), Smith's Garage Fiddle Band, 03/1929, San Antonio, TX, Vocalion 5306

MRS. LOUISE LONG

Source: Unknown
Collector: Mrs. Louise Long
Location: Carroll Co.

Carve Dat Possum

Authors' comments: The source transcription was in B♭, I suspect reflecting that the fiddle was tuned low. This is not the usual melody that accompanies this title. Mrs. Long may have been the source for this tune. She was a music teacher for the WPA, widowed with two daughters and living in Vaiden as of the 1940 census.

MRS. R. S. LOVE

Source: Mrs. R. S. Love
Collector: Mrs. W. F. Townsend
Location: Itta Bena, Leflore Co.

White Cat, Black Cat

When you catch a white cat, shave him, shave him When you catch a black cat, shave him, tail and all

White cat, black cat,   any cat at   all, Any kind of old   cat, shave him tail and   all

---

Authors' comments: The source transcription was in B♭, I suspect reflecting that the fiddle was tuned low.

Comparable versions:
Phil. Rice, *The Correct Method for the Banjo, with or without a master* (Boston: Oliver Ditson, 1886), 35

BILLIE MANSFIELD AND CHRIS MARTIN

Source: Billie Mansfield and Chris Martin
Collector: Mrs. A. B. Newman
Location: Cleveland, Bolivar Co.

Fisher's Hornpipe

Authors' comments: This original transcriber was not clear or had trouble notating time. There is no time signature but 12/8 seems to encompass most of the measures. m8 seems to be comprised of three quarter notes followed by two eighths. In m9–11 the transcriber seems to have miscounted by one eighth, and does not indicate the rests.

Comparable versions:
"Fisher's Hornpipe," J. Fishar (ca. 1780), *A New & Highly Improved Violin Preceptor* (Utica, NY: William Williams, 1817), 23
"Old Zip Coon and Medley Reels" (GE 13833), Doc Roberts & Asa Martin, 05/15/1928, Richmond, IN, Gennett 6495
"Fisher's Hornpipe" (E 3972W), The Hillbillies, 10/21/1926, NYC, Vocalion 5017
"Fisher's Hornpipe" (6713-), Clayton McMichen, Hoyt "Slim" Bryant & Jerry Wallace, 06/01/1939, NYC, Decca 2649
"Texas Breakdown" (W 404065-B). W. T. Narmour & S. W. Smith, 06/06/1930, San Antonio, TX, OKeh 45492 (has only the "A" part in common)
Other versions of "Fisher's Hornpipe" in this book by Alvis Massengale, Mr. N. Odom, Stephen B. Tucker, and "Unknown."

Goose Girl Waltz

Comparable versions:

"Lauterbach Waltz," Boettger, Theo. G. (Philadelphia: G. Andre & Co., 1870) (www.loc.gov/item/sm1870.05557/)

Ford, Ira, *Traditional Music of America* (New York: Dutton, 1940), 139

"Lauterbach Waltz" (E 34422-A), Kessinger Brothers, 09/15/1930, NYC, Brunswick 567

"Where Has My Little Dog Gone" (C 2434-), Hoosier Hot Shots, 02/02/1939, Chicago, IL, Vocalion 04688

Other versions in this book by Richard Scovel ("Little Dog"), Charlie Edmondson ("Dutch Waltz"), and Rev. J. E. Williams ("Polly Put the Kettle On").

Irish Washerwoman

Comparable versions:

Neil Gow, *A Third Collection of Strathspey Reels &c for the Piano-forte, Violin and Violoncello* (1792), 31 imslp.org/
wiki/A_Third_Collection_of_Strathspey_Reels,_etc._(Gow,_Niel)

"Medley of Jigs: Irish Washerwoman" (BVE 34528-4), Mellie Dunham, 02/03/1926, Camden, NJ, Victor 20537

"Irish Washerwoman" (GE 13836), Doc Roberts & Asa Martin (as Jim Burke), 05/14/1928, Richmond IN, Silvertone 8176

Other versions of "Irish Washerwoman" in this book by Mr. T. W. Cooper and unknown ("Virginia Reel").

MR. JOHN McCARTIE

Source: Mr. John McCartie
Collector: Anna Wallace
Location: Forrest Co.

Billy Boy Waltz

Authors' comments: The source transcription was in E♭. Judging by the double stops, I have moved it to F. This song was very popular in the Mississippi Department of Archives and History song collection, with twenty-five versions. My mother sang it to me when I was a child.

Comparable versions:
The Naughty Naughty Girls Songster, 1867, 22
Billy Cotton's Old Black Joe Songster, 1873
"Billy Boy" (BVE 33653), Frank Crummit, 12/22/1925, Camden, NJ, Victor 19945
"Charming Billy" (9600-A), Andrew Jenkins & Mary Lee Eskew, ca. 03/1926, Atlanta, GA, OKeh 6204
"Billy Boy" (WC 2846-A), Louise Massey & the Westerners, 12/09/1939, Chicago, IL, Vocalion 15358

Run Nigger, Run

Manuscript comments: He heard it played in Civil War days when Paderoles were the order of the day."

Comparable versions:
"Run Nigger, Run," Allen, William, Francis, *Slave Songs of the United States* (New York: A. Simpson, 1867) #110, 89
"Run Nigger, Run" (8709-A), Fiddling John Carson, 08/27/1924, Atlanta, GA, OKeh 40230
"Run Nigger, Run" (667/668), Uncle Dave Macon, 04/13/1925, NYC, Vocalion 15032
"Run Boy, Run" (BVE 56361-2), Eck Robertson & Dr. J. B. Cranfill, 10/10/1929, Dallas, TX, Victor V40205
Other versions of "Run Nigger, Run" in this book by Mrs. M. B. Brister, W. E. Claunch, Stephen B. Tucker, Mrs. A. Tynes, Mrs. Louise Walker Wallace, and Thaddeus Willingham.

HENRY McCLATCHING

Source: Henry McClatching
Collector: Dalton Brantley
Location: Wyatte, Tate Co.

Nigger in the Tater House

I fooled old Master seven years I'spect to fool him seven more Pooh, Pooh— Pooh

I shucked the corn in the loft
I slop the hogs in the trough
Pooh, Pooh

Manuscript comments: "Melody and words were learned by Mr. Dalton Brantly of Wyette from Henry McClatching, 80 year-old negro of Wyette. Written down with assistance of Raymond Williams of Senatoba."

Possum Up the Simmon Tree

Possum up the simmon tree, racoon on the ground

Wrap your tail around a limb and shake some simmons down

Nigger in the cotton patch, White man in the
   house
Nigger said white man don't mind you will take
   the gout

The sun shines all day, the moon shines all night
De sun and moon both makes so suits the nigger
   all right

De squirrel he run up the tree, the rabbit he runs
   in a hole
De squirrel and rabbit can't beat the mole

Manuscript comments: African American source.

MRS. JOE McCOY

Source: Mrs. Joe McCoy
Collector: Mrs. H. H. Weldy
Location: McLain, Greene Co.

Her Cheeks Are Like the Cherry

Authors' comments: A Mrs. Jae B. McCoy is listed in the 1940 census as born 1892, white, with six children and a husband, working in a dry cleaning shop as a presser.

Comparable versions:
"Cindy in the Meadows" (81706-1), Samantha Bumgarner & Eva Davis, 4/22/1924, NYC, Columbia 167-D
"Cindy" (W 143867-), Riley Puckett & Clayton McMichen, 04/02/1927, Atlanta, GA, Columbia 15232-D
"Get Along Home, Miss Cindy" (BVE 41853-2), Pope's Arkansas Mountaineers, 02/06/1928, Memphis, TN, Victor 21577
Other versions in this book by Charlie Addison ("Want to Go to Meeting"), John Brown ("Cindy"), W. E. Claunch ("Cindy"), Enos Canoy ("Where'd You Get Your Whiskey"), Mrs. R. C. Clifton ("Miss Cindy"), B. M. Guilette ("Liza Jane"), Frank Kittrell ("Cindy Jane"), Hardy Sharp ("Liza Jane"), Rev. J. E. Williams ("Cindy Waltz"), and Thaddeus Willingham ("Miss Cindy").

I'm Gwine to My Shanty

Chorus

Serenade

Authors' comments: In the manuscript m6 totaled three beats, so I have indicated a time change, although the manuscript
did not.

The Music Transcriptions

J. W. McDonough

Source: J. W. McDonough
Collector: Charlie F. South
Location: Ripley, Tippah Co.

My Old Coon Dog

Once I had an old coon dog as blind as he could be but ev-ry night at su-per time I believe that dog could

see Whoa Mule I tell you, Whoa Mule I say Tie a knot in that mare's ta-il and he'll run a-way

Somebody stole my old coon dog. I wish they'd
bring him back
To run the big hog over the fence the little ones
thru the crack
Whoa Mule I tell you, Whoa Mule I say
Tie a knot in that mare's tail and he'll run away

Possum up a simmon tree, a raccoon on the
ground
The raccoon said you son-of-a-gun shake them
simmons down
Whoa Mule I tell you, Whoa Mule I say
Tie a knot in that mare's tail and he'll run away

Watch that mule go around the hill, Watch him
how he sails
Watch him how he shakes his ears and how he
shakes his tail
Whoa Mule I tell you, Whoa Mule I say
Tie a knot in that mare's tail and he'll run away

Comparable versions:
"Whoa Mule" (1487/8/9), Bill Chitwood and Bud Landress, 11/21/1924, NYC, Brunswick 2811
"Whoa, Mule" (S 73120-A), The Hillbillies, 01/15/1925, NYC, OKeh 40376
"Hold on to the Sleigh" (E 3720/21), Uncle Dave Macon, 09/09/1926, NYC, Brunswick 114
Other versions in this book by Mrs. R. L. Halberg ("Whoa Mule") and Thaddeus Willingham ("Humpbacked Mule").

VERTIS McFARLAND

Source: Vertis McFarland
Collector: Mrs. Ava White
Location: Bovina, Warren Co.

Liza Jane

Law, Law, Wil‑ly, Liz‑a Jane, Liz‑a Jane, Law, Law, Wil‑ly, Liz‑a Jane, Liz‑a Jane,

The rea‑son I love old Wil‑ly, so, he make five dol‑lahs and he give me fouh, Liz‑a Jane, Liz‑a Jane

Law, Law, Wil‑ly, Liz‑a Jane, Liz‑a Jane, Law, Law, Wil‑ly, Liz‑a Jane, Liz‑a Jane,

Authors' comments: This is an unfamiliar tune for a well-known title.

EVERETT MITCHELL

Source: Everett Mitchell, 13 years old
Collector: Leona R. Vinson
Location: Aberdeen, Monroe Co.

Liza Jane

Whoo-pee Li-za, Pretty little girl. Whoo-pee Li-za Jane Whoo-pee

Li-za, Pretty little girl. she come down on the train

Comparable versions:

"Old Liza Jane" (13302), Uncle Am Stuart, 06/1924, NYC, Vocalion 14846

"Liza Jane" (140018-1), Riley Puckett, 09/11/1924, NYC, Columbia 15014-D

"Goodbye Liza Jane" (9596-A), Fiddlin' John Carson & His Virginia Reelers, 03/11/1926, Atlanta, GA, OKeh 45049

Other versions of "Liza Jane" in this book by Enos Canoy ("Where'd You Get Your Whiskey"), Horace Kinard, Everett Mitchell, J. P. Reece ("I Ain't Gonna Leave Her by Herself"), and Thaddeus Willingham ("Liza Jane" and "Want a Little Water Johnny").

J. E. MOORMAN

Source: J. E. Moorman
Collector: Mrs. Jeff Purcell, Itta Bena
Location: Webb, Tallahatchie Co.

Billie in the Low Ground

Authors' comments: The source transcription was in E♭, I suspect reflecting that the fiddle was tuned high.

Black Eyed Susan

Comparable versions:

"Black Eyed Susie" (81635-1), Gid Tanner and Riley Puckett, 03/08/1924, NYC, Columbia 119-D

"Black Eyed Susie" (GE 13040), Fiddlin' Doc Roberts, 09/1927, Richmond, IN, Gennett 6257

"Black Eyed Susie" (BVE 39747), J. P. Nestor, 08/01/1927, Bristol, TN, Victor 21070

Other versions of "Black Eyed Susan" in this book by John Brown, W. E. Claunch ("Black Eyed Susie"), John Hatcher, and Thaddeus Willingham ("Black Eyed Susie") in this book.

Eighth of January

Manuscript comments: "The following old fiddler's tunes were supplied by J.A. Moorman, Webb. Miss, age 43. All of these, he learned from his father who was a fiddler."

Comparable versions of "Eighth of January":
Ford, Ira, *Traditional Music of America* (New York: Dutton, 1940), 63
Arkansas Barefoot Boys (W 400229-B), 02/11/1928, Memphis, TN, OKeh 45217
Fox Chasers (W 5404166-A), 06/11/1930, San Antonio, TX, OKeh 45496
Ted Gossett's Band (GN 17041), 09/16/1930, Richmond, IN, Champion 16160
Other versions of "Eighth of January" in this book by Enos Canoy, W. E. Claunch, Charlie Edmundson, John Hatcher, and Hardy Sharp.

Fannie Logan

Honey Babe

Comparable version:

"If I Lose I Don't Care" (W 144509-1), Charlie Poole & the North Carolina Ramblers, 07/25/1927, NYC, Columbia 15215

Lazy Kate

Authors' comments: This version is unrelated to others by this name.

Old Kicking Mule

Old Mollie Hare

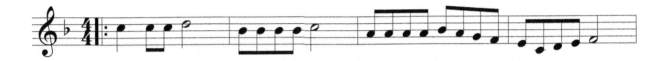

Comparable versions:

"Largo's Fairy Dance," Gow, John and Andrew, *A Collection of Slow Airs, Strathspeys & Reels*, vol. 5 (London: Wm. Campbell, ca. 1795), 19

Christy's Panorama Songster (New York: W.H. Murphy, ca. 1850s)

"Old Molly Hare," Fiddling Power & Family, 9/28/1927, Winston-Salem, NC, OKeh 45628

Other versions in this book by W. A. Bledsoe, Mrs. M. B. Brister, W. E. Claunch, J. A. Moorman, J. E. Shoemaker, and two by "Unknown."

Picayune Butler

Authors' comments: John "Picayune" Butler of New Orleans may well have been the originator of the Jim Crow song, dance, and character. He was known in the Mississippi and Ohio River regions in the 1850s. See Andy Kuntz's article in *Fiddler Magazine*, Summer 2012, 31 for more info on Picayune Butler, the man.

Comparable versions:
"Old Granny Rattletrap" (13322), Uncle Am Stuart, 06/1924, NYC, Vocalion 14888
"Fire in the Mountain" (9845-A), Fiddlin' John Carson & His Virginia Reelers, 11/21/1926, Atlanta, GA, OKeh 45068
"Hog Eye" (BVE 41858-2), Pope's Arkansas Mountaineers, 02/06/1928, Memphis, TN, Victor 21295
"Mississippi Square Dance, Pt. 1" (W 404740-B), Freeny's Barn Dance Band, 12/16/1930, Jackson, MS, OKeh 45533

MR. N. ODOM

Source: Mr. N. Odom
Collector: Mrs. S. A. Jones
Location: Cleveland, Bolivar Co.

Fisher's Hornpipe

Manuscript comments: "Written from memory as I used to play accompaniment for Mr. N. Odom on violin."

Comparable versions:
"Fisher's Hornpipe," J. Fishar (ca. 1780) *A New & Highly Improved Violin Preceptor* (Utica, NY: William Williams, 1817), 23
"Old Zip Coon and Medley Reels" (GE 13833), Doc Roberts & Asa Martin, 05/15/1928, Richmond, IN, Gennett 6495
"Fisher's Hornpipe" (E 3972W), The Hillbillies, 10/21/1926, NYC, Vocalion 5017
"Fisher's Hornpipe" (6713-), Clayton McMichen, Hoyt "Slim" Bryant & Jerry Wallace, 06/01/1939, NYC, Decca 2649
"Texas Breakdown" (W 404065-B), W. T. Narmour & S. W. Smith, 06/06/1930, San Antonio, TX, OKeh 45492 (has only the "A" part in common)
Other versions of "Fisher's Hornpipe" in this book by Billie Mansfield, Alvis Massengale, Stephen B. Tucker, and "Unknown."

MRS. DELLA PATTERSON

Source: Unknown
Collector: Mrs. Della Patterson
Location: Humphreys Co.

Turkey in the Straw

As I went dri-ving down the road, I met Mr. Hopper and I met Mr. Toad

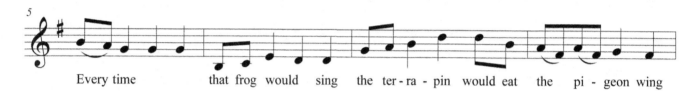

Every time that frog would sing the ter-ra-pin would eat the pi-geon wing

Tur-key in the Straw Tur-key in the Hay Turkey in the high grass, git out of my way

High ball, low ball, no ball at all Whistle up a tune called Turkey in the Straw

---

Authors' comments: The source transcription was in F, I suspect reflecting that the fiddle was tuned low. A widely known minstrel song from the 1800s purported to come from the lower section of Vicksburg known as Natchez Under-the-Hill, where a rough crowd danced, drank, and amused themselves.

Comparable versions:

"Zip Coon" (New York: Thos. Birch, 1834) (www.loc.gov/item/sm1834.360780/)

"Natchez on the Hill," Knauff, George, *Virginia Reels*, vol. 1 (Baltimore: George Willig Jr., 1839) (dc.lib.unc.edu/cdm/ref/collection/sheetmusic/id/9230)

"Turkey in the Straw" (B 26663-2), Henry Gilliland & A. C. "Eck" Robertson, 06/30/1922, NYC, Gennett 4974

"Turkey in the Straw" (1790-1), Dr. D.D. Dix Hollis, 06/1924, NYC, Paramount 33153

Other versions of "Old Zip Coon" in this book by Sinclair Crocker and Berlon Flynt.

MRS. EDWIN PEASE

Source: Mrs. Edwin Pease
Collector: Mrs. Renfro Seaton
Location: Gunnison, Bolivar Co.

Run Liza Jane

Heap Big Taters on Sand-y Land Run Liza Jane Heap Big Taters on Sandy Land

Run Liza Jane Run, Run, Run Run Liza Jane

Manuscript comments: "This was sung to her when a child by her grandfather."

MRS. JEFF PURCELL

Source: Mrs. Jeff Purcell
Collector: Mrs. E. M. Purcell
Location: Iuka, Tallahatchie Co.

I Love Somebody

I love some-body, yes I do, and I know some-body loves me too.

Manuscript comments: "This is an old fiddler's tune I heard when a small child. There are words also but I recall just those I have written. The tune was not new when I heard it but I do not know it's age."

Authors' comments: The source transcription from a singer was in E♭, so I have moved it to a more fiddle-friendly key.

Comparable versions:
"College Hornpipe," *A New & Highly Improved Violin Preceptor* (Utica, NY: William Williams, 1817), 11
"Richmond Blues," George P. Knauff, *Virginia Reels*, vol. 2 (Baltimore: George Willig Jr., 1839), 13
"Sailor's Hornpipe" (9261), Jasper Bisbee, 12/1923, NYC, Edison 51382
"Charleston #3" (W 404069-A), Narmour and Smith, 06/06/1930, San Antonio, TX, OKeh 45459

Rochester Schottische

Manuscript comments: "My mother played this 50 years ago."

Comparable versions:
"Rochester Schottische," Howe, Elias, *Musician's Omnibus* (Boston: Elias Howe, 1863–82), 56
"Rochester Schottische," Ford, Ira, *Traditional Music of America* (New York: Dutton, 1940), 60
"Patrick County Blues" (W 403123-A), John W. Spangler & Dave Pearson, the Old Virginia Fiddlers, 10/14/1929, Richmond, IN, OKeh 45387
Other versions of "Rochester Schottische" in this book by Charlie Edmundson and Mrs. Ben Walker ("Schattiche #2").

WILLIAM E. RAY

Source: Unknown or from the collector
Collector: William E. Ray
Location: Chester, Choctaw Co.

Soldier's Joy

Authors' comments: This whole tune appears to have the bar lines misplaced. If you move bar lines one beat to the left, the usual version of this widely known tune emerges.

Comparable versions:
Aird, James, *A Selection of Scotch, English, Irish and Foreign Airs*, vol. 1, no. 109 (1778)
"Soldier's Joy" (9189-A), Fiddlin' John Carson & His Virginia Reelers, 06/30/1925, Atlanta, GA, OKeh 45011
"Soldier's Joy" (GE 12747), Taylor's Kentucky Boys, 06/27, Richmond, IN, Silvertone 5060
"Soldier's Joy" (E29273), Kessinger Brothers, 02/05/1929, NYC, Brunswick 341
See other versions in this book by W. A. Bledsoe ("Farewell Mary Ann"), Dalton Brantley, W. E. Claunch, Charlie Edmondson, John Hatcher, Stephen B. Tucker, and Rev. J. E. Williams ("Rickets Hornpipe").

TOM REDDITT

Source: Tom Redditt
Collector: Mrs. Juliette Baab
Location: Oak Ridge, Warren Co.

Dan Tucker [Money Musk]

Authors' comments: This tune is actually "Money Musk." The 1940 census lists a Thomas J. Redditt as a white farmer, age 54, living with his wife, granddaughter, and son, T. J. Redditt, age 27, working as a bus driver.

Comparable versions:
"Money Musk," Howe, Elias, *Howe's School for the Violin* (Boston: Oliver Ditson, 1851), 29
"Money Musk" (9259), Jasper Bisbee, 11/24/1923, NYC, Edison 51381
"Money Musk" (BVE 34335-4), Henry Ford's Old Time Dance Orchestra, 01/18/1926, NYC, Victor 19964

J. P. REECE

Source: Unknown
Collector: J. P. Reece
Location: Lauderdale Co.

I' Ain't Goin to Leave Her By Herself

Manuscript comments: "This is a fiddle tune."

Comparable versions:
"Old Liza Jane" (13302) Uncle Am Stuart, 06/1924, NYC, Vocalion 14846
"Liza Jane" (140018-1), Riley Puckett, 09/11/1924, NYC, Columbia 15014-D
"Goodbye Liza Jane" (9596-A), Fiddlin' John Carson & His Virginia Reelers, 03/11/1926, Atlanta, GA, OKeh 45049
Other versions in this book by Enos Canoy ("Where'd You Get Your Whiskey"), Horace Kinard ("Liza Jane"), Everett Mitchell ("Liza Jane"), and Thaddeus Willingham.

W. S. ROBERTSON

Source: W. S. Robertson
Collector: Mrs. E. R. Andrews
Location: Oxford, Lafayette Co.

Roll Them Simelons

Oh, Miss Mary, I'm so sorry,
Bound for Texas, I'm so sorry
Roll them simelons, roll em around
Keep them simelons rollin' around
Roll them simelons, roll em around
All them pretty girls down town

Comparable versions:
"Roll them Simelons," A. P. Hudson, *Folk Tunes from Mississippi* (National Service Bureau pamphlet, NYC, 1937)
Other version in this book by J. H. Johnson ("Possum Up a Simmon Tree").

RICHARD SCOVEL

Source: Richard Scovel
Collector: Miss Elizabeth Gordon
Location: Pascagoula, Jackson Co.

Little Dog

Manuscript comments: "Played on the violin by Richard Scovel, Pascagoula, Jackson County, Mississippi. He said his mother sang it in French, as given above. His older brothers, nor he remember the words, as they never learned French. They say it is the same as the tune given below, which is copied from 'Ryan's True Violin Instructor' published by the John Church Co;, in 1872, Page 36. The book is owned by Bennie Scovel, Pascagoula, Jackson Co. Miss., brother of Richard. The 1940 census lists Richard, age 64, as born 1876, married with five children working as a WPA road construction laborer. When the writer (collector) was a little girl, she picked up a song to this same tune, but all the words she remembers are:

'Oh where, oh where, has my little dog gone
Oh where, oh where, can he be?
With his tail cut short and his ears out long,
Oh where, oh where can he be?'

'Oh, tra, la, la, tra, la, la . . .' through the second part."

Comparable versions:
"Lauterbach Waltz," Boettger, Theo. G. (Philadelphia: G. Andre & Co., 1870) (www.loc.gov/item/sm1870.05557/)
Ford, Ira, *Traditional Music of America* (New York: Dutton, 1940), 139
"Lauterbach Waltz" (E 34422-A), Kessinger Brothers, 09/15/1930, NYC, Brunswick 567
"Where Has My Little Dog Gone" (C 2434-), Hoosier Hot Shots, 02/02/1939, Chicago, IL, Vocalion 04688
Other versions in this book by Charlie Edmondson ("Dutch Waltz"), Billie Mansfield ("The Goose Girl"), and Rev. J. E. Williams ("Polly Put the Kettle On").

Red Wing

Authors' comments: This the first half of the usual two-part tune. The original lyrics concern the Indian maiden "Red Wing" and her love for an Indian warrior. Kerry Mills also wrote "Georgia Camp Meeting" and "Whistling Rufus."

Comparable versions, which contain both halves of the tune:
"Red Wing," Kerry Mills/Thurland Chattaway (New York: F.A. Mills, ca. 1907) (contentdm.baylor.edu/cdm/ref/collection/fa-spnc/id/9342)
"Red Wing" (81730-), Ernest Thompson, 04/25/1934, NYC, Columbia 190-D
"Red Wing" (2861-2), Blue Ridge Highballers, 09/1927, Chicago, IL, Paramount 3083
"Red Wing" (W 145043-2), Riley Puckett, 01/31/1927, Atlanta, GA, Columbia 15226-D

J. E. SHOEMAKER

Source: J. E. Shoemaker
Collector: Miss Olive Bryan
Location: Moss, Jasper Co.

Darling I'm Crazy 'Bout You

Authors' comments: In addition to the fiddle tunes collected from Shoemaker there was one song, "I'm a Roving Little Darky,"
which was nearly identical to Chubby Parker's recording of September 17, 1927, in Richmond, Indiana, matrix 13088, Gennett
6374. It is not included here.

Comparable versions:
Lew Sully, "I Don't Love Nobody" (Rhode Island: Howley, Haviland & Co., 1896) (lcweb2.loc.gov/diglib/ihas/loc.award.
rpbaasm.0971/default.html)
"I Don't Love Nobody" (81628-1), Gid Tanner, 03/07/1926, NYC, Columbia 150-D
"I Don't Love Nobody" (11579-), Fiddlin' Doc Roberts, 03/25/1932, NYC, Banner 32818

Gulfport

Comparable versions:

"Karo" (W 143004-), Uncle Jimmy Thompson, 11/01/1926, Atlanta, GA, Vocalion 15368

"The Long Eared Mule" (S 73378), Emmett Lundy & Ernest Stoneman, 05/27/1925, NYC, OKeh 40405

"Old Virginia Reel, Pt. 2" (W 81644-A), Fiddlin' John Powers & Family, 09/28/1927, Winston-Salem, NC, OKeh 45154

Other versions in this book by Cleve Bass ("Flop Eared Mule"), Mrs. Maud Freeman ("G & C Schottiche"), and John Hatcher
  ("Long Eared Mule or Baldin").

Ladies Fancy

Comparable versions:

"Molly Put the Kettle On," White, Charles, *White's New Illustrated Melodeon Song Book* (New York: H. Lond & Brother, 1851), 29

"Molly Put the Kettle On" (W 147631-), Leake County Revelers, 12/13/1928, New Orleans, LA, Columbia 15380

"Molly Put the Kettle On" (W 151918-1), Gid Tanner & His Skillet Lickers, 10/24/1931, Atlanta, GA, Columbia 15746-D

Other versions in this book by John Brown ("Molly Put the Kettle On") and Mr. T. W. Cooper ("Mollie Bring the Kettle").

Mississippi Sawyer

Comparable versions:

"Love from the Heart," George P. Knauff, *Virginia Reels*, vol. 4, no. 4 (Baltimore, 1839)

"Mississippi Sawyer" (W 148200-1), Gid Tanner and His Skillet Lickers, 04/08/1929, Atlanta, GA, Columbia 15420-D

"Mississippi Sawyer" (E 29271-), Kessinger Brothers, 02/05/1929, NYC, Brunswick 309

"Old Time Corn Shuckin' pt. 1" (BVE 39270-2), Ernest Stoneman & the Blue Ridge Corn Shuckers, 07/27/1927, Bristol, TN, Victor 20835

Other versions of "Mississippi Sawyer" in this book by W. E. Claunch, Sinclair Crocker, Hardy Sharp, Stephen B. Tucker, Rev. J. H. Wheeler, and Rev. J. E. Williams.

Old Mollie Hare

Authors' comments: The tune was obviously in D, but in the original notation the key signature was G. This could be a simple omission, but it certainly is more interesting to play with the C natural.

Comparable versions:

"Largo's Fairy Dance," Gow, John and Andrew, *A Collection of Slow Airs, Strathspeys & Reels*, vol. 5 (London: Wm. Campbell, ca. 1795), 19

Christy's Panorama Songster (New York: W. H. Murphy, ca. 1850s)

"Old Molly Hare," Fiddling Power & Family, 9/28/1927, Winston-Salem, NC, OKeh 45628

Other versions in this book by W. A. Bledsoe, Mrs. M. B. Brister, W. E. Claunch, J. A. Moorman, and two versions by "Unknown."

Sally Goodin

Comparable versions:

"Sally Goodwin," Ford, Ira, *Traditional Music of America* (New York: Dutton, 1940), 64, 209 (calls), 419 (verses)

"Sally Gooden" (B 26664-1), Eck Robertson, 07/01/1922, NYC, Victor 18956

"Old Sally Goodman" (S 72-015-A), Fiddlin' John Carson, 11/07/1923, NYC, OKeh 40095

"Sally Goodin" (E 29275-), Kessinger Brothers, 02/05/1929, NYC, Brunswick 308

Other versions of "Sally Goodin" in this book by John, Brown, W. E. Claunch ("Sally Goodin" and the "A" part of "Bear Creek's Up"), and Thaddeus Willingham.

Tom Tit

Authors' comments: This tune is named after a bird, which is also known as a chickadee or a titmouse.

Way Late Last Night When Peter Went A-Fishing

Comparable versions:

"Georgia Railroad" (140019-1), Gid Tanner, 09/11/1924, NYC, Columbia 15019-D

"Peter Went A-Fishin'" (65712-A), Clayton McMichen, 06/01/1939, NYC, Decca 2649

"Peter Went A-Fishing" (9846-A), John Carson & His Virginia Reelers, 11/21/1926, Atlanta, GA, OKeh 45068

White Hat

The Music Transcriptions

MRS. J. SMITH

Source: Mrs. J. Smith
Collector: Anna Wallace
Location: Poplarsville, Pearl River Co.

Flirtin' Song

Oh Come, my Love and go with me Oh Come, my Love and go with me Oh

Come, my Love and go with me And see what care I'll take of thee

I am too young, I cannot go
I am too young, I cannot go
I am too young, I cannot go
I cannot leave my mother so

You are sixteen or twenty-two
You are sixteen or twenty-two
You are sixteen or twenty-two
And I am sure that that will do

If you won't go, then fare you well.
If you won't go, then fare you well.
If you won't go, then fare you well.
I love you more than tongue can tell.

Manuscript comments: "A 'play Song' sung by soldiers to their sweethearts before going off to war about 1861 from Pearl River Settlement."

DR. FRANK SMITH

Source: Dr. Frank Smith
Collector: Mrs. Florence Hawkins
Location: Greenwood, Leflore Co.

Jaybird Died

Oh, the jay bird died with the whooping cough and the black bird died with the

col - ic I met a frog with a fid - le on his back In - quiring his way to the frol - ic

Comparable versions:
"The Gal I Left Behind," Ford, Ira, *Traditional Music of America* (New York: E.P. Dutton, 1940), 417
"The Girl I Left Behind Me" (705/06 W), Uncle Dave Macon & Sid Harkreader, 04/15/1925, NYC, Vocalion 15034
"The Girl I Left Behind Me" (W 143797-2), Gid Tanner & His Skillet Lickers, 03/29/1927, Atlanta, GA, Columbia 15170-D
"Girl I Left Behind Me" (AL 226/27), Kessinger Brothers, 04/26/1928, Ashland KY, Brunswick 267

Old Hen Cackled

The old hen cackled. She cackled in the lot The next time she cackled she cackled in the pot. The

pul - let cackled she cackled in the millet the next time she cackled, she cackled in the skillet. The

old hen cackled, the young one laid, the next time she cackled the rooster crowed

and the gobbler gobbled and the guinea said all the little niggers love short'nin bread

---

Authors' comments: The last few measures resemble "Shortenin' Bread."

Comparable versions:
"The Old Hen Cackled and the Rooster is Going to Crow" (8375-A-B), John Carson, 06/14/1923, Atlanta, GA, OKeh 4890
"Hen Cackle" (81630-2), Gid Tanner & Riley Puckett, 03/08/1924, NYC, Columbia 110-D
"Cackling Hen" (9307-A), J. D. Harris, 1925, Asheville, NC, OKeh 45024
"Shortenin' Bread" (E 21837), Dykes Magic City Trio, 03/10/1927, NYC, Brunswick 125
"Shortenin' Bread" (GE-13655-A), Tweedy Brothers, 03/1928, Richmond, IN, Gennett 6529
Other versions of "Old Hen Cackled" in this book by Mrs. M. B. Brister ("Old Hen Cackled on the Pot"), John Brown, W. M. Collom ("Rabbit in a Ditch"), and Jim Gooch.

Possum Up De Simmon Tree

Possum up the Simmon tree, coonie on de ground   Coonie say "You son of a gun"

fling some   Simmons   down   Squirrel am a pretty bird.   He's got a bushy tail

He eats up all my daddies corn   and sits on a rail   Red bird sitting on   a swing limb,

Jay-bird say "Yore Liar"   Red-bird say "Don't you say that again,   I'll scratch your eyes   wid a briar

Rac-coon got a bushy tail,   Possum tail am bare   Rabbit got no tail at all   just a bunch of hair.

Comparable versions:
"Sandy Boy," *Phil Rice's Correct Method for the Banjo with or without a Master* (Boston: Oliver Ditson & Co., 1857), 50
"Sandy Boys," *Edden Hammons Collection* (LP, West Virginia University Press, 1984)

WILBUR SNOWDEN

Wilbur Snowden

Collector: Mrs. W. A. Harbour

Location: Bailey, Lauderdale Co.

Washpot Blues

MR. J. E. TARTT

Source: Mr. J. E. Tartt
Collector: Mrs. Willie Davis
Location: Lauderdale Co.

Go Long Liza

You go up the new cut road and I'll come down the lane   Go Long Su-san, Git 'long Li-za Jane

Comparable versions:
Other version in this book by Mrs. W. J. Bonds.

E. THOMAS

Source: E. Thomas
Collector: L. Silas Virgil
Location: Gulfport, Harrison Co.

Chicken in Bread Tray

Manuscript comments: "This is a negro frolic tune in the early 18th century it was slap for them to dance by, at all the frolic and was a popular dance tune at that time, music fixed by L.S. Virgil Sep 11, 1936 Gulfport, Miss."

Authors' comments: The source was African American.

Horse Shoe of the Battle

Whiskey O Bra-ndy no friend of mine you kill my old father and trouble my mind

Eat when I'm hungry and drink when 'm dry.
Think of Little Willie set down and cry

Your cheeks are inviting, your tongue bid me to
    come
First time I saw you won my heart.

My foot in my stirrup and whip in my hand
Farewell my darling, my horse will not stand.

Manuscript comments: "Tune by E. Thomas 66 years ago he play this tune on his violin and his grandfather sing it when he was
    a boy he say this is an Indian's war song in 1752."

MRS. BETTIE THORNTON

Source: Unknown

Collector: Mrs. Bettie Thornton

Location: West, Holmes Co.

Swinging Neath the Red Apple Tree

MRS. A. TYNES

Source: Mrs. A. Tynes
Collector: Mrs. Vivian Skinner, 1936
Location: Shuqualak, Noxubee Co

Run, Nigger, Run

Run nigger run, the patty-ro'll ___ catch you Run nigger run, it's almost day

Comparable versions:

"Run Nigger, Run," Allen, William Francis, *Slave Songs of the United States* (New York: A. Simpson & Co., 1867), #110, 89

"Run Nigger, Run" (8709-A), Fiddling John Carson, 08/27/1924, Atlanta, GA, OKeh 40230

"Run Nigger, Run" (667/668), Uncle Dave Macon, 04/13/1925, NYC, Vocalion 15032

"Run Boy, Run" (BVE 56361-2), Eck Robertson & Dr. J. B. Cranfill, 10/10/1929, Dallas, TX, Victor V40205

Other versions of "Run Nigger, Run" in this book by Mrs. M. B. Brister, W. E. Claunch, Mr. John McCartie, Jr., Stephen B. Tucker, Mrs. Louise Walker Wallace, and Thaddeus Willingham.

UNKNOWN

Source: Unknown
Collector: Unknown
Location: Mississippi

Coon

Comparable versions:

"Hot Time in the Old Town Tonight," Theodore Metz, words and music (New York: Willis Woodward; Milwaukee: Joseph Flanner, 1896) (library.duke.edu/digitalcollections/hasm_b0570/)

"Hot Time in the Old Town Tonight" (W 149279-), Gid Tanner & His Skillet Lickers, 01/29/1929, Atlanta, GA, Columbia 15695-D

Fisher's Hornpipe

Comparable versions:

"Fisher's Hornpipe," J. Fishar (ca. 1780), *A New & Highly Improved Violin Preceptor* (Utica, NY: William Williams, 1817), 23

"Old Zip Coon and Medley Reels" (GE 13833), Doc Roberts & Asa Martin, 05/15/1928, Richmond, IN, Gennett 6495

"Fisher's Hornpipe" (E 3972W), The Hillbillies, 10/21/1926, NYC, Vocalion 5017

"Fisher's Hornpipe" (6713-), Clayton McMichen, Hoyt "Slim: Bryant & Jerry Wallace, 06/01/1939. NYC, Decca 2649

"Texas Breakdown" (W 404065-B), W. T. Narmour & S. W. Smith, 06/06/1930, San Antonio, TX, OKeh 45492 (has only the "A" part in common)

Other versions of "Fisher's Hornpipe" in this book by Billie Mansfield, Alvis Massengale, Mr. N. Odom, and Stephen B. Tucker.

Make Me a Bed On the Floor

Comparable versions:

"Make Me a Pallet on De Flo," Odum, Howard W., and Guy B. Johnson, *The Negro and His Songs* (Chapel Hill: University of North Carolina Press, 1925), 183 (lyrics only)

"Make me a Bed on the Floor" (W 146210-3), Leake County Revelers, 04/27/1928, New Orleans, LA, Columbia 15264

"Pallet on the Floor" (60693-), Stripling Brothers, 03/12/1936, New Orleans, LA, Decca 5267

Murilla's Lesson

Authors' comments: The source transcription was in D♭, I suspect reflecting that the fiddle was tuned low. The manuscript took no notice of the extra beat in m4. I suspect a counting error on the part of the transcriber.

Comparable versions:
"Murillo's Lesson," McCurry, John G., *The Social Harp* (Philadelphia: T.K. Collin's Jr., 1855; reprinted 1973), 358
Howe, Elias, *Complete Preceptor for the Accordeon* (1843), 12
"Murillo's Lesson" (GE 13777), J. T. Allison's Sacred Harp Singers, 05/07/1928, Richmond, IN, Gennett 6564
"Murillo's Lesson" (W 402056-B), Charles Butt's Sacred Harp Singers, 08/03/1928, Atlanta, GA, OKeh 45251

Old Mollie Hare #1

Authors' comments: The source transcription was in E♭, I suspect reflecting that the fiddle was tuned high. Though only a crude outline, the "A" part of this version is clearly related to the versions below.

Comparable versions:
"Largo's Fairy Dance," Gow, John and Andrew, *A Collection of Slow Airs, Strathspeys & Reels*, vol. 5 (London: Wm. Campbell, ca. 1795), 19
Christy's Panorama Songster (New York: W.H. Murphy, ca. 1850s)
"Old Molly Hare," Fiddling Power & Family, 9/28/1927, Winston-Salem, NC, OKeh 45628
Other versions in this book by W. A. Bledsoe, Mrs. M. B. Brister, W. E. Claunch, J. A. Moorman, J. E. Shoemaker, and two versions by "Unknown."

Old Mollie Hare #2

Old Moll-y Hare What you doing there, trotting cross the cotton patch as fast as you can tear

Ta da, ta da, Ta da, da, Ta da, ta da, Ta da, da, Ta da, ta da, Ta da, da, Ta da, ta da, Ta da, da

Authors' comments: The "A" part of this version is strongly related to the versions below.

Comparable versions:
"Largo's Fairy Dance," Gow, John and Andrew, *A Collection of Slow Airs, Strathspeys & Reels*, vol. 5 (London: Wm. Campbell, ca. 1795), 19
Christy's Panorama Songster (New York: W.H. Murphy, ca. 1850s)
"Old Molly Hare," Fiddling Power & Family, 9/28/1927, Winston-Salem, NC, OKeh 45628
Other versions in this book by W. A. Bledsoe, Mrs. M. B. Brister, W. E. Claunch, J. A. Moorman, J. E. Shoemaker, and two versions by "Unknown."

Untitled (Bonny Blue Flag)

9 Chorus

Comparable versions:
"Bonny Blue Flag," Kerr, *Merry Melodies* vol. 3, no. 292, 32.
"Bonny Blue Flag," O'Neill, *Waifs and Strays of Gaelic Melody* (1922), No. 70; Sweet, *Fifer's Delight* (1964), 28.
"Bonny Blue Flag," Hoyt Ming and His Pep Steppers, *New Hot Times!* LP, (Homestead Records 103, 1975)

Virginia Reel

Authors' comments: First tune is "Irish Washerwoman" and the second is the "White Cockade."

Comparable versions:

"Irish Washerwoman":

Niel Gow, *A Third Collection of Strathspey Reels &c for the Piano-forte, Violin and Violoncello* (1792), 31 (imslp.org/wiki/A_Third_Collection_of_Strathspey_Reels,_etc._(Gow,_Niel))

"Medley of Jigs: Irish Washerwoman" (BVE 34528-4), Mellie Dunham, 02/03/1926, Camden, NJ, Victor 20537

"Irish Washerwoman" (GE 13836), Doc Roberts & Asa Martin (as Jim Burke), 05/14/1928, Richmond, IN, Silvertone 8176

Other versions of "Irish Washerwoman" in this book by Billie Mansfield/Chris Martin.

"White Cockade":

A Jacobite song from the eighteenth century written by Muiris mac Daibhi mac Gerailt (Maurice FitzDavid FitzGerald)

Elias Howe, *Complete Preceptor for the Accordeon* (ca. 1843), 6 imslp.org/wiki/The_Complete_Preceptor_for_the_Accordeon_(Howe,_Elias)

"Medley of Reels" (BVE 34389-4), Mellie Dunham's Orchestra, 02/03/1926, NYC, Victor 20537

"Medley: White Cockade" (N 106562), Uncle Joe Shippee "Winner New England Contest," 02/1926, NYC, Path 21164

MRS. BEN WALKER

Source: Mrs. Ben Walker
Collector: Mrs. Renfro Seaton
Location: Gunnison, Bolivar Co.

Put Your Big Foot Right There

Authors' comments: The source transcription was in B♭, I suspect reflecting that the fiddle was tuned low.

Comparable versions:
"Varsovienne," Francisco Alonso, 1853, originally with eight parts
Ford, Ira, *Traditional Music of America* (New York: Dutton, 1940), 151
"Varsovienne" (BVE 34000-3), Henry Ford's Old Time Dance Orchestra, 12/02/1925, Dearborn, MI, Victor 19910
"Varsovienne" (W 400498-), Bob Skiles' Four Old Tuners, 03/13/1928, San Antonio, TX,OKeh 45243
"Varsovienne" (C 842-1), The Westerners, 11/14/1934, Chicago, IL, Vocalion 05401

Schattische #1

8
Chorus

Authors' comments: Schottische is spelled "Schattische" in the manuscript.

Schattische #2

Authors' comments: Schottische is spelled "Schattische" in the manuscript.

Comparable versions:
"Rochester Schottische," Howe, Elias, *Musician's Omnibus* (Boston: Elias Howe, 1863–82), 56
"Rochester Schottische," Ford, Ira, *Traditional Music of America* (New York: Dutton, 1940), 60
"Patrick County Blues" (W 403123-A), John W. Spangler & Dave Pearson, The Old Virginia Fiddlers, 10/14/1929, Richmond, IN, OKeh 45387
Other versions of "Rochester Schottische" in this book by Charlie Edmundson and Mrs. E. M. Purcell.

MRS. L. A. WALKER

Source: Mrs. L. A. Walker
Collector: Miss Ceola Walker
Location: Water Valley, Yalobusha Co.

Smokey Moke

Manuscript comments: "The triplets are like a slide on a trombone."

Authors' comments: The source transcription was in C, with the notes falling below violin range. Abe Holtzman wrote a cakewalk in 1899 sharing this title, but little else.

The 1940 census lists a Loveless Al Walker as a 57-year-old white husband of Lura Walker, age 49, and lists his occupation as barber.

Comparable versions:

"Whistling Rufus," words by Kerry Mills (New York: F.A. Mills Music, 1899) (clio.lib.olemiss.edu/cdm/ref/collection/sharris/id/1663)

"Rufus Blossom" (E 5026/27W). Sam & Kirk McGee w/Maizi Todd, 05/11/1927, NYC, Vocalion 5170

"Whistling Rufus" (E 30193-), Kessinger Brothers, 06/25/1929, NYC, Brunswick 521

"Whistling Rufus" (W 151921), Gid Tanner & His Skillet Lickers, 10/24/1930, Atlanta, GA, Columbia 15730-D

BEN WALL

Source: Ben Wall

Collector: Florence Hawkins and Mrs. Everett Hemphill

Location: Hemingway, Leflore Co.

Buffalo Gals

Buf-fa-lo gals won't you come out to night? Won't you come out to night? Come out, to night?

Buf-fa-lo gals won't you come out to night, an we'll dance by the light of the moon

Chorus

Buf-fa-lo gals won't you come out to night? Won't you come out to night? Come out, to night?

Buf-fa-lo gals won't you come out to night, an we dance by the light of the moon

Danced with a gal with a hole in her stocking,
a hole in her stocking, a hole in her stocking
Danced with a gal with a hole in her stocking,
a hole in her stocking, a hole in her stocking
as we dance by the light of the moon

Comparable versions:

"Midnight Serenade," Knauff, George P., *Virginia Reels*, vol. 1, no. 4 (Baltimore, ca. 1839)

"Round Town Gals" (GEX 498-A), Ernest V. Stoneman & His Grayson County Boys, 02/02/1927, NYC, Gennett 6052

"Buffalo Gals" (8514-1-2), Pickard Family, 01/31/1929, NYC, Banner 6371

Versions of "Buffalo Gals" in this book by Babe Casey ("Grasshopper On a Sweet Tater Vine"), R. H. Ellis, John Hatcher ("Buffalo Girl"), A. J. Howell ("Buffalo Girl"), and Edward Kittrell.

Do Johnny Booker, Do

Do, John-ny Booker Can you mend my ring? Yes, I can mend most any little thing. Do, John-ny

Book-er, Do Do, John-ny Book-er, Can you help that nig - ger? Do, John - ny Booker,

Now, Mr. Booker, Can you mend my yoke?
Yes, I think I can mend that yoke
Do, Johnny Booker, Do
He built up a fire and started a smoke
Do, Johnny Booker, Do

Comparable versions:
"Jonny Boker, or, De Broken Yoke in de Coaling Ground," *Sweeny's Virginia Melodies* (1840) https://jscholarship.library.jhu.edu/handle/1774.2/13246
"Old Johnny Bucker Wouldn't Do" (GE 14942), Walter Smith, 03/10/1928, Richmond, IN, Gennett 6825

MRS. LOUISE WALKER WALLACE

Source: Unknown
Collector: Mrs. Louise Walker Wallace
Location: Mississippi

Run Nigger Run

Run nigger run, the pat-ty-ro will catch you Run nigger run, it's almost day

that nigger run, that nigger flew that nigger lost his wed-ding shoe

---

Authors' comments: It is not clear from the manuscript if the Mrs. Wallace is the collector or the source, or both.

Comparable versions:

"Run Nigger, Run," Allen, William Francis, *Slave Songs of the United States* (New York: A. Simpson & Co., 1867), #110, 89

"Run Nigger, Run" (8709-A), Fiddling John Carson, 08/27/1924, Atlanta, GA, OKeh 40230

"Run Nigger, Run" (667/668), Uncle Dave Macon, 04/13/1925, NYC, Vocalion 15032

"Run Boy, Run" (BVE 56361-2), Eck Robertson & Dr. J. B. Cranfill, 10/10/1929, Dallas, TX, Victor V40205

Other versions of "Run Nigger, Run" in this book by Mrs. M. B. Brister, W. E. Claunch, Mr. John McCartie, Jr., Stephen B. Tucker, Mrs. A. Tynes, and Thaddeus Willingham.

MR. J. H. WHEELER

Source: Mr. J. H. Wheeler, 90 years old.
Collector: Mrs. E. M. Purcell
Location: Tutwiler, Tutwiler Co.

Leather Breeches

Comparable versions:

"Lord McDonald's Reel," Niel & Nathaniel Gow, *Third Collection of Niel Gow's Reels* (ca. 1792), 9

M. M. Cole, *One Thousand Fiddle Tunes* (Chicago: M. M. Cole, 1940; reprinted from *Ryan's Mammoth Collection*, 1883), 22

"Leather Breeches" (N 839-), Carter Brothers & Son, 11/22/1928, Memphis, TN, Vocalion 5295

"Leather Breeches" (W 143968-2), Leake County Revelers, 04/13/1927, New Orleans, LA, Columbia 15149-D

Other versions of "Leather Breeches" in this book by John Hatcher, Hardy Sharp, and Stephen B. Tucker.

Mississippi Sawyer

Manuscript comments: "J. H. Wheeler - Tutwiler, 90 yrs. ld. "Mr. Wheeler did not know the name of the following tune but 'caught it by ear' when a small boy from an old fiddler living in his neighborhood."

Authors' comments: The source transcription was in B♭, I suspect reflecting that the fiddle was tuned very low.

Comparable versions:

"Love from the Heart," George P. Knauff, *Virginia Reels*, vol. 4, no. 4 (Baltimore, 1839)

"Mississippi Sawyer" (W 148200-1), Gid Tanner and His Skillet Lickers, 04/08/1929, Atlanta, GA, Columbia 15420-D

"Mississippi Sawyer" (E 29271-), Kessinger Brothers, 02/05/1929, NYC, Brunswick 309

"Old Time Corn Shuckin' Pt. 1" (BVE 39270-2), Ernest Stoneman & the Blue Ridge Corn Shuckers, 07/27/1927, Bristol, TN, Victor 20835

Other versions of "Mississippi Sawyer" in this book by W. E. Claunch, Sinclair Crocker, Hardy Sharp, J. E. Shoemaker, Stephen B. Tucker, and Rev. J. E. Williams.

MISS MAE BELLE WILLIAMS

Source: not documented

Collector: Miss Mae Belle Williams

Location: Iuka, Tishomingo Co.

Bear Creek

Bear Creek's up and Bear Creek's mud-dy I'll swim Bear Creek to see my hon-ey

Bear Creek's up and Bear Creek's mud - dy I'm so drunk that I can't keep stead - y

Authors' comments: This collector also collected tunes from John A. Brown who lived in Bear Creek; perhaps this is also from him. Most of his tunes were in the key of A as well.

Comparable versions (only the "B" part of the above tune):

"Sally Goodwin," Ford, Ira, *Traditional Music of America* (New York: Dutton, 1940), 64, 209 (calls), 419 (verses)

"Sally Gooden" (B 26664-1), Eck Robertson, 07/01/1922, NYC, Victor 18956

"Old Sally Goodman" (S 72-015-A), Fiddlin' John Carson 11/07/1923, NYC, OKeh 40095

"Sally Goodin" (E 29275-), Kessinger Brothers, 02/05/1929, NYC, Brunswick 308

Other versions of "Sally Goodin" in this book by John Brown, W. E. Claunch ("Sally Goodin" and the "A" part of "Bear Creek's Up"), and Thaddeus Willingham.

Bear Creek Waltz

Bear Creek's up and Bear Creek's mud-dy I'll swim Bear Creek to see my

hon-ey   Bear   Creek's up and   Bear Creek's muddy

I'm   so   drunk that   I   can't   keep   stead - y

Manuscript comments: "My version"

Authors' comments: This appears to be an awkward adaptation of the previous "Bear Creek," perhaps created by Miss Williams.

REV. J. E. WILLIAMS

Source: Rev. J. E. Williams
Collector: Anna Wallace
Location: Poplarsville, Pearl River Co.

Cindy Waltz

Her eyes are like a cher-ry, Her cheeks are like a

rose, and how I love my Cindy there's no - body knows

Manuscript comments: "Rev. Williams heard this played in 1886 by Richard Gray of Rankin County."
Authors' comments: The portion of this version with lyrics is related to the versions below.

Comparable versions:
"Cindy in the Meadows" (81706-1), Samantha Bumgarner & Eva Davis, 4/22/1924, NYC, Columbia 167-D
"Cindy" (W 143867-), Riley Puckett & Clayton McMichen, 04/02/1927, Atlanta, GA, Columbia 15232-D
"Get Along Home, Miss Cindy" (BVE 41853-2), Pope's Arkansas Mountaineers, 02/06/1928, Memphis, TN, Victor 21577
Other versions in this book by Charlie Addison ("Want to Go to Meeting"), John Brown ("Cindy"), W. E. Claunch ("Cindy"),
     Enos Canoy ("Where'd You Get Your Whiskey"), Mrs. R. C. Clifton ("Miss Cindy"), B. M. Guilette ("Liza Jane"), Frank Kittrell
     ("Cindy Jane"), Mrs. Joe McCoy ("Her Cheeks Are Like the Cherry"), Hardy Sharp ("Liza Jane"), and Thaddeus Willingham
     ("Miss Cindy").

Cotton Eyed Joe

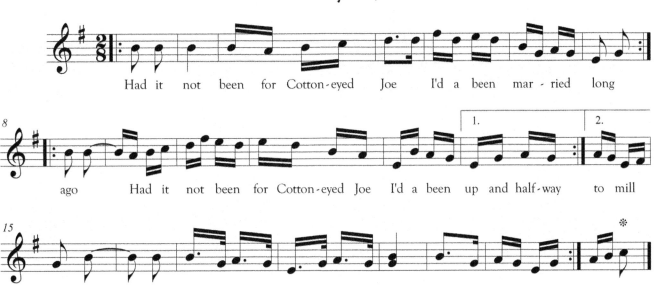

Had it not been for Cotton-eyed Joe I'd a been mar-ried long ago Had it not been for Cotton-eyed Joe I'd a been up and half-way to mill

Manuscript comments: "A Negro Tune, Breakdown, from Smith County played at dances."
Authors' comments: * m22, the last measure leads into the "A" part of the tune and the tune ends on m8 with the last note held.

Comparable versions:
Ford, Ira, *Traditional Music of America* (New York: Dutton, 1940), 60
"Cotton-Eyed Joe" (M836-), Carter Brothers and Son, 11/22/1928, Memphis, TN, Vocalion 5349
"Cotton-Eyed Joe" (W146002-2), Gid Tanner & His Skillet Lickers, 04/10/1928, Atlanta, GA, Columbia 15283-D
"Cotton-Eyed Joe" (BVE 41852-2), Pope's Arkansas Mountaineers, 02/06/1928, Memphis, TN, Victor 21469
Allen Alsop's version in this book.

Cotton Field Song

Pos-sum and a rac-coon in a chim-ney cor-ner. Pos-sum say to Racoon Don't you want to
mar-ry I'm too young to mar-ry Take me back to mam-my!
I'm to young to mar-ry Take me back to mam-my!

Manuscript comments: "Used in Dances 50 years ago."
Authors' comments: This song has familiar lyrics but an unfamiliar tune. The G♯ in m19–20 was a G natural in the manuscript and appeared to be a mistake.

Mississippi Sawyer

Authors' comments: The manuscript had this tune in 2/8. I have transferred it to 2/4 to make it a bit easier to read.

Comparable versions:

"Love from the Heart," George P. Knauff, *Virginia Reels*, vol. 4, no. 4 (Baltimore, 1839)

"Mississippi Sawyer" (W 148200-1), Gid Tanner and His Skillet Lickers, 04/08/1929, Atlanta, GA, Columbia 15420-D

"Mississippi Sawyer" (E 29271-), Kessinger Brothers, 02/05/1929, NYC, Brunswick 309

"Old Time Corn Shuckin' pt. 1" (BVE 39270-2), Ernest Stoneman & the Blue Ridge Corn Shuckers, 07/27/1927, Bristol, TN, Victor 20835

Other versions of "Mississippi Sawyer" in this book by W. E. Claunch, Sinclair Crocker, Hardy Sharp, J. E. Shoemaker, Stephen B. Tucker, and Rev. J. H. Wheeler.

Polly Put the Kettle On

The source transcription was in E♭, I suspect reflecting that the fiddle was tuned high.

Comparable versions:
"Lauterbach Waltz," Boettger, Theo. G. (Philadelphia: G. Andre & Co., 1870) (www.loc.gov/item/sm1870.05557/)
Ford, Ira, *Traditional Music of America* (New York: Dutton, 1940), 139
"Lauterbach Waltz" (E 34422-A), Kessinger Brothers, 09/15/1930, NYC, Brunswick 567
"Where Has My Little Dog Gone" (C 2434-), Hoosier Hot Shots, 02/02/1939, Chicago, IL, Vocalion 04688
Other versions in this book by Richard Scovel ("Little Dog"), Charlie Edmondson ("Dutch Waltz"), and Billie Mansfield ("The Goose Girl").

Rickett's

animato

Manuscript comments: "Heard 1886 by a roving fiddler."

Comparable versions:

Aird, James, *A Selection of Scotch, English, Irish and Foreign Airs*, vol. 1, no. 109 (1778)

"Soldier's Joy" (9189-A), Fiddlin' John Carson & His Virginia Reelers, 06/30/1925, Atlanta, GA, OKeh 45011

"Soldier's Joy" (GE 12747), Taylor's Kentucky Boys, 06/27, Richmond, IN, Silvertone 5060

"Soldier's Joy" (E29273), Kessinger Brothers, 02/05/1929, NYC, Brunswick 341

Other versions in this book by W. A. Bledsoe ("Farewell Mary Ann"), Dalton Brantley, W. E. Claunch, Charlie Edmondson, John Hatcher, W. E. Ray, and Stephen B. Tucker.

Scotch Hornpipe

Manuscript comments: "Heard many 50, years ago played by Mr. Foreman, Glosted, Miss, Amite County."

Comparable versions:
"Mrs. Mclouds Reel," O'Neil, Francis, *The Dance Music of Ireland* (Chicago: Lyon and Healey, 1907), no. 1418, 263
"Hop Out Ladies" (S 72-348-A), Henry Whitter, 2/1924, NYC, OKeh 40064
"Hop Light Lady" (9186-A), Fiddlin' John Carson & His Virginia Reelers, 06/30/1925, Atlanta, GA, OKeh 45011
"Hop High Ladies, The Cakes All Dough" (E 4933/34W), Uncle Dave Macon & His Fruit Jar Drinkers, 05/07/1927, NYC, Vocalion 5154
"McCloud's Reel" (E 30191), Kessinger Brothers, 06/25/1929, NYC, Brunswick 580
Other version in this book by Sinclair Crocker ("Fiddlers Reel").

Soldier's Joy Hornpipe

Comparable versions:
"Rickett's Hornpipe," *One Thousand Fiddle Tunes* (Chicago: M. M. Cole, 1940), 89
"Rickett's Hornpipe" (11922-), Tweedy Brothers, 06/14/1924, Atlanta, GA, Gennett 5613
"Rickett's Hornpipe" (GS 17036), Green's String Band, 09/15/1930, Richmond, IN, Champion 16489
"Rickett's Hornpipe" (W 151027-2), Gid Tanner & His Skillet Lickers, 12/04/1930, Atlanta, GA, Columbia 15682-D
Other versions in this book by Charles Long ("Fisher's Hornpipe") and Stephen B. Tucker ("Raker's Hornpipe").

MRS. JOSIE GAUTIER WINTERTON

Source: Mrs. Josie Gautier Winterton

Collector: Mrs. E. Gordon and Mrs. R. A. Farnsworth

Location: Gautier, Jackson Co.

Johnny Get Your Hair Cut Polka

Authors' comments: In the 1940 census a Mrs. Winterton, born 1900, is listed as married to Lester C. a civil engineer.

MRS. W. E. WOOD

Source: Mrs. W. E. Wood
Collector: Lockie Moore
Location: Corinth, Alcorn Co.

Joplin Girl

I went down to Joplin boys, to stay two weeks or
three.
I fell in love with a Joplin girl and her in love
with me,
been all around this world

The new railroad's finished boys, the cars are on
the track.
The new railroad's finished boys, the cars are on
the track.
She takes me away from my baby boys, my
money will bring me back
I been all around this world

Lord they're gonna hang me, the death I dread
to die
Lord they're gonna hang me, between this earth
and sky,

Been accused of murder boys, How I hate to die,
I been all around this world

Out on the Ozark mountain boys, there'll I take
my stand
Out on the Ozark mountain boys, there'll I take
my stand
Rifle on my shoulder and a six shooter in my
hand, I been all around this world

When you see me coming girls, Go raise your
window high
When you see me coming girls, Go raise your
window high
When you see me leaving girls, Go bow your
head and cry.
I been all around this world

Manuscript comments: The manuscript of this melody was marked "unusable."

Comparable versions:
Justus Begley, of Hazard, Perry County, Kentucky, recorded by Alan Lomax for the Library of Congress on October 17, 1937. AFS
1531 A1
"Been All Around this World," Highwoods Stringband, *Dance All Night*, (LP, Rounder 0045, 1974)

3

Music Collected in 1939

W. A. BLEDSOE

Meridian, Lauderdale Co.

Fiddle and Song

From Abbott Ferriss's field notes:

Mr. Bledsoe is Deputy Circuit Clerk. He was reared in Lincoln County, Tennessee, where he learned to play the fiddle from his father. His father was twelve years old during the Civil War. Bledsoe "slipped the fiddle out" and learned to play.

"The old time music have two turns. One combination of tunes is followed by another with rearrangement of the noting."

He spoke of an article he read in *Etude.* He came to Meridian in 1905.

On the 1939 recording he commented:

"I was born and reared in Lincoln County Tenn. I am 58 years of age. I came to Meridian in 1905. My father had a fiddle. He was twelve years old during the Civil War and he didn't have a chance to go to school, but he had a fiddle. And his father fiddled. And about ten or twelve years old I began to get the fiddle out and play and he caught me playing one day and he told me that I—he didn't have a chance to go to school—that he'd do the

fiddling for the family. Wanted me to let the fiddle alone. But I continued to slip the fiddle out when he wasn't there. And by the time he was due home. I'd slip the fiddle back under the bed. And it wasn't long till I could play just about as good as he could."

Big Footed Nigger in a Sandy Lot

Field notes: "This is one of the first pieces he learned from his father. His father is the only one he ever heard play it."

Bill Cheatum

Comparable versions:

"Quayside Hornpipe," Keith Norman McDonald, *The Skye Collection of the Best Reels & Strathspeys Extant* (1887; reprinted 1979 by P. S. Cranford), 174 (only the "A" part of the tune)

"Brilliancy Medley" (B 26665-), Eck Robertson, 10/11/1929, Dallas, TX, Victor 40298

"Bill Cheatem" (IND 651-), James Cole String Band, 06/1928, Indianapolis, IN, Vocalion 5226

"Bill Cheatham" (BVE 47154-3), Blind Joe Mangrum & Fred Schriver, 10/06/1928, Nashville, TN, Victor 40018

Farewell Mary Anne

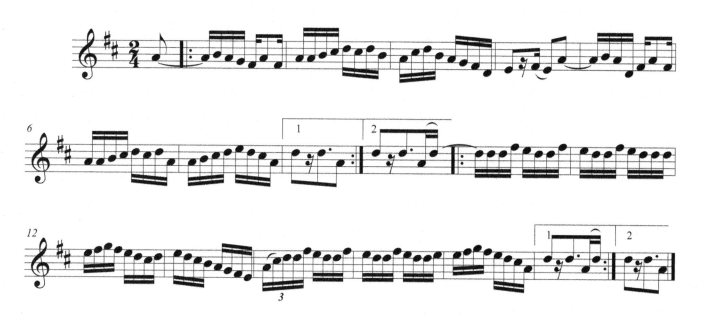

Field notes: Bledsoe learned the piece "from an uncle of mine."

Comparable versions:

Aird, James, *A Selection of Scotch, English, Irish and Foreign Airs*, vol. 1, no. 109 (1778)

"Soldier's Joy" (9189-A), Fiddlin' John Carson & His Virginia Reelers, 06/30/1925, Atlanta, GA, OKeh 45011

"Soldier's Joy" (GE 12747), Taylor's Kentucky Boys, 06/27, Richmond, IN, Silvertone 5060

"Soldier's Joy" (E29273), Kessinger Brothers, 02/05/1929, NYC, Brunswick 341

See other versions in this book by Dalton Brantley, W. E. Claunch, Charlie Edmondson, John Hatcher, W. E. Ray, Stephen B. Tucker, and Rev. J. E. Williams ("Rickets Hornpipe").

Old Molly Hare

Field notes: Bledsoe has known the piece "ever since I was a kid."

Comparable versions:
"Largo's Fairy Dance," Gow, John and Andrew, *A Collection of Slow Airs, Strathspeys & Reels*, vol. 5 (London: Wm. Campbell, ca. 1795), 19
Christy's Panorama Songster (New York: W.H. Murphy, ca. 1850s)
"Old Molly Hare," Fiddling Power & Family, 9/28/1927, Winston-Salem, NC, OKeh 45628
Other versions in this book by Mrs. M. B. Brister, W. E. Claunch, J. A. Moorman, J. E. Shoemaker, and two versions by "Unknown."

Purtiest Little Girl in the County

Authors' comments: For the slides in this tune, the open A is played, then the finger immediately slides from B♭ to B, giving the sound of a smooth slide from A to B.

Comparable versions:
"Dandy Jim of Caroline," Thomas "Daddy" Rice of the Virginia Minstrels, (Philadelphia: A. Fiot, 1844) (www.loc.gov/item/ sm1844.391720/)
"Prettiest Little Girl in the County" (W 146004-3), Skillet Lickers, 04/10/1928, Atlanta, GA, Columbia 15315-D
"Little More Sugar in The Coffee" (W 404626-B), Fiddlin' John Carson & His Virginia Reelers, 12/09/1930, Atlanta, GA, OKeh 45542
Other version in this book by Allen Alsop, 1936 ("Pretty Little Girls in the County").

Stoney Point

Field notes: "Bledsoe has known it for 45 years. When Kinard plays he closes his eyes, wobbles from side to side."
Authors' comments: * Note the three "Ghost notes," indicated by "X" note heads in measures 2, 6, and 18.

JOHN ALEXANDER BROWN

Iuka, Tishomingo Co. (12/28/1872–10/27/1944)

From Abbott Ferriss's field notes:

John Alexander Brown, 67 years old, lives 4 miles east of Iuka on Rural Route 3. He wore faded blue overalls and a soiled jumper that was wet from the rain. He had a healthy ruddy complexion and sparkling blue eyes above a hoary beard. His beard was 6 or 8 inches long, but three strands of white hair extended below the beard for 4 or 5 additional inches. Music animated his eyes, he swayed from side to side with his shoulders and head. His interest, his enthusiasm to everything that he said, and his kindly attitude toward others made him delightful.

When someone spoke of a man being thrown into jail, Brown said, "It's a pity, he ought to learnt Farewell Whisky."

Brown has eight sons, only one of which plays fiddle. Brown moved to Tishomingo County from Itawamba County where his father lived. He has lived in Tishomingo County for forty years. His slightly Roman nose suggests English origin.

"I just picked fiddling up from my daddy, just practiced the sounds of it, I just listened. I heard a piece and went back home and played it. I can't play and sing both."

His pleasure both in listening to his own music and to the music of others is shown by his open

John Alexander Brown. Photo by Abbott Ferris, 1939, courtesy Mississippi Department of Archives and History.

mouth, heavy breathing, laughing, patting feet, and dancing eyes. It is the innocent enjoyment of a child. The life of a farmer in Tishomingo County is not easy, but Brown's clear skin has not a wrinkle.

John and Annie Brown. Courtesy Ruby Brown Smith.

John Alexander Brown. Courtesy Ruby Brown Smith.

After recording Brown said he had to hurry home. "Left my oxen out in the field."

His tunes are played in A.

Authors' comments: John Brown's father, Samuel Houston Brown, was originally from South Carolina. He and his two brothers fought in the Civil War, but only he survived. After the war he moved to Dumas, Tippah County, Mississippi, and married Betty Pickens, one of the twenty-four children of Israel Pickens, who had migrated from Jackson County, Alabama.

Samuel and Betty settled in Dumas, where they had a peach orchard and made peach brandy. Around 1875 they fled to Brown Hollow near Bear Creek and Iuka when the authorities became

aware of their distilling activities. They had four children.

John Brown was born December 28, 1872, in Dumas and died October 27, 1944. He married Annie Kathryn Campbell (1882–1962) on April 13, 1902. John Brown was redheaded, fair, had blue eyes and was around 6'3" in height. Five of his children had red hair as well. His wife, Annie, was very much Dutch, five feet tall with dark skin and black hair. They lived near Bear Creek for the first couple of years of their marriage before moving to Mill Creek, where all thirteen children were born.

John Brown learned fiddle from his father and was well known for his playing in Alabama, Mississippi, and Tennessee. He entered and won several fiddle contests. His favorite hymn was "The Unclouded Day," which he would play and he would ask his wife, Annie to sing. He would on occasion ask traveling preachers to stay the night with his family, thereby displacing the children from their bed.

His neighbors Bob Nix and Fed Booker were known to accompany him on banjo and two of his older children, Bill and Mary Lou, accompanied him on guitar for dances and other activities. His other children Elizabeth, Bob, Owen, Lile Mae, and John Henry played guitar and sang. Bob and Charlie played fiddle. Charlie inherited John's fiddle and passed it to his son Alec, who played French harp and hung the fiddle on his wall.

Brown loved his oxen, which he raised and trained to plow and work with the wagon. He planted cotton, trying to raise a bale a year, sometimes selling it by the sack. He raised corn and vegetables and did not believe in buying fertilizer.

John Brown is the only fiddler who both had his music notated in 1936 and had audio recordings made in 1939.

See the 1936 section for five of his tunes collected that year.

Cindy

Tuning: AEAE

Authors' comments: We include two versions of this tune, this simpler notation and the following highly detailed one that shows the double notes, bowing, and fingering. Most of our transcriptions fall somewhere between these extremes, attempting to strike the right balance between readability and accuracy.

Comparable versions:

"Cindy in the Meadows" (81706-1), Samantha Bumgarner & Eva Davis, 4/22/1924, NYC, Columbia 167-D

"Cindy" (W 143867-), Riley Puckett & Clayton McMichen, 04/02/1927, Atlanta, GA, Columbia 15232-D

"Get Along Home, Miss Cindy" (BVE 41853-2), Pope's Arkansas Mountaineers, 02/06/1928, Memphis, TN, Victor 21577

Other versions in this book by Charlie Addison ("Want to Go to Meeting"), W. E. Claunch ("Cindy"), Enos Canoy ("Where'd You Get Your Whiskey"), Mrs. R. C. Clifton ("Miss Cindy"), B. M. Guilette ("Liza Jane"), Frank Kittrell ("Cindy Jane"), Mrs. Joe McCoy ("Her Cheeks Are Like the Cherry"), Hardy Sharp ("Liza Jane"), Rev. J. E. Williams ("Cindy Waltz"), and Thaddeus Willingham ("Miss Cindy").

Cindy – full version

Authors' comments: Please note the common old-time technique of holding a unison and then noting on the higher of the adjacent strings

The Music Transcriptions

Dusty Miller

Tuning: AEAE modal

Recording comments: "That's where I can't quit, my father played it afore me."

Authors' comments: This is a well-known title, but not the familiar tune. Note that this tune is modal, with an indeterminate third which falls between C and C♯. Brown uses the third finger for slides.

The long held E note at the start of the "B" part shifts the downbeat to the second beat of the thirteenth measure. The rhythmic pulse is not disrupted.

This shifting of the downbeat while retaining the underlying pulse is what gives a polyrhythmic flavor. This type of syncopation is not unique to Mississippi, but is used frequently.

Comparable versions:

The first few measures of this tune resemble "Indian War Whoop" by Frank Kittrell in this book.

"Cotton Eyed Joe" (80557-A), Fiddlin' John Carson, 03/27/1927, Atlanta, GA, OKeh 45122

"Cotton Eyed Joe," Marcus Martin, Asheville, NC, Library of Congress LP AFS L62

Froggy Went A-Courtin'

Tuning: AEAE.

Comparable versions:

William, Alfred, *Folk Songs of the Upper Thames* (London: Augener, 1913), 133–34

Mackenzie, W. Roy, *Ballads and Seas Songs from Nova Scotia* (Cambridge, MA, 1928), 373–74

"Sugar Babe," Sharp, Cecil J., and Maud Karpeles, *English Folk Songs from the Southern Appalachians* (Oxford University Press, 1932), 312–20

"Froggie Went A-Courting," Bradley Kincaid, 02/27/1928, Chicago, IL, Gennett 6462

"King Kong Kitchie Kitchie Ki-Me-O" (GN 17176), Chubby Parker, 10/20/1931, Richmond, IN, Champion 16211

The Music Transcriptions

Give the Fiddler a Dram

Comparable versions:
Carter Brothers and Son, "Give the Fiddler a Dram," 1928 ("B" part)
Other versions in this book by John Brown ("A" part), W. E. Claunch ("A" part), and Stephen B. Tucker ("Calico," "B" part).

Not A-Gonna Have No Supper Here Tonight

Saddle old gray, let's run away Ain't gonna have no sup-per here today

From John Hatcher:
Saddle old gray, let's run away
Ain't gonna have no supper here today

From Mrs. Vivian Skinner:
Boys all drunk and the girls all tight
Ain't gonna have no supper here tonight

Tuning: GDAD

Comparable versions:
"Saddle Up the Gray" (W 400336-A), Carter Brothers & Son, 02/24/1928, Memphis, TN, OKeh 45202

Rats in the Meal Barrel

Tuning: GDAD

Recording comments: "learned from his father."

Authors' comments: In the first strain, the third finger holds down the D on the A string while the melody is played on the tuned-down E string. Note that the E string is tuned down to D when you are reading the fingering numbers.

Comparable versions:

T. A. Bickerstaff collected the tune title from Tishomingo Co. in the early 1920s.

Sally Goodin

Tuning: AEAE

Recorded comments: Mr. Brown said, "I believe I'm pretty good on it. You can prove it on that machine." Tune was learned from his father.

Authors' comments: Here is another crooked tune in which Brown lengthens the opening phrase with drawn out mournful E notes, shifting the downbeat to the second beat in m5; the pulse is maintained, things "come round right" by the end of the first part, and the second part is square.

Comparable versions:
"Sally Goodwin," Ford, Ira, *Traditional Music of America* (New York: Dutton, 1940), 64, 209 (calls), 419 (verses)
"Sally Gooden" (B 26664-1), Eck Robertson, 07/01/1922, NYC, Victor 18956
"Old Sally Goodman" (S 72-015-A), Fiddlin' John Carson, 11/07/1923, NYC, OKeh 40095
"Sally Goodin" (E 29275-), Kessinger Brothers, 02/05/1929, NYC, Brunswick 308
Other versions of "Sally Goodin" in this book by W. E. Claunch, J. E. Shoemaker, and Thaddeus Willingham.

Wolves A-Howlin'

Don't you hear them wolves a-howlin'
All around my poor little darlin'
Don't you see then blue clouds flyin'
Poor little darling haulin' and a-cryin'

Wo-o-olves a-howlin', howlin', howlin',
O-o-oh them wolves a-howlin', howlin', howlin'

Don't you hear them wolves a-howlin,
Poor little darling bawlin' and a-cryin'
Don't you see them blue clouds a-flying
All around my poor little darling

Tuning: AEAE

Authors' comments: * Indicates that the A at the end of m3 is a pulsed or divided upbow.

    The tune is non-square with the equivalent of three extra measures added to the first part, so that the expected location of the down beat shifts in the first part, but then comes around to the right place in the second part. The shifting of the beat back and forth throughout the tune is a form of syncopation, which I find both artful and satisfying for the listener.

    This type of syncopation/polyrhythm occurs with noticeable frequency in the collection, especially Brown and Kittrell.

Comparable versions:
Thede, Marion, *The Fiddle Book* (Oak Publication NY, 1970), 133
"Wolves Howling," (C 4135-) Stripling Brothers, 08/19/1929 Chicago, IL, Vocalion 5412
Other version in the book by: W. E. Claunch.

CANOY FAMILY

Magee, Simpson Co.

From Abbott Ferriss's field notes:

Tim Canoy, thirty-seven years old plays mandolin. "The first guitar I ever had, I wanted so bad when I was a little boy 'till I taken a cheese box, put strings on it, and learned to tune it. None of my family played. I like music. Whenever a piece of music is played, I quit work and listen."

Mrs. Lola Canoy, wife of Tim Canoy, and sister of Grover Bishop, plays guitar. "This is just a jumped up piece of business for me."

Enos Canoy, thirty years old and born in Simpson County. He has played the fiddle since he was twelve years old. His first fiddle he constructed from a pine box. He had two uncles and one brother who played. His father fiddled but he died when Enos was four years old. He has used as accompaniment to his fiddle, straws. He plays with one tuning only. His fiddle was decorated with hand-tooled figures that were painted in various colors—the work of Canoy himself. Canoy lives in a small, four-room tenant house with a front porch. There is no chimney. "The house has what we in the back woods call wood shutters, that is the windows are constructed of pine lumber and made to slide back and forth." The house is located on the Magee and Rawleigh road. Born one mile east of Magee, March 8th, 1909. Family: wife and two children. Lived in Simpson County all his life. A farmer with very little education. Baptist. Five feet seven inches tall; 145 pounds in weight, brown eyes and black hair. He has made a bass fiddle, which resembles a factory made product. He constructed his first fiddle.

The three have played together for about two years, calling themselves the Canoy Band.

Authors' comments: The band played for schools, political rallies, town fairs, and dances. A later version of the band that played into the 1950s was named Enos and the Canoy Wildcats, adding a weekly radio show on WRBC from Jackson to their musical outlets.

Buck Dancing Charlie

Field notes: Enos Canoy said, "just a-fooling with my fiddle. I made it up just pranking."
Authors' comments: Canoy varies the repeats of the parts in the tune each time he plays it.

Comparable versions:
"Buckin' Mule" (1963-), J. D. Harris, 11 or 12/1924, Asheville, NC, Broadway 1963
"Buckin' Mule" (W 145053-2), Gid Tanner & the Skillet Lickers, 10/21/1927, Atlanta, GA, Victor 21534

Eighth of January

Authors' comments: Originally titled "Jackson's Victory" after Andrew Jackson's defeat of the British at New Orleans on January 8, 1815. With the later decline in his reputation, the tune was renamed "Eighth of January."

Comparable versions:
Ford, Ira, *Traditional Music of America* (New York: Dutton, 1940), 63
Arkansas Barefoot Boys (W 400229-B), 02/11/1928, Memphis, TN, OKeh 45217
Fox Chasers (W 5404166-A), 06/11/1930, San Antonio, TX, OKeh 45496
Ted Gossett's Band (GN 17041), 09/16/1930, Richmond, IN, Champion 16160
Other versions of "Eighth of January" in this book by Enos Canoy, W. E. Claunch, Charlie Edmundson, John Hatcher, Hardy Sharp, and J. A. Moorman.

Henry Holmes' Holla

ho   ho ho ho   ho ho ho ho ho ho   hu ho   ha ho ha ho huh ha ho ha   ho

Authors' comments: This was sung in A. The fiddle was playing G tuned up a whole step. The first eight measures were sung by Jim Myers, the rest fiddled by Enos Canoy.

Lost John

Field notes: "Enos Canoy says he learned the piece from hearing it played on the French harp. He has never heard it played on the fiddle. He said, 'I've heard old people speak about Lost John, so we're going to see if we can find him.' After playing, he said, 'I found him!'"

This tune seems loosely related to:
"Lost John" (C 4122-B), Stripling Brothers, 08/19/1929, Chicago, IL, Vocalion 5441
"Lost John" (143092-2), Burnett & Rutherford, 11/06/1926, Atlanta, GA, Columbia 15122-D

Old Blue Sow

Field notes: "Enos Canoy learned this tune from his uncle, an old-time fiddler, who says it is an old tune. He called certain figures, which he had heard at square dances. Usually, he says, separate callers, not the fiddler, give the call. However, earlier fiddlers both furnished the music and calls."

Authors' comments: Mr. Canoy varies the length of each part on each pass through the tune.

Measures 13–18 are a shuffle played on the first and second strings—the C♯ note is held down and the bow remains in contact with both strings, which are sounded continuously throughout the passage. The bow is rocked very slightly between the first and second strings. The alternate transcript shows it "as if" one were playing single notes, to give the sense of the rocking motion.

Pearl Bryan

Deep, deep in yonder valley	Down in these woods I have you
Where the growing flowers bloom	From me you cannot fly
There lies a lone Pearl Brown	No human hands can save you
In a cold and silent tomb	Pearl Brown you're bound to die
She died not broken hearted	What have I done dear darling
Nor of an illness will	That you should take my life
But she grieved to leave her mother	I have always been your sweetheart
And the home she loved so well	And would have been your wife
That night the moon shone brightly	Down on her knees before him
And the stars were shining too	She begged to save her life
Into the cottage window	Into her snow white bosom
Her jealous lover grew	He plunged a fatal knife
Come darling lets go walking	But I'll forgive you darlin'
Down through the meadow gate	Was her last dying word
Where we disturb none other	They found her dead next morning
And name our wedding day	Lying on the ground.

Source: Lola Canoy, vocal; Jim Meyers, fiddle

Field notes: "Meyers said he played the alto part to the song for the first time. Mrs. Canoy said she thought it was a true song. She believes someone made the song up from a true happening. She says most songs are composed from something that happened, like 'Kenny Wagoner,' 'Jesse James.' I like sad love songs. When I take the blues, I like to sing sad songs."

Comparable versions:
Melody:
"I'll Be All Smiles Tonight," T. B. Ransom, words and music, 1879
"I'll Be All Smiles Tonight" (BE 47174-3), Allen Brothers, 10/15/1928, Atlanta, GA, Victor V40210
"I'll Be All Smiles Tonight" (BS 83130-1), Carter Family, 5/08/1934, Camden, NJ, Brunswick B5529
Lyrics:
"Pearl Bryan" (W 143097-2), Dick Burnett & Leonard Rutherford, 11/6/1926, Atlanta, GA, Columbia 15113-D
"Pearl Bryant" (GEX 14028-B), Roy Harvey & Bob Hoke & the North Carolina Ramblers, 7/28/1927, NYC, Silvertone 5181a

Pickin' the Devil's Eye

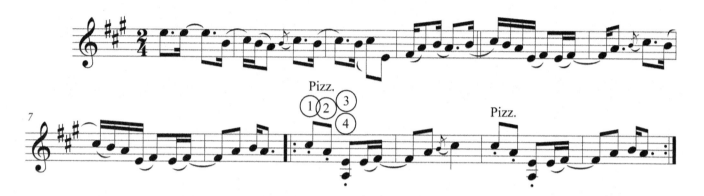

Tuning: AEAC♯

Field notes: "Fiddle Enos Canoy. Straws Jim Meyers. Canoy learned it from hearing Love Kennaday play it 'a long time ago.' Two
    straws were used. In the piece the plucking of the strings, according to Canoy, is 'picking' his eye, 'trying to get it out.'"

Poor Little Mary Settin' in the Corner

Alt versions of m7-10

Tuning: AEAE
Field notes: Learned from Love Kennaday and Robert Runnels.
Authors' comments: The basic tune is stated in the first two parts; the following measures show Canoy's variations.

Possom and Coon

Possom   and   the   coonie   Racoon   on

the   hill Possom said to   coonie Give me dollar bill

Possum up a simmon tree
Coonie on the ground
Coonie said to the possum
Shake them simmons down

Field notes: "The fiddler, contrary to the majority of informants who play violin, calls his instrument the 'violin.' The tune he learned from L. D. Kennaday, a local old-timer fiddler, about 12 years ago. The text was communicated by Grover Bishop, FWP."

Comparable versions:

Belden, H. M. and Arthur Palmer Hudson, *Frank C. Brown Collection of North Carolina Folklore*; *Vol. 3: Folk Songs* (Durham, NC: Duke University Press, 1952), 510, 565

"Been to the East Been to the West" (W 146208-2), Leake County Revelers, 04/27/1928, New Orleans, LA, Columbia 15318-D

"Share 'Em" (W 402127-A), Scottsdale String Band, 08/10/1928, Atlanta, GA, OKeh 45256

"Shear the Sheep Bobbie" (W 147647-1), Gatwood Square Dance Band, 12/15/1928, New Orleans, LA, Columbia 15363

"Take Me Back to Tulsa" (Dal 1180-1), Bob Wills & His Texas Playboys, 02/25/1941, Dallas, TX, OKeh 06101

Other versions in this book by W. E. Claunch ("Chicken Pie" and "Miss Sally at the Party"), Ruby Costello ("Want To Go To Meeting"), John Hatcher ("Old Miss Sally"), Charles Long ("Jones County" and "Steamboat"), and Hardy Sharp ("Great Big Yam Potatoes").

Where'd You Get Your Whiskey

Where'd you git yor whiskey Where'd you git your dram Stole it from a

bootlegger Way down in bootlegger town Got a little home to go to Got a little home to

go to Got a little home to go to Way down in jailhouse now

Tuning: AEAC♯
Field notes: Canoy learned the piece from Robert Runnels who was raised in Simpson County.
Authors' comments: The "A" part of this tune is related to "Liza Jane" and the "B" part resembles the "B" part of "Cindy."

Comparable versions:
Cindy:
"Cindy in the Meadows" (81706-1), Samantha Bumgarner & Eva Davis, 4/22/1924, NYC, Columbia 167-D
"Cindy" (W 143867-), Riley Puckett & Clayton McMichen 04/02/1927, Atlanta, GA, Columbia 15232-D
"Get Along Home, Miss Cindy" (BVE 41853-2), Pope's Arkansas Mountaineers, 02/06/1928, Memphis, TN, Victor 21577
Other versions in this book by Charlie Addison ("Want to Go to Meeting"), John Brown ("Cindy"), W. E. Claunch ("Cindy"),
    Mrs. R. C. Clifton ("Miss Cindy"), B. M. Guilette ("Liza Jane"), Frank Kittrell ("Cindy Jane"), Mrs. Joe McCoy ("Her Cheeks
    Are Like the Cherry"), Hardy Sharp ("Liza Jane"), Rev. J. E. Williams ("Cindy Waltz"), and Thaddeus Willingham ("Miss
    Cindy").
Liza Jane:
"Old Liza Jane" (13302), Uncle Am Stuart, 06/1924, NYC, Vocalion 14846
"Liza Jane" (140018-1), Riley Puckett, 09/11/1924, NYC, Columbia 15014-D
"Goodbye Liza Jane" (9596-A), Fiddlin' John Carson & His Virginia Reelers, 03/11/1926, Atlanta, GA, OKeh 45049
Other versions in this book by Horace Kinard ("Liza Jane"), Everett Mitchell ("Liza Jane"), J. P. Reece ("I Ain't Gonna Leave Her
    by Herself"), and Thaddeus Willingham.

W. E. CLAUNCH

Guntown, Lee Co.

From Abbott Ferriss's field notes:
Recordings and interviews made May 10, 1939—
at home of W. E. Claunch.

W. E. Claunch, forty-five years old, is over six feet in height. "Don't know one note from another." He learned to play the fiddle from his father when he was very young. His four brothers also play the fiddle, are all farmers. His grandfather, who came from England, also played. "Every Claunch there ever was could play." He also picks the five-string banjo, plays the piano. For ten or twelve years he "Trooped" with a circus. "My hair still gets kinky and I want to go," he said. "I followed shows and carnivals all my life, 'till I got murdered—married I mean." He said that his father had given him three farms, and that he spent them all. At present he plays regularly at a theatre at Baldwin.

The three-room house is bare but clean. It has no wallpaper, no screens, few pictures, but a radio. He has been married for twenty-five years. He has one daughter who plays the guitar and one son. His son was plowing in the field while we were recording. Claunch had some difficulty making his son stay in the field. He wanted to hear music.

Claunch, who is a World War veteran, is a thirty-third degree Mason.

W. E. Claunch. Photo by Abbott Ferriss, 1939, courtesy Mississippi Department of Archives and History.

Claunch's daughter, Mrs. Christine Haygood 22 years old, accompanied him on many of the recordings. Claunch said he played better with an accompaniment.

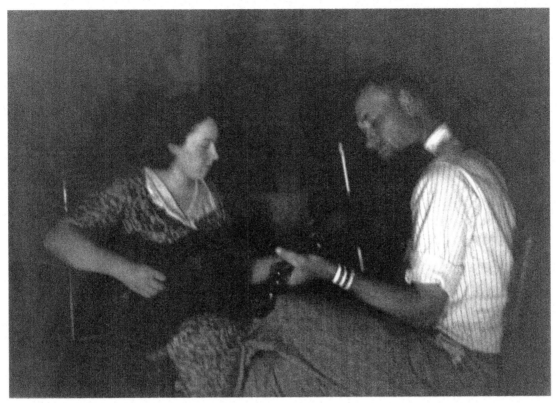

W. E. Claunch and his daughter, Christina Heygood. Photo by Abbott Ferriss, 1939, courtesy Mississippi Department of Archives and History.

Besides playing at a theatre, his experience included performances at schools, dances, and over the radio with a band. On the twenty five acres he farms, last year Claunch devoted five acres to cotton, harvested three bales of cotton. "I can live without the crop," he said. Between 1928 and 1937, he said, he spent $16,000— evidently given him by his father. "The banks ruined me," he said. He is most proud, however, of the fact that during his "trooping" days, he visited seven states.

Authors' comments: W. E. Claunch was born in 1894 near Guntown, Mississippi, and died on November 10, 1958. Claunch was a well-known local dance and contest fiddler and played often at a theater in Baldwyn, to attract patrons for the movies. His daughter Christine recalled family gatherings, often weekly, when much of family played. Claunch's friend and guitarist Algie

Surratt described Ernest as a "fastidious" man who would go to great lengths to keep clean and presentable. He described Ernest opening doors while keeping his hand in his pocket when grabbing the doorknob so as to avoid actually touching the doorknob or by reaching to the top edge of a door to open it.

All of the tunes recorded in 1939 are included in this book along with two transcriptions from the 1950s home recordings.

Christine seems to have been playing D and A tunes with a capo at the second fret and fingering in C and G.

A list of fiddle tunes played by Ernest Claunch, Age 43, Guntown Miss. Rural Route #3, Dec 29, 1938, by Lee County collector Fletcher Stokes:

Chicken Pie
Chicken Reel

Sailor's Hornpipe
Forked Deer
Gooseberry Pie
Fire in the Mountain
Frost-bitten Peas
Goin' On Down Town
Grandfather's Old Brown Pants
Gray Eagle
The Great Titanic
Natchez on the Hillside
New York Gas Light
Oh, My Little Indian, Don't Get Drunk
One-Eyed Square
Pass around the bottle
Rabbit in the Pea patch
Rat Time Annie
Texas Belle
Well Done Davy
Wolves A Howlin'

He also plays most of the following ballads, etc. but couldn't give much help on the words:

Bring My Willie Back to Me
Coon, Coon, Coon, Wish My Color
Dance by the Light of the Moon
Darling Clementine
Dear Lawd, Remember
Dublin Bay
Doan Yo' Cry, My Honey
Hello, Central, Give Me Heaven
In Dat Great Risin' Day
I'se Gwine to Heaven When I Die
Lawd, Thy Prayer Like a Wheel A Rollin'
Little Brown Jug
Mulberry Bush
Maid of Monterey (Mexican War Song)
Possum Up A 'Simmon Tree
Sweet Bird, Sweet Bird
'Taint Gonna Rain No Mo'
Time Enough Yet
Way Down in the Cornfield

Recorded in 1950:
As part of a Tupelo 6 a.m. radio show, *Sunrise Salute.* They were billed as the Mississippi Melody

Boys and were promoting that night's concert at the Joy Theater in Nettleton, Mississippi, performing a set between two western movies:

Good Night Waltz
Grey Eagle
Old Joe Clark
Tennessee Wagoner
Unannounced (I Don't Love Nobody)
Unknown, Claunch attempted to play a "little jitterbug tune" that he composed, but Algie asked him to play a waltz instead.

A 1950 rehearsal tape-recorded on a wire recorder at the Claunch home with guitarist Algie Surratt, all tunes unannounced so the titles may have been different:

Arkansas Traveler
Billy in Lowground
Carroll County Blues
Chicken Reel
Down Yonder
Eighth of January
I Don't Love Nobody
Little Star
Sitting on Top of the World
Soldier's Joy
Something perhaps derived from St. Louis Blues.
Untitled, similar to Walk Along John—One can only wonder what he called it.
Wagoneer

Arkansas Traveler

I don't think too much fair m' fool are ya?
No just a fence is all there's between me and you

Mister your corn looks mighty yeller
I reckon so, I planted a yellow crop

Don't look like you're gonna make more'n half a
   crop
No sir, I planted on the share

Say mister head that ox out there a way
Well he's got a better head'n I can put on 'im

Well I mean turn 'im
Well he's got the right side out

well I mean talk to 'im
Hello ox!

Come in mister supper's about ready
What'll you have
Well I'll take a knife
Well I ain't got that

Well I'll take a spoon
Well I ain't got that

Well I'll take a fork
Well I ain't got that

Well how in the devil do you do here?
Oh pretty well, thank you, how're y'all?

Say mister where's this road out here go to out
   here?
Well I don't know, been livin' here forty year,
And ain't went nowhere yet, oh yeah

Tuning: ADAE

Field notes: Claunch said that his father spoke the words, just as he did on the record and "that this was the old-timey way."
   He said he could talk the Arkansas Traveller "two hours." His wife said some of the verses were "things they made up
   themselves."

Authors' comments: Note the fingering for the low part; this section is essentially a double shuffle on the low strings. Claunch
   was one of the younger fiddlers at 45 years old, and this may represent a more "modern" technique that he absorbed.

Comparable versions:

"The Arkansas Traveler," *The Arkansas Traveller's Songster* (New York: Dick & Fitzgerald, 1864), 5–9 imslp.org/wiki/
   The_Arkansas_Traveler's_Songster_(Various)

"Arkansas Traveler" (B 26660-2), Henry C. Gilliland and A. C. "Eck" Robertson, 06/30/1922, NYC, Victor 18956

"Arkansas Traveler" (8613-A), Fiddlin' John Carson & His Virginia Reelers, 03/1924, Atlanta, GA, OKeh 40108

"Arkansas Traveler" (AL 228), Kessinger Brothers, 02/11/1928, Ashland, KY, Brunswick 247

Other versions of "Arkansas Traveler" in this book by John Hatcher and Stephen B. Tucker.

Bear Creek's Up

Bear Creek's up and Bear Creek's muddy When a man gets drunk he can't (stand) studdy

Authors' comments: A regional variant of "Sally Goodin," which he also plays. T. A. Bickerstaff includes the title in a seminar paper in 1927. There is a Bear Creek in Tishomingo County.

Comparable versions:
"Sally Goodwin," Ford, Ira, *Traditional Music of America* (New York: Dutton, 1940), 64, 209 (calls), 419 (verses)
"Sally Gooden" (B 26664-1), Eck Robertson, 07/01/1922, NYC, Victor 18956
"Old Sally Goodman" (S 72-015-A), Fiddlin' John Carson 11/07/1923, NYC, OKeh 40095
"Give Me a Chaw of Tobacco" (M 833-), Carter Brothers & Son, 11/22/1928, Memphis, TN, Vocalion 5295
"Sally Goodin" (E 29275-), Kessinger Brothers, 02/05/1929, NYC, Brunswick 308
The "A" part of the tune above resembles versions of "Sally Goodin" in this book by John Brown, W. E. Claunch, and Thaddeus Willingham; the "B" part resembles "Bear Creek" by Mae Belle Williams.

Black Eyed Susie

Love my mammy, love my daddy Love my flip-flop turned in gravy

Oh, my pretty little black-eyed Susie Oh, my pretty little black-eyed Susie

Love my mammy, I love my daddy
And I love my sweetheart better'n anybody (or
    possibly "I love my sweetheart settin' in the
    parlor")

Tuning: ADAE

Authors' comments: The third finger holds the D note on the A string while the first finger notes on the E string, where
    necessary.

Comparable versions:

"Black Eyed Susie" (81635-1), Gid Tanner and Riley Puckett, 03/08/1924, NYC, Columbia 119-D

"Black Eyed Susie" (GE 13040), Fiddlin' Doc Roberts, 09/1927, Richmond, IN, Gennett 6257

"Black Eyed Susie" (BVE 39747), J. P. Nestor, 08/01/1927, Bristol, TN, Victor 21070

Other versions of "Black Eyed Susan" in this book by John Brown, John Hatcher, J. A. Moorman, and Thaddeus Willingham
    ("Black Eyed Susie").

Chicken Pie

Comparable versions:

Belden, H. M., and Arthur Palmer Hudson, *Frank C. Brown Collection of North Carolina Folklore; Vol. 3: Folk Songs* (Durham, NC: Duke University Press, 1952), 510, 565

"Been to the East Been to the West" (W 146208-2), Leake County Revelers, 04/27/1928, New Orleans, LA, Columbia 15318-D

"Share 'Em" (W 402127-A), Scottsdale String Band, 08/10/1928, Atlanta, GA, OKeh 45256

"Shear the Sheep Bobbie" (W 147647-1), Gatwood Square Dance Band, 12/15/1928, New Orleans, LA, Columbia 15363

"Take Me Back to Tulsa" (Dal 1180-1), Bob Wills & His Texas Playboys, 02/25/1941, Dallas, TX, OKeh 06101

Other versions in this book by Enos Canoy ("Possum and Coon"), W. E. Claunch ("Miss Sally at the Party"), Ruby Costello ("Want To Go To Meeting"), John Hatcher ("Old Miss Sally"), Charles Long ("Jones County" and "Steamboat"), and Hardy Sharp ("Great Big Yam Potatoes").

(right page)

Tuning: ADAE

Authors' comments: On the recording Claunch sings "Kiss me, girl" and then squeaks his bow across the strings, perhaps behind the bridge, repeats with "Kiss me again," plays the next vocal line on fiddle, squeaks, and then sings the last line.

Comparable versions:

"Cindy in the Meadows" (81706-1), Samantha Bumgarner & Eva Davis, 4/22/1924, NYC, Columbia 167-D

"Cindy" (W 143867-), Riley Puckett & Clayton McMichen, 04/02/1927, Atlanta, GA, Columbia 15232-D

"Get Along Home, Miss Cindy" (BVE 41853-2), Pope's Arkansas Mountaineers, 02/06/1928, Memphis, TN, Victor 21577

Other versions in this book by Charlie Addison ("Want to Go to Meeting"), John Brown ("Cindy"), Enos Canoy ("Where'd You Get Your Whiskey"), Mrs. R. C. Clifton ("Miss Cindy"), B. M. Guilette ("Liza Jane"), Frank Kittrell ("Cindy Jane"), Mrs. Joe McCoy ("Her Cheeks Are Like the Cherry"), Hardy Sharp ("Liza Jane"), Rev. J. E. Williams ("Cindy Waltz"), and Thaddeus Willingham ("Miss Cindy").

Cindy

Once

I had a pretty girl, name was Katie Brown ev-ry where that Katie went I was-a hangin' a-round kiss

me girl, kiss me again hug my neck la - w - d hold-in' on!

kiss

me kiss me a-gain la - w - d hold-in' on!

Devil's Dream

Tuning: AEAE

Authors' comments: The "B" part starts with a wild slide on the first six notes, a rather bluesy intrusion into this Scottish tune.

Comparable versions:

Howe, Elias, *Howe's School for the Violin* (Boston: Oliver Ditson, 1851), 29

"Devil's Dream" (AL 213), Kessinger Bros, 02/10/1928, Ashland, KY, Brunswick 256

"Devil's Dream" (65713-A), Clayton McMichen, 06/01/1931, NYC, Decca 2649

Other versions of "Devil's Dream" in this book by Mr. T. W. Cooper ("Untitled") and Stephen B. Tucker.

Drunken Hiccups

Tuning: AEAC♯

Field notes: Claunch said learned this from his father, "The picking is he-cupping."

Comparable versions:

"Jack of Diamonds" (12783-A), Ben Jarrell with Da Costa Woltz's Southern Broadcasters, 04/1927, Richmond, IN, Herwin 75561

"Drunkard's Hiccups" (S 73-878-A), Fiddlin' John Carson, 12/1925, NYC, OKeh 45032

"Way Up On Clinch Mountain" (BVE 42491-2), Jilson Setters (J. W. Day), 02/27/1928, NYC, Victor 21635

Other versions in this book by Charles Long and John Hatcher ("Farewell Whiskey").

Eighth of January

Tuning: ADAE

Field notes: Learned from Jim Claunch.

Authors' comments: According to Andy Kuntz at the Traditional Tune Archive [tunearch.org/wiki/Annotation: Eighth_of_January_(1)], the tune was originally titled "Jackson's Victory" after Andrew Jackson's defeat of the British at New Orleans on January 8, 1815. With the later decline in his reputation, the tune was renamed "The Eighth of January."

Comparable versions of "Eighth of January":

Ford, Ira, *Traditional Music of America* (New York: Dutton, 1940), 63

Arkansas Barefoot Boys (W 400229-B), 02/11/1928, Memphis, TN, OKeh 45217

Fox Chasers (W 5404166-A), 06/11/1930, San Antonio, TX, OKeh 45496

Ted Gossett's Band (GN 17041), 09/16/1930, Richmond, IN, Champion 16160

Other versions of "Eighth of January" in this book by Enos Canoy, Charlie Edmundson, John Hatcher, Hardy Sharp, and J. A. Moorman.

Give the Fiddler a Dram

Hey, give the fiddler a dram, the fiddler a dram
Come boy, come boy, give the fiddler a dram.

Tuning: ADAE

Comparable versions:
Carter Brothers and Son, "Give the Fiddler a Dram," 1928 ("B" part)
Other versions in this book by John Brown ("A" part), W. E. Claunch ("A" part), and Stephen B. Tucker ("Calico," "B" part).

Great Titanic

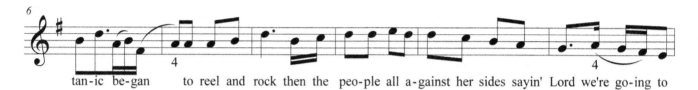

One Tues - day morn ing a bout two O' - clock when the gre - at ship Ti -

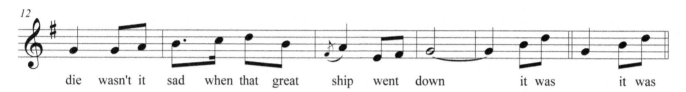

tan-ic be-gan to reel and rock then the peo-ple all a-gainst her sides sayin' Lord we're go-ing to

die wasn't it sad when that great ship went down it was it was

Chorus

sad when that great ship went down it was sad when that gr-eat ship went down

hus-bands and wives and all the lit-tle ba-bies lost th-eir lives it was sad wh-en that great ship went down

They said when they built the great Titanic
What else could they do
They said they'd build a ship that water could not
    go through
But God with his mighty hand
Showed the world it could not stand

Authors' comments: On April 14, 1912, the *Titanic* struck an iceberg in the Atlantic and sank, killing over a thousand passengers.
    Over one hundred and sixty songs were published in the next few months describing the event.

Comparable versions:
"Sinking of the Titanic" (W 140646-), Vernon Dalhart, 6/04/1925, NYC, Columbia 15032-D
"The Titanic" (S 72-788-B), Ernest Stoneman, 09/24/1924, NYC, OKeh 40288
"When That Great Ship Went Down" (4685-728), William & Versey Smith, ca. 06/1927, Chicago, IL, Paramount 12505

Grey Eagle

Authors' comments: The famous Tennessee racing horse Wagner beat Grey Eagle in a race in 1839. Both horses have fiddle tunes named for them.

Comparable versions:
"Grey Eagle" (13310/*09), Uncle "Am" Stuart, 07/1924, NYC, Vocalion 14843

Grub Springs

Tuning: ADAE

Authors' comments: While playing, Claunch announces several square dance calls: "up four," "all sides circle," and "all of them swing."

Comparable versions:
"Get Up in the Cool" by Eck Robertson, 1965, County LP 202

How Old Are You My Pretty Little Miss

How old are you, my   pretty little miss How   old are you, my   honey I'm old enough for - to

kiss all day I'll   be sixteen next   Sunday   Oh   Fad - de - li - dank - tum Dod - de - la - da

Tuning: AEAE

Field notes: Claunch said he learned the tune from an "old grey-headed darkey. It's an old war song."

Authors' comments: Note how Claunch varies the slurs and shuffles, never playing it exactly the same. For a simpler notion of the setting, see the singing part.

Comparable versions:

"Black Jack Davy" (C 3361-), Carter Family, 10/04/1940, Chicago, IL, OKeh 06313

Mississippi Sawyer

Field notes: "He also knew the tune as 'The Downfall of Paris.'"

Comparable versions:

"Love from the Heart," George P. Knauff, *Virginia Reels*, vol. 4, no. 4 (Baltimore, 1839)

"Mississippi Sawyer" (W 148200-1), Gid Tanner and His Skillet Lickers, 04/08/1929, Atlanta, GA, Columbia 15420-D

"Mississippi Sawyer" (E 29271-), Kessinger Brothers, 02/05/1929, NYC, Brunswick 309

"Old Time Corn Shuckin' pt. 1" (BVE 39270-2). Ernest Stoneman & the Blue Ridge Corn Shuckers, 07/27/1927, Bristol, TN, Victor 20835

Other versions of "Mississippi Sawyer" in this book by Sinclair Crocker, Hardy Sharp, J. E. Shoemaker, Stephen B. Tucker, Rev. J. H. Wheeler, and Rev. J. E. Williams.

Miss Sally at the Party

asked Mis' Sally to be my wife She stuck at me with a bowie knife

I asked Mis' Sally to be my wife
She stuck at me with a bowie knife
Mis' Sally, Mis' Sally
Mis' Sally at the party-o

Comparable versions:

Belden, H. M., and Arthur Palmer Hudson, *Frank C. Brown Collection of North Carolina Folklore; Vol. 3: Folk Songs* (Durham, NC: Duke University Press, 1952), 510, 565

"Been to the East Been to the West" (W 146208-2), Leake Co. Revelers, 04/27/1928, New Orleans, LA, Columbia 15318-D

"Share 'Em" (W 402127-A), Scottsdale String Band, 08/10/1928, Atlanta, GA, OKeh 45256

"Shear The Sheep Bobbie" (W 147647-1), Gatwood Square Dance Band, 12/15/1928, New Orleans, LA, Columbia 15363

"Take Me Back to Tulsa" (Dal 1180-1), Bob Wills & His Texas Playboys, 02/25/1941, Dallas, TX, OKeh 06101

Other versions in this book by Enos Canoy ("Possum and Coon"), W. E. Claunch ("Chicken Pie"), Ruby Costello ("Want to Go to Meeting"), John Hatcher ("Old Miss Sally"), Charles Long ("Jones County" and "Steamboat"), and Hardy Sharp ("Great Big Yam Potatoes").

Oh Yes, Mammy Look at Sam

Oh, yes, Mammy, look at Sam Eatin' up the biscuits And soppin' out the pan

I never heard the like since I been born Old folks a-shuckin' and a - shellin' corn

---

Tuning: AEAE

Field notes: Claunch said, "That's when they had them old-time parties, when the boy that found the red ear of corn got to hug and kiss any girl that he wanted."

"I learned this from my father."

Comparable versions:

"Old Granny Rattletrap" (13322), Uncle "Am" Stuart, 06/1924, NYC, Vocalion 14888

"Hog Eye" (BVE 41858-2), Pope's Arkansas Mountaineers, 02/06/1928, Memphis, TN, Victor 21295

"Far in the Mountain," Red Headed Fiddlers, 10/28/1929, Dallas, TX, Brunswick 470

"Mississippi Square Dance, Pt. 1," Freeny's Barn Dance Band, 12/16/1930, Jackson, MS, OKeh 45533

Old Molly Hare

Old Molly Hare whatcha doin' there
Runnin' through the cotton patch as hard as I
    can tear
Knockin' out the cotton and knockin' out the
    corn
Never seen the like since I been born

Tuning: ADAE
Field notes: Learned from his grandfather.

Comparable versions:
"Largo's Fairy Dance," Gow, John and Andrew, *A Collection of Slow Airs, Strathspeys & Reels*, vol. 5 (London: Wm. Campbell, ca.
    1795), 19
Christy's Panorama Songster (New York: W.H. Murphy, ca. 1850s)
"Old Molly Hare," Fiddling Power & Family, 9/28/1927, Winston-Salem, NC, OKeh 45628
Other versions in this book by W. A. Bledsoe, Mrs. M. B. Brister, J. A. Moorman, J. E. Shoemaker, and two versions by "Unknown."

Pass Around the Bottle

Hang Jeff Davis to a sour apple tree
Hang Jeff Davis to a sour apple tree
Hang Jeff Davis to a sour apple tree
As we go marching on

Field notes: Claunch "guesses it's fifty year old." He says he does not know another song to the same tune.

Authors' comments: Claunch drops a beat each time through for instrumental and start of the first verse, then switches to regular eight-bar structure.

Comparable versions:

"John Brown's Song," Simonds, Phillip (Boston: Russell & Patee, 1861) www.loc.gov/item/ihas.200001979

"The Battle Hymn of the Republic," H. N. Hempsted (Milwaukee, 1861–65) www.loc.gov/item/ihas.200000179/

Rabbit in the Pea Patch

Tuning: ADAE

Comparable versions:
"The Rabbit in the Pea Patch" (E 4960), Uncle Dave Macon & the Fruit Jar Drinkers, 05/091927, NYC, Vocalion 5156

Raise Big Taters

Sift the meal and
save the bran Goodbye gals I'm going in

Sift the meal and save the bran
Goodbye gals I'm going in
Raise big 'taters on sandy land
Raise big 'taters on sandy land

Comparable versions:

"Sail Away Ladies" (W 141876-1-2), Uncle Bunt Stephens, 03/29/1926, NYC, Columbia 15071-D

"Sail Away Ladies" (GE 14361-), H. L. Bandy, 10/17/1928, Richmond, IN, *Kentucky Mountain Music* (CD), Yazoo Records 2200, 2003

"Great Big Taters in Sandy Land" (BVE 56360-2), Eck Robertson & J. B. Cranfill, 10/10/1929, Dallas, TX, Victor V 40205

Run Nigger Run

Run, nigger, run Patteroller'll git you   Run, nigger, run Better git away

Nigger   run, nigger   flew Nigger   tore   his   shoe   in   two

---

Tuning: ADAE

Comparable versions:

"Run Nigger, Run," Allen, William Francis, *Slave Songs of the United States* (New York: A. Simpson, 1867), #110, 89

"Run Nigger, Run" (8709-A), Fiddling John Carson, 08/27/1924, Atlanta, GA, OKeh 40230

"Run Nigger, Run" (667/668), Uncle Dave Macon, 04/13/1925, NYC, Vocalion 15032

"Run Boy, Run" (BVE 56361-2), Eck Robertson & Dr. J. B. Cranfill, 10/10/1929, Dallas, TX, Victor V40205

Other versions of "Run Nigger, Run" in this book by Mrs. M. B. Brister, Mr. John McCartie, Jr., Stephen B. Tucker, Mrs. A. Tynes, Mrs. Louise Walker Wallace, and Thaddeus Willingham.

Sally Goodin

Alt. m.11

Ex. - fingering for mm.9,10
a similar pattern is used for mm. 4,8&11.

Had a piece of pie and I had piece of puddin'
And I give it all away to see Sally Goodin

Looked up a road and saw my Sally a-comin'
I thought to my soul I'd kill myself runnin'

Went to the creek but the creek was muddy
I hugged Sally Goodin til I couldn't stand study

Tuning: AEAE

Comparable versions:

"Sally Goodwin," Ford, Ira, *Traditional Music of America* (New York: Dutton, 1940), 64, 209 (calls), 419 (verses)

"Sally Gooden" (B 26664-1), Eck Robertson, 07/01/1922, NYC, Victor 18956

"Old Sally Goodman" (S 72-015-A), Fiddlin' John Carson, 11/07/1923, NYC, OKeh 40095

"Sally Goodin" (E 29275-), Kessinger Brothers, 02/05/1929, NYC, Brunswick 308

Other versions of "Sally Goodin" in this book by John Brown, W. E. Claunch ("A" part of "Bear Creek's Up"), J. E. Shoemaker, and
  Thaddeus Willingham.

(right page)

Tuning ADAE

Field notes: Claunch says he ends all pieces with "Tippy get your hair cut, fifteen cents."

Comparable versions:

Aird, James, *A Selection of Scotch, English, Irish and Foreign Airs*, vol. 1, no. 109 (1778)

"Soldier's Joy" (9189-A), Fiddlin' John Carson & His Virginia Reelers, 06/30/1925, Atlanta, GA, OKeh 45011

"Soldier's Joy" (GE 12747), Taylor's Kentucky Boys, 06/27, Richmond, IN, Silvertone 5060

"Soldier's Joy" (E29273), Kessinger Brothers, 02/05/1929, NYC, Brunswick 341

Other versions in this book by W. A. Bledsoe ("Farewell Mary Ann"), Dalton Brantley, Charlie Edmondson, John Hatcher, W. E.
  Ray, Stephen B. Tucker, and Rev. J. E. Williams ("Rickets Hornpipe").

Soldier's Joy

Texas Bells

Tuning: AEAC#

Field notes: "The picking of the strings represents the bells."

Untitled (1950)

Collector: Home recording with Algie Surratt on guitar, 1950
Location: Guntown, Lee Co.
Authors' comments: None of the tune titles from that session were identified on the recording.

Comparable versions:
"Walk Along John" (M 832-), Luke Highnight & His Ozark Strutters, 00/22/1928, Memphis, TN, Vocalion 5339

Untitled (Twinkle, Twinkle Little Star, 1950)

Collector: Home recording with Algie Surratt on guitar, 1950

Location: Guntown, Lee Co.

Authors' comments: None of the tunes from this session were titled.

   Judging by his repertoire lists (see Appendix), Claunch seems to have learned some of his tunes from 78s by Mississippi fiddle bands, but this version is closer to the other comparable versions below.

Comparable versions:

"Little Star" (W 400236-B), W. T. Narmour & S. W. Smith, 02/14/1928, Memphis, TN, OKeh 45276

"Twinkle, Twinkle Little Star" (DAL 737-), Smith's Garage Fiddle Band, 12/1928, Dallas, TX, Vocalion 5268

"Twinkle, Twinkle Little Star" (DAL 622-1), Bob Wills and His Texas Playboys, 11/28/1938, Dallas, TX, Vocalion 05401

Wagoner

* Example m 1, 8, 9, 17, 18

Authors' comments: The famous Tennessee racing horse Wagner beat Grey Eagle in a race in 1839. Both horses have fiddle tunes named for them.

* In measures 1, 8, 9, 17, and 18, the E's drone against the melody as in the example measure below.

Comparable versions:
"The Hero," Knauff, George P., *Virginia Reels*, vol. 2, no. 5 (Baltimore, 1839)
"Waggoner" (13308), Uncle Am Stuart, 06/1924, NYC, Vocalion 14840
"Kentucky Wagoners" (10220), Allen Sission, 02/25/1925, NYC, Edison 51720
"The Waggoner" (10462-2), Fiddlin Doc Roberts Trio, 03/05/1931, NYC, Banner 32309
"Northeast Texas" (MEM 755-), Milner & Curtis with the Magnolia Ramblers, 02/1930, Memphis, TN, Vocalion 5246
Other version in this book by Stephen B. Tucker ("Texas Wagon").

Walking in the Parlor

Alt m4-6   sl   sl

Tuning: ADAE

Wolves A-Howlin'

Don't you hear them __ wolves a-howlin' Settin in the corner talking' to my darlin'

Alt m2-4 Alt m8 another Alt m8

Tuning: AEAE

Comparable versions:
Thede, Marion, *The Fiddle Book* (New York: Oak Publications, 1970), 133
"Wolves Howling" (C 4135-), Stripling Brothers, 08/19/1929, Chicago, IL, Vocalion 5412
Other version in the book by John Brown.

MRS. BIRMAH HILL GRISSOM

Mooreville, Lee Co.

From Abbott Ferriss's field notes:
Mrs. Birmah Hill Grissom is a niece of Mrs. Theodosia Bonnett Long.

Mrs. Birmah Hill Grissom, Route 1, Mooreville, Lee County, visited Theodosia Bonnett Long, Saltillo, who is a relative, that she might record her songs. She has farmed and has lived in Lee County all her life. Her family came from Itawamba County, near Oak Grove. Of ten children, six are living, and she has twenty-two grandchildren. She is 64 years old. According to Miss Long, she is "of Irish, English, Welsh, and Dutch ancestry."

Mrs. Grissom and her husband farm 81 acres, of which 13 are in cotton. They own cows and horses.

Mrs. Grissom proved a good singer, having a high, twangy voice.

Authors' comments: Mrs. Grissom was one of A. P. Hudson's informants. Many of her song texts are in *Folksongs of Mississippi and Their Background*, which led to her being recorded by Herbert Halpert.

Her songs:

Charlie Guiteau
Coffee
George Collum
Hog Eye
Here We Go In A Ring So Straight
Hog Drovers
Jesse James
Jen-a-Lin
London Bridge
Nebby-Cad-Nazer (Nebuchadnezzar)
Old Mexico
Old Morgan
Old Pharaoh
The Boatman
The Brown Girl
The Comely Youth
The Fight in Mexico
The Irish Girl
The Judgment
The Little Brown Jug
The Little Family
The Lost Child
The Silver Dagger
The Texas Ranger
Weevily Wheat
We're Marching 'Round the Lily
Willy

Location: Saltillo, Lee Co.

Mrs. Birmah Grissom. Photo by Abbott Ferriss, 1939, Courtesy Mississippi Department of Archives and History.

Hog-Eye

I dreamt a dream the other night I dreamt I was a-jumping I dreamt I eat a mushy-room

As big as any pumpkin. Roll a boat a-shore and a hogeye, Pretty little girl and a hogeyed man.

I dreamt a dream the other night
It was a very droll one
I dreamt I had a brand new coat
Made out of my daddy's old one
Roll a boat ashore and a hog-eye,
Pretty little girl and a hog-eyed man.

I dreamt a dream the other night
It was a very droll one
I dreamt I had a brand new dress
Made out of my mammy's old one
Roll a boat ashore and a hog-eye,
Pretty little girl and a hog-eyed man.

Authors' comments: A hogeye is a type of fish.

Comparable versions: All four of the tunes in the collection that mention "Hog Eye" have a few measures that sound related.
   In Stephen B. Tucker's 1939 version, the "B" part is related to the measures marked "Chorus" in Mittie Lee Adams 1936 "All I Wants a Hogeye," Charlie Addison's 1936 "Hog Eye," and Birmah Grissom's 1939 "Hog-eye."

Old Morgan

Mor - gan's wife loved butter and cheese And Morgan drank the whey. It came a storm last

Friday night And blowed old Morgan away, And blowed old Morgan away___

I went to hunt old Morgan up
And where do you reckon I found 'im
Away down yonder in a blackjack thicket
With the buzzards all around him
With the buzzards all around him

I'se plowing along the other day
I'se plowing a very poor horse
Had to stop ever once in a while
To beat them buzzards off
To beat them buzzards off

I went to the house to get my gun
And I didn't stay very long.
Before I could get back to save my life
They'd eat 'im up and gone
They'd eat 'im up and gone

Sixteen cents a pound a week
Get whiskey here for sale
How can the young boys stay away
When the pretty girls look so gay
When the pretty girls look so gay

If I marry a scolding wife
I'll whip her sure's she's born
I'll carry her down to New Orleans
And swap her off for corn
And swap her off for corn

JOHN HATCHER

Iuka, Tishomingo County (Sept. 1, 1886–1958)

From Abbott Ferriss's field notes:

John Hatcher lives six miles southwest of Burnsville, Tishomingo County. He says he plays "old fiddlums." He was reared by his grandfather and learned to play from two old fiddlers, Dick Brown and George Cheek. He heard fiddling at neighbor's homes during the evening, and "picked it up because I like them."

"I still like the old-time music." He has played at dances, always using a "second." He has played with bands at Jackson, Tennessee over the radio and at Sheffield, Alabama.

"It was pretty late in the year, crop time, and it was three of us fellows farming. We got up a band. Usually we git paid. They pay so much a set, depends upon how many dancing. Sometimes they give us what they take in."

Hatcher plays the high bass (fourth string, G) and the counter, D, "run up about a step." E and A of the first and second string, he said. He said that most old pieces were tuned in a high key.

"Guitar players prefer to pick in lower keys, and for that reason many of the old-time pieces are played in A, but have been changed."

He is fifty-three years old, owns forty-nine acres, which he describes as "a little rabbit ranch." He is over six feet in height, complexion very dark, and has discolored teeth, curly hair parted in the middle, rough hands. When he recorded and when the picture was taken he was dressed in his best clothes, wore a blue spotted necktie.

John Hatcher. Photo by Abbott Ferriss, 1939, courtesy Mississippi Department of Archives and History.

His grandfather on his mother's side of the family came to Tishomingo Co. from Georgia.

Authors' comments: Mr. Hatcher, a farmer and wood hauler, was an orphan raised by his grandfather and learned to play fiddle from two local fiddlers, Dick Brown and George Cheek. He attended nearby fiddle contests, fiddled with the Tishomingo County Jamboree Boys on their weekly radio show, but was perhaps best known locally as a dance fiddler. He sings on his 1939 recording of "Up the Road" and John Brown's "Wolves a Howling."

Recording location: Iuka, Tishomingo Co.

Arkansas Traveler

The Music Transcriptions

"B" modulates to key of A

Tuning: ADAE
Authors' comments: "Ghost" notes in measures 31, 62, and 63.

Comparable versions:
"The Arkansas Traveler," *The Arkansas Traveller's Songster* (New York: Dick & Fitzgerald, 1864), 5–9 imslp.org/wiki/
    The_Arkansas_Traveler's_Songster_(Various)
"Arkansas Traveler" (B 26660-2), Henry C. Gilliland and A. C. "Eck" Robertson, 06/30/1922, NYC, Victor 18956
"Arkansas Traveler" (8613-A), Fiddlin' John Carson & His Virginia Reelers, 03/1924, Atlanta, GA, OKeh 40108
"Arkansas Traveler" (AL 228), Kessinger Brothers, 02/11/1928, Ashland, KY, Brunswick 247
Other versions of "Arkansas Traveler" in this book by W. E. Claunch and Stephen B. Tucker.

Billy in the Lowground

The Music Transcriptions

Black Eyed Susie

Rain come wet me,
Sun come dry me,
Said stand back pretty little girl
Don't come nigh me.

All I want to make me happy,
Two little boys to call me pappy,
One name Sope, one named Gravy,
I love my wife and I love my baby.

Comparable versions:

"Black Eyed Susie" (81635-1), Gid Tanner and Riley Puckett, 03/08/1924, NYC, Columbia 119-D

"Black Eyed Susie" (GE 13040), Fiddlin' Doc Roberts, 09/1927, Richmond, IN, Gennett 6257

"Black Eyed Susie" (BVE 39747), J. P. Nestor, 08/01/1927, Bristol, TN, Victor 21070

Other versions of "Black Eyed Susan" in this book by John Brown, W. E. Claunch ("Black Eyed Susie"), J. A. Moorman, and Thaddeus Willingham ("Black Eyed Susie").

(left page)

Authors' comments: John Hatcher's version seems to be based on, or very closely related to, the 1924 Eck Robertson version. Notice how Hatcher treats the repeat of the "A" part by holding the C and shifting the melody forward by a beat. Alt m17 is a more accurate version of the rhythm.

Comparable versions:

"The Braes of Auchtertyre," Gow 1799 I, 20

"Beaus of Albany," Howe 1843, II, 37

"Billy in the Low Ground" (W 145089-1), Burnett and Rutherford, 11/03/1927, Atlanta, GA, Columbia 15209-D

"Billy in the Low Ground" (W 150207-), Lowe Stokes & Riley Puckett, 04/14/1930, Atlanta, GA, Columbia 15620-D)

"Billy in the Lowground" (B 26666-1), A. C. Eck Robertson, 07/01/1922, NYC, Victor 19372

"Billy in the Lowground" (S 72-013-B), Fiddlin' John Carson, 11/07/1923, NYC, OKeh 40020

Bonaparte's Retreat

Tuning: DDAD

Field notes: "Hatcher said his grandfather told him that the piece was played during the Civil War."

Comparable versions:

"Bumblebee in the Pumpkin Patch," Elias Howe, *Musician's Omnibus* (Boston: Elias Howe, 1864), #162

"Bonaparte's Retreat" (8591-), A. A. Gray, 03/21/1924, Atlanta, GA, OKeh 40110

"Bonaparte's Retreat" (C 4018-), Crockett's Kentucky Mountaineers, 08/1929, Chicago, IL, Brunswick 353

"Bonaparte's Retreat" (W 149280-2), Gid Tanner & His Skillet Lickers, 10/29/1929, Atlanta, GA, Columbia 15485-D

Buffalo Girl

Tuning: AEAE

Comparable versions:
"Midnight Serenade," Knauff, George P., *Virginia Reels*, vol. 1, no. 4 (Baltimore, ca. 1839)
"Round Town Gals" (GEX 498-A), Ernest V. Stoneman & His Grayson County Boys, 02/02/1927, NYC, Gennett 6052
"Buffalo Gals" (8514-1-2), Pickard Family, 01/31/1929, NYC, Banner 6371
Versions of "Buffalo Gals" in this book by Babe Casey ("Grasshopper on a Sweet Tater Vine"), R. H. Ellis, A. J. Howell ("Buffalo Girl"), Edward Kittrell, and Ben Wall.

Music Collected in 1939

Down Yonder

Field notes: Learned from his son.

Comparable versions:

L. Wolf Gilbert, words and music, 1921

"Down Yonder" (B-25310/3), Peerless Quartet, 05/19/1921, Camden, NJ, Victor 18775 www.loc.gov/jukebox/recordings/detail/id/7910/

"Down Yonder" (W 143091-2), McMichen's Melody Men, 11/06/1926, Atlanta, GA, Columbia 15130-D

"Down Yonder" (13811-), Fiddlin' Doc Roberts Trio, 08/16/1933, NYC, Banner 32889

Eighth of January

Authors' comments: Hatcher recorded two versions of this tune.

The alt measures are from the second version.

He tends to play the "A" part once and the "B" part three times.

The * indicates a divided up-bow, or bow rock.

Comparable versions of "Eighth of January":

Ford, Ira, *Traditional Music of America* (New York: Dutton, 1940), 63

Arkansas Barefoot Boys (W 400229-B), 02/11/1928, Memphis, TN, OKeh 45217

Fox Chasers (W 5404166-A), 06/11/1930, San Antonio, TX, OKeh 45496

Ted Gossett's Band (GN 17041), 09/16/1930, Richmond, IN, Champion 16160

Other versions of "Eighth of January" in this book by Enos Canoy, W. E. Claunch, Charlie Edmundson, Hardy Sharp, and
   J. A. Moorman.

Farewell Whiskey

Tuning: AEAE

Field notes: Mr. John Brown said, "When he hits over in that bass, you can hear pouring out of the bottle."

Authors' comments: Harmonics are produced by lightly touching the string, not depressing it to the fingerboard. The circled number indicates the string to play. The small number is the finger to use. The lower note shows the note that would be produced if the finger pressed down, the higher note is the actual pitch of the harmonic note. For example, for the first harmonic, slide the second finger up to position of the E note on the fourth string (third position). The hand would then remain in this position to play all of the harmonics above.

Comparable versions:

"Jack of Diamonds" (12783-A), Ben Jarrell with Da Costa Woltz's Southern Broadcasters, 04/1927, Richmond, IN, Herwin 75561

"Drunkard's Hiccups" (S 73-878-A), Fiddlin' John Carson, 12/1925, NYC, OKeh 45032

"Way Up on Clinch Mountain" (BVE 42491-2), Jilson Setters (J. W. Day), 02/27/1928, NYC, Victor 21635

Other versions in this book by W. E. Claunch and Charles Long.

Going Up to Hamburg

swi - i - ing   cha - nge   goin up to Ham-burg

pret-ty lit-tle la-dy goin up to Ham-burg yes I am goin up to Ham-burg pret-ty lit-tle la-dy goin up to Ham-burg

get me'a dram

Recorded comments: Hatcher said, "That's an awful old piece."
Authors' comments: The verse is sung on the second time through, then the first part variation played, and end. Note the "ghost" notes, indicated as "x" note heads, in measures 1, 3, 5 and 7.

Grub Springs

Authors' comments: This tune is modal. Note that m8 ends on a down-bow, facilitating the string crossing for the syncopated up-bow in m9. Also note the unisons in m4, which also are used in m8.

Leather Britches

Recording comments: Hatcher said before playing, "I'm going to play one leg of them now, and the other when I come back."

Authors' comments: Hatcher plays the repeats A, B, C, D, B, B, C, D, A, first half of B, and then ends.

Comparable versions:

"Lord McDonald's Reel," Niel & Nathaniel Gow, *Third Collection of Niel Gow's Reels* (ca. 1792), 9

M. M. Cole, *One Thousand Fiddle Tunes* (Chicago: M. M. Cole, 1940; reprinted from *Ryan's Mammoth Collection*, 1883) pg22

"Leather Breeches" (N 839-), Carter Brothers & Son, 11/22/1928, Memphis, TN, Vocalion 5295

"Leather Breeches" (W 143968-2), Leake County Revelers, 04/13/1927, New Orleans, LA, Columbia 15149-D

Other versions of "Leather Britches" in this book by Hardy Sharp, Stephen B. Tucker, and J. H. Wheeler ("Leather Breeches").

Little Danville Girl

As I got off in Danville I met a little Danville girl
And you bet your, she was out of sight
And she wore a Danville curl.
She wore the curl of fashion and the city too,
And as that Danville train rolled out (of Danville)
I bid the little girl adieu.

All around that platform awaiting for that train,
As I laid down so cold and hungry with our a bit to eat,
Thinking of those good old days and hoping they'd come again.
Ten thousand miles away beating a local train,

Drinking and gambling brought me before the court.

The juror found me guilty and the judge passed the fine,
And they gave me six months in the Corinth Jail
And the rest in the Coal-Bury mines.
My father was a gambler he learned me how to play,
He learned me how to deal my ace, deuce, jack and trey.
The jack is neither big and the trey is neither low,
But I've got the ace and deuce both in my hand,
and I'm bound to play high, low.

Comparable versions:
"Wild and Reckless Hobo" (10624-B), Charlie Powers, 10/07/1925, NYC, Edison 5131
"Danville Girl" (E 21812), Doc Boggs, 1927
"Ramblin' Reckless Hobo" (W 145085-1), Burnett & Rutherford, 11/03/1927, Atlanta, GA, Columbia 15240-D

Long Eared Mule

Comparable versions:

"Karo" (W 143004-), Uncle Jimmy Thompson, 11/01/1926, Atlanta, GA, Vocalion 15368

"The Long Eared Mule" (S 73378), Emmett Lundy & Ernest Stoneman, 05/27/1925, NYC, OKeh 40405

"Old Virginia Reel, Pt. 2" (W 81644-A), Fiddlin' John Powers & Family, 09/28/1927, Winston-Salem, NC, OKeh 45154

Other versions in this book by Cleve Bass ("Flop Eared Mule"), Mrs. Maud Freeman ("G & C Schottiche"), and J. E. Shoemaker ("Gulfport").

Music Collected in 1939

Old Miss Sally

I ask Miss Sally for to be my wife, She run'ed at me with a butcher knife Oh

Miss Sally - Sally-o, Oh   Miss Sally - Sally - o Oh   Miss Sally - Sal-ly   go   in' to the

par ty - o   Miss Sal-ly   Sal-ly-o   Miss Sal-ly   Sal-ly - o.

Alt m6-7

Oh Miss Sally-Sally-o
Going to the partie-o
Ask Miss Sally for to be my beau,
And she run at me with the grubbing hoe.

Oh Miss Sally-Sally-o, Oh Miss Sally-Sally-o
I ask Miss Sally for to be my wife,

And she run at me with a butcher knife
Oh Miss Sally-Sally-o, Oh Miss Sally-Sally-o

Oh Miss Sally-Sally-o, Oh Miss Sally-Sally-o
I ask Miss Sally for to be my wife,
Said she wouldn't to save my life
Oh Miss Sally-Sally-o, Oh Miss Sally-Sally-o

Authors' comments: Hatcher plays the "C" part when he is singing and the "B" part when he is not.

Comparable versions:

Belden, H. M., and Arthur Palmer Hudson, *Frank C. Brown Collection of North Carolina Folklore; Vol. 3: Folk Songs* (Durham, NC: Duke University Press, 1952), 510, 565

"Been to the East Been to the West" (W 146208-2), Leake County Revelers, 04/27/1928, New Orleans, LA, Columbia 15318-D

"Share 'Em" (W 402127-A), Scottsdale String Band, 08/10/1928, Atlanta, GA, OKeh 45256

"Shear the Sheep Bobbie" (W 147647-1), Gatwood Square Dance Band, 12/15/1928, New Orleans, LA, Columbia 15363

"Take Me Back to Tulsa" (Dal 1180-1), Bob Wills & His Texas Playboys, 02/25/1941, Dallas, TX, OKeh 06101

Other versions in this book by Enos Canoy ("Possum and Coon"), W. E. Claunch ("Chicken Pie" and "Miss Sally at the Party"), Ruby Costello ("Want to Go to Meeting"), Charles Long ("Jones County" and "Steamboat"), and Hardy Sharp ("Great Big Yam Potatoes").

Pretty Little Girl All Around Town

Tuning: AEAE

Recording comments: Mr. Hatcher said, "I'm old enough for to kiss all day, I'll be sixteen next Sunday!"

Comparable versions:

"The Girl I Left Behind Me" (W 143797-2), Gid Tanner and His Skillet Lickers, 03/29/1927, Atlanta, GA, Columbia 15170-D

"Girl I Left Behind Me" (AL 226/27), Kessinger Brothers, 04/26/1928, Ashland, KY, Brunswick 267

"The Girl I Left Behind Me" (GE 14913), Doc Roberts & Asa Martin, 03/15/1929, Richmond, IN, Gennett 6826

Scott No. 2

Authors' comments: This is an attempt to simplify Mr. Hatcher's somewhat fluid approach to length of parts. Hatcher plays the parts: A, B, C, D, C, D, A, B, C, D, E.

Soldier's Joy

Authors' comments: Hatcher plays the repeats as A, B, A, 1/2 B, C, 1/2 B

Comparable versions:

Aird, James, *A Selection of Scotch, English, Irish and Foreign Airs*, vol. 1, no. 109 (1778)

"Soldier's Joy" (9189-A), Fiddlin' John Carson & His Virginia Reelers, 06/30/1925, Atlanta, GA, OKeh 45011

"Soldier's Joy" (GE 12747), Taylor's Kentucky Boys, 06/27, Richmond, IN, Silvertone 5060

"Soldier's Joy" (E29273), Kessinger Brothers, 02/05/1929, NYC, Brunswick 341

See other versions in this book by W. A. Bledsoe ("Farewell Mary Ann"), Dalton Brantley, W. E. Claunch, Charlie Edmondson,
  W. E. Ray, Stephen B. Tucker, and Rev. J. E. Williams ("Rickets Hornpipe").

Tishomingo County Blues (2 versions)

Tuning: ADAE

Recording comments: Mr. Hatcher said: "All counties have blues. I felt that Tishomingo County was blue enough and ought to have one. I picked up notes from other tunes and made one up of my own. It took me time, not all at once." No words although he said he might "git up some words."

Authors' comments: I suspect that Hatcher was inspired to create a blues by Willie T. Narmour's success with the "Carroll County Blues." Hatcher's performance does not easily lend itself to accompaniment, so an alternate, simplified version is shown below.

Version #2

Authors' comments: This is a simplified version with a consistent beat suitable for playing with accompaniment.

Tom and Jerry

Tuning: AEAE

Comparable versions:
Elias Howe, *Musician's Omnibus* (Boston: Elias Howe, 1864), 46
"Tom and Jerry" (E 4959), Uncle Dave Macon & His Fruit Jar Drinkers, 05/09/1927, NYC, Vocalion 5165
"Tom and Jerry" (DAL 526-), Smiths Garage Fiddle Band, 10/29/1929, Dallas, TX, Vocalion 5375
Other version in this book by Stephen B. Tucker.

Up the Road

Oh up the road, its up the road, Oh up the road boys as far as I can see, I

has that lone - some dove going from vine Mourning for its own true love Just like I mourn mine.

Oh up the road, it's up the road,
Oh up the road boys as far as I can see,
I has that lonesome dove going from vine
Mourning for its own true love
Just like I mourn for mine.

What you gonna do boys?
Oh what you gonna do
Oh what you gonna do, when the work's all
    done?
I'm going back home, boys, I'm going back home,
It's never to return

An apple like a cherry
And a cherry like a rose
And how I love my honey
They ain't no-body knows

There's something on her finger
That shines more than like gold,

I'm going to see my darling girl
Before she gets too awful old.

I went up on the mountain
To get a load of cane,
To make a barrel of lasses
To sweeten up Liza Jane.

Miss Liza went down the new cut road
And I went down the lane
And I throwed my hat in the corner of the fence
And scared poor Liza Jane

Perhaps you may have a brother
And perhaps a sister too
And perhaps you may have a sweetheart
To weep and mourn for you.

Recorded comments: Mr. Hatcher said, "It may be too old, I can't remember all of it".

FRANK T. KITTRELL

Lauderdale Co. (April 12, 1872–April 11, 1953)

From Abbott Ferriss's field notes:
Meridian, Mississippi, Lauderdale Co. Accompanied by Mrs. Kittrell on straws.

Mr. Kittrell has farmed most of his life, but now works for the WPA. He wore a blue shirt with white stripes and a blue tie with a small metal piece pinned on. His heavy dark pants were attached to suspenders and a white belt. He wore black low-quarters. His face was florid; he had a white mustache, and grey hair around a bald spot. He is 68 years old.

"My two uncles were the best fiddlers in Mississippi. I learned from them."

His uncle, who played the fiddle 15 or 20 years before Frank T. took it up, was born in Lauderdale County. His grandfather, of Scotch and Irish ancestry, came to Mississippi from Charleston, S.C.

At the first party he attended when he was 10 years old, he remembers his uncle playing "I Want To Go To Meetin' and I Got No Shoes." "My cousin was beating straws. Nowadays, they are playing 'Turkey in the Straw' and all this classical stuff."

At the age of 14 he had heard enough fiddle pieces to want to play himself. After hearing his uncle, David Kittrell, he "just picked up the fiddle and played them. He never told me how." He says he began playing about 53 years ago. When 17 he lost interest, and picked it up again when he was 22 years old. He has been fiddling "off and on" ever since.

He plays 118 pieces, he says, and used three tunings: Flat key, Natural and Cross note.

"I could play the fiddle a lot better if I didn't have to work in the field—makes my fingers sore. If I could, I'd play fiddle all the time."

At present, he plays mostly around the house. But he has organized seven bands in Meridian. "I fired them all because they drank. I won't play with a man who drinks."

"I could take that banjo man over there and that guitar, and challenge the State of Mississippi." He pointed to the two men waiting to record.
But at the time he was "raised" near Lockhart, Mississippi, the fiddle was not "seconded" by either banjo or guitar. The accompaniment was a straw. "Just a broom straw. Grows in the old fields."

Mrs. Kittrell's straw was heavy and about 18 inches long. She sat beside her husband and leaned forward when "beating." She was very large, wore a solid blue dress, brown stockings, black substantial patent leather shoes, and a black hat with a brim and a white band. As Mrs. Kittrell beat the straw, she chewed gum. She has only two upper front teeth.

Mrs. Kittrell: "I just picked it up and went to knocking."

She holds the straw in the left hand, using index and thumb. The thumb of her right hand is held underneath the straw and below the left hand. In "knocking," Mrs. Kittrell makes deft up-down motions with her right hand. Her whole body shakes.

She "knocks straws" on the one or two strings that the fiddler does not use in playing the piece. The straw falls directly on the D and on the G strings. If the fiddler plays on the D and G strings, she "knocks" on the other strings. The straw falls on the upper portion to the handle of the fiddle.

Mrs. Kittrell can use two straws as well as one. In doing this, she has one in each hand.

Mr. Kittrell said, "When I was a boy the only instruments they had to go with a violin was a broom straw. Later, we had a homemade banjo, and then a guitar. That brought company."

"If someone whistled a tune, I'd whistle it and go home and start playing. I might not learn it all then, but I'd keep playing and whistling until I learned it. It took a long time learning what I did learn."

Both are Baptists and have five living children, all residing nearby. Kittrell said that he hadn't played a violin in over two months. His violin was made by hand according to the date, stated in figures, 1736. He says some Louisiana music people offered him $2,500 for it. He purchased it from a man in Meridian ten or twelve years ago. It is not a Stradivarius, although it is constructed in that tradition, according to Halpert.

According to Halpert, he is a good fiddler.

Authors' comments: Mr. Kittrell continued to play into the 1950s, performing in local bands. He also played the following uncollected tunes:
Ain't That Handsome
Dolly-O
Ridin' in the Buggy

Recording location: Meridian, Lauderdale Co.

Cindy Jane

etc

Tuning: AEAE

Field notes: "Learned from uncle 'way back yonder'. Ain't tried to play that in forty years."

Authors' comments: This is a fifteen-measure tune. The eighth measure is both the last measure of the first strain and the first measure of the second strain, which shifts the expected location of the downbeat in the second strain. This is a frequently employed type of syncopation in Mississippi fiddling.

Comparable versions:

"Cindy in the Meadows" (81706-1), Samantha Bumgarner & Eva Davis 4/22/1924, NYC, Columbia 167-D

"Cindy" (W 143867-), Riley Puckett & Clayton McMichen, 04/02/1927, Atlanta, GA, Columbia 15232-D

"Get Along Home, Miss Cindy" (BVE 41853-2), Pope's Arkansas Mountaineers, 02/06/1928, Memphis, TN, Victor 21577

Other versions in this book by Charlie Addison ("Want to Go to Meeting"), John Brown ("Cindy"), W. E. Claunch ("Cindy"), Enos Canoy ("Where'd You Get Your Whiskey"), Mrs. R. C. Clifton ("Miss Cindy"), B. M. Guilette ("Liza Jane"), Mrs. Joe McCoy ("Her Cheeks Are Like the Cherry"), Hardy Sharp ("Liza Jane"), Rev. J. E. Williams ("Cindy Waltz"), and Thaddeus Willingham ("Miss Cindy").

Corn Stalk Fiddle

Tuning: AEAE

Field notes: "I learned it from an uncle of mine."

Authors' comments: Note the "ghost" notes, indicated as "x" note heads, in measures 1, 3, and 7.

Going to the Wedding

Tuning: AEAE

Field notes: "Learned from the same uncle from whom he got practically all his pieces."

Comparable versions:
"Sally Ann" (S 73-121-A), The Hillbillies, 01/15/1925, NYC, OKeh 40336
"Sally Ann" (S 73-456-A), Fiddlin' John Carson, 06/24/1925, NYC, OKeh 40419
"Great Big Taters in Sandy Land" (BVE 56360-2), Eck Robertson & J. B. Cranfill, 10/10/1929, Dallas, TX, Victor V40205
"Mississippi Square Dance Pt. 2" (W 404741-B), Freeny's Barn Dance Band, 1930, Jackson, MS, OKeh 45533
"Going to the Wedding to Get Some Cake," Newton County Hillbillies, 12/16/1930, Jackson, MS, OKeh 45533

Hell After Yearlings

Tuning: ADAE

Field notes: Kittrell explained that the title meant a "cow yearling."

Comparable versions:

"Going Down the River" (47017-1), Dr. Smith's Champion Hoss Hair Pullers, 09/12/1928, Memphis, TN, Victor 21711

"Davy" (145355-2), Weems String Band, 12/09/1927, Memphis, TN, Columbia 15300-D

"Boatin' Up Sandy" (E 23148/49), Al Hopkins & His Buckle Busters, 05/14/1927, NYC, Brunswick 182

Indian War Whoop

Tuning: AEAE

Recording comments: Mr. Kittrell said, "My wife's gonna knock straws on the violin."

    After hearing the piece replayed he was very pleased and said, "That's extra good, ain't it. I learnt him quick."

Comparable versions:

The first few measures of this tune resemble "Dusty Miller" by John Brown in this book.

Little Boy Went A-Courtin'

_____

Tuning: AEAE

Authors' comments: More interesting syncopation from Kittrell, here the final note of the "B" part becomes the first note of the
"A" part, causing the expected position of the downbeat to continuously shift as the piece goes around.

Rye Straw

Alt m 5-6

Tuning: ADAE

Field notes: Mr. Kittrell said, "this was a dancing old piece when I was a kid, They swung it."

Comparable versions:
"Rye Straw (The Unfortunate Pup)" (13329), Uncle Am Stuart, 06/1924, NYC, Vocalion 14843
"Rye Straw" (W 149290-2), Clayton McMichen & Riley Puckett, 10/29/1929, Atlanta, GA, Columbia 15524-D
"Rye Straw" (GE 16086), Doc Roberts & Asa Martin, 01/13/1930, Richmond, IN, Gennett 7221
Other versions in this book by Charles Long ("Alabama Waltz") and Stephen B. Tucker ("Joke on the Puppy").

Want to Go to Meeting and I Got No Shoes

Tuning: AEAC♯

Field notes: "Mr. Kittrell is not pleased with his own tuning and asks another fiddler to tune it for him. He plucks the strings with his fingers and appears pleased. 'It'll let you know when you get it right—see there.'"

Authors' comments: This is a common tune title in Mississippi, but this is not the usual melody.

CHARLES LONG

Quitman, Clarke Co.

From Abbott Ferriss's field notes:

Mr. Long borrowed the fiddle he played on. His own was about fifteen years old and was slightly battered up by his children. But he had to whittle keys for the one he was tuning. "Pore folks have to have pore ways," his large wife said.

"I learned to play a little from other fiddlers. My pap couldn't carry a tune. Learned when I was fifteen or sixteen. But I never could do nothing much good."

Mr. C. L. Long, farmer will be seventy years old in August. He first began playing in Choctaw County, Alabama. "First, I used to pick at a 'juse' harp. Then I blowed a French harp. Next thing you knowed, I was trying to pick out on a fiddle the tunes I'd hear. I bought four fiddles before I got one I liked. Some of them are soft, some are hard. I like the hard-toned ones."

"The fiddle I got in the house ain't no good. One of the children bought it in Jackson."

One of Long's children, a young man, said: "I learned to play the organ and can't tune a fiddle. I can't no more get his tuning than a 'haint."

Charlie Long moved to Clarke County from Alabama about thirty-five years ago. "Line don't make much difference—we're about the same," he said. "About the same" means that he lives in hill country. There a few signs of erosion, very few. The surrounding acres are covered with timber. The soil, some of it newly-cleared, is productive soil. The nearest town is Quitman, seven and one half miles to the west. The graveled road is about two miles north.

Long says he "don't fool with cotton much." He has four acres in cotton, fifteen acres in corn. He has sheep, hogs, cows and a garden. His wife was trying to persuade him to not plant any more potatoes.

He has reared nine children. Two learned to play the organ at "singing school." One son, who lives "about two miles up the road," is now trying to learn to play the fiddle by notes. "But he can't do that," said Charlie who plays by ear. No one else in the family plays the fiddle. Long owns an organ, phonograph, and radio. For the past three weeks, since Long knew the recordings would be made, he has kept the radio turned off, to the discomfort of his daughter, so that he might practice on the fiddle and recall old tunes. He played last in an Old Fiddlers Contest in March. He says that he doesn't play much now.

"When they got lined up for the dancing, is when I started playing."

"I guess we've played many a-night and never played the same piece twice."

Charles Long and Sam Neal. Photo by Abbott Ferriss, 1939, courtesy Mississippi Department of Archives and History.

Charlie showed, in saying he did not know words to certain pieces, a streak of modesty. His son said of him: "He just got sorter like a little Nigger preacher. He's shamed at the face."

Charlie said: "There's two things a fiddler would get at a frolic. Whiskey and a chair. Wasn't much trouble for a fiddler to get a partner, neither. Scared he'd quit."

"I used to could sing and play it—can't no more."

"In my day, didn't have no banjo. Used straw."

Sam Neal, a neighbor who once played the fiddle, "kept time with the straw." He used one straw, but had used two, and worked exactly as did Mrs. Kittrell, except for a wrist instead of an arm motion. Neal said he was "seconding" Charlie Long. Neal, another farmer, is 60 years old. He came from Choctaw County, Alabama about twenty-five years ago. He said he used to play one hundred forty fiddle pieces; didn't play much now.

Several references to the records of Jimmie Rogers were made by the gathering of twenty five men, women and children who were standing and sitting on Long's front porch and in his "dog trot" to watch the proceedings. Several men stood in the yard. Long's daughter, probably about twenty years old, said that Jimmie Rogers probably wasn't as good as his records.

When we left, Long's wife expressed her appreciation for our making recordings. She was anxious to obtain copies of the records. "It means so much to us," she said.

As we left, she walked into the house and said to her two daughters, "I'm too tired to milk the cow, tonight." The daughters said they would not milk her either.

Charlie Long said: "Stay all night with us and we'll show you how pore folks live."

Recording location: Quitman, Clarke Co.

Alabama Waltz

Tuning: ADAE

Authors' comments: On the recording, Mr. Neal takes a drumming break with measures of Mr. Long only holding the fiddle. See the "C" part notated here. The number of repetitions in the low phrase is somewhat random in each pass through the tune.

Comparable versions:
"Rye Straw (The Unfortunate Pup)" (13329), Uncle Am Stuart, 06/1924, NYC, Vocalion 14843
"Rye Straw" (W 149290-2), Clayton McMichen & Riley Puckett, 10/29/1929, Atlanta, GA, Columbia 15524-D
"Rye Straw" (GE 16086), Doc Roberts & Asa Martin, 01/13/1930, Richmond, IN, Gennett 7221
Other versions in this book by Stephen B. Tucker ("Joke on the Puppy") and Frank Kittrell ("Rye Straw").

Big Eyed Rabbit

Big eyed rabbit, who boys who   Big eyed rabbit, who boys who

Ol' Mister Rabbit you look might shy.
Yes, by God, I got a big eye.

Ol' Mister Rabbit you look might cunning.
Yes, by God, and I do good running.

Ol' Mister Rabbit you look might thin
Yes, by God, been cutting through the wind.

Tuning: ADAE

Field notes: "After playing, Charlie Long said: 'I saw a man the other day who said he hit a rabbit six time, and the rabbit got up and walked off.' No one would 'bite', so I asked; 'Where'd he shoot the rabbit?' Charlie: 'He don't know—the rabbit went on!'"

Comparable versions:

"Black Eyed Susie" (81635-1), Gid Tanner and Riley Puckett, 03/08/1924, NYC, Columbia 119-D

"Black Eyed Susie" (GE 13040), Fiddlin' Doc Roberts, 09/1927, Richmond, IN, Gennett 6257

"Black Eyed Susie" (BVE 39747) J. P. Nestor, 08/01/1927, Bristol, TN, Victor 21070

Other versions of "Black Eyed Susan" in this book by John Brown, W. E. Claunch ("Black Eyed Susie"), John Hatcher, J. A. Moorman, and Thaddeus Willingham ("Black Eyed Susie").

Drunken Hiccups

Tuning: AEAE modal

Authors' comments: The G in m3 and m7 may be played sharp or natural.

Comparable versions:

"Jack of Diamonds" (12783-A), Ben Jarrell with Da Costa Woltz's Southern Broadcasters, 04/1927, Richmond, IN, Herwin 75561

"Drunkard's Hiccups" (S 73-878-A), Fiddlin' John Carson, 12/1925, NYC, OKeh 45032

"Way Up on Clinch Mountain" (BVE 42491-2), Jilson Setters (J. W. Day), 02/27/1928, NYC, Victor 21635

Other versions in this book by W. E. Claunch and John Hatcher ("Farewell Whiskey").

Fisher's Hornpipe

Tuning: ADAE

Comparable versions:

"Rickett's Hornpipe," *One Thousand Fiddle Tunes* (Chicago, IL: M. M. Cole 1940), 89

"Rickett's Hornpipe" (11922-), Tweedy Brothers, 06/14/1924, Atlanta, GA, Gennett 5613

"Rickett's Hornpipe" (GS 17036), Green's String Band, 09/15/1930, Richmond, IN, Champion 16489

"Rickett's Hornpipe" (W 151027-2), Gid Tanner & His Skillet Lickers, 12/04/1930, Atlanta, GA, Columbia 15682-D

Other versions in this book by Stephen B. Tucker ("Raker's Hornpipe") and Reverend J. E. Williams ("Soldier's Joy Hornpipe").

Hard Road to Texas

Tuning: AEAE modal

Authors' comments: Mr. Long plays G in a range of pitches between G and G♯. To properly learn this tune, one really needs to refer to the recording.

Jones County

Gone a whole week   to see my love Down   in Jones County

Gone a   whole week to   see my love Down   in Jones County

Goin' away good-bye, oh
Down in Jones County
Goin' away good-bye, oh
Down in Jones County

Fare you well and good-bye, too
Down in Jones County
Fare you well and good-bye, too
Down in Jones County

Prettiest little girl I ever did see
Down in Jones County
Prettiest little girl I ever did see
Down in Jones County

Tuning: AEAE
Field notes: Charlie said, "It takes a little elbow juice for this."
Authors' comments: The "B" part of this tune resembles the versions below.

Comparable versions:

Belden, H. M., and Arthur Palmer Hudson, *Frank C. Brown Collection of North Carolina Folklore; Vol. 3: Folk Songs* (Durham, NC: Duke University Press, 1952), 510, 565

"Been to the East Been to the West" (W 146208-2), Leake County Revelers, 04/27/1928, New Orleans, LA, Columbia 15318-D

"Share 'Em" (W 402127-A), Scottsdale String Band, 08/10/1928, Atlanta, GA, OKeh 45256

"Shear the Sheep Bobbie" (W 147647-1), Gatwood Square Dance Band, 12/15/1928, New Orleans, LA, Columbia 15363

"Take Me Back to Tulsa" (Dal 1180-1), Bob Wills & His Texas Playboys, 02/25/1941, Dallas, TX, OKeh 06101

Other versions in this book by Enos Canoy ("Possum and Coon"), W. E. Claunch ("Chicken Pie" and "Miss Sally at the Party"), Ruby Costello ("Want to Go to Meeting"), John Hatcher ("Old Miss Sally"), Charles Long ("Steamboat"), and Hardy Sharp ("Great Big Yam Potatoes").

Little Willie

Tuning: ADAE

Comparable versions:

"Richmond Blues," Knauff, George P., *Virginia Reels*, vol. 1, no. 4 (Baltimore, c. 1839), 13 (dc.lib.unc.edu/cdm/ref/collection/
   sheetmusic/id/33599)
"Love Somebody" (13362), Sid Harkreader & Uncle Dave Macon, 06/10/1924, NYC, Vocalion 14887
"Too Young to Marry" (W-142641-1), North Carolina Ramblers, 9/18/1926, NYC, Columbia 15127-D

My Little Dony

Eyes just like a cherry Cheek just like a rose How I love my

Dony God in heaven knows

Alt. mm.11-13.

Fare you well, my Dony
Fare you well, I say
Fare you well, my Dony
Come another day.

You can ride the old gray horse
I will ride the roan.
When you go a-courtin'
Let my Dony alone.

Preacher in the pulpit
Bible in his hand
Said he won't preach no more

Till he gets another dram,
(After singing this verse, Long said:
"That's the way they do, ain't it")

Wish I had a band box
Put my Dony in
Take her out and kiss her
Put her back in again.

Tuning: AEAE modal
Field note comments: "After the record is re-played from the disc, Mrs. Long said, 'I don't believe that was Charlie.'"

Comparable versions:
Other version in this book by Thaddeus Willingham ("Oh, My Little Darling").

My Old Dog Trailing Up a Squirrel

My ol' dog's trailin' up a   squirrel My ol' gal's the   beauty of the world.

<hr />

Tuning: AEAE modal

Authors' comments: The "A" part is played with and without repeats. The "B" part is played three times.

Rock Candy

Tuning: AEAE modal

Sally-O

Tuning: AEAE

Steamboat

Yonder   come   the   steamboat Floating

down   the   river   Eatin'   a   rine   of hog meat   Court my   little widow

Don't care how you share 'em
Don't care how you share 'em
Don't care how you share 'em
Just so you share 'em even.

Big bee suck the blossom
Little bee makes the honey
Nigger works the cornfield
White man totes the money.

Don' you whip the baby
Don' you whip the baby
'Cause don't have no pappy
Don' you whip the baby

Tuning: ADAE

Authors' comments: The first eight measures are only played the first time. Mr. Long's version is rudimentary and is only loosely
  related to the comparable versions listed below.

Comparable versions:

Belden, H. M., and Arthur Palmer Hudson, *Frank C. Brown Collection of North Carolina Folklore; Vol. 3: Folk Songs* (Durham,
  NC: Duke University Press, 1952), 510, 565

"Been to the East Been to the West" (W 146208-2), Leake County Revelers, 04/27/1928, New Orleans, LA, Columbia 15318-D

"Share 'Em" (W 402127-A), Scottsdale String Band, 08/10/1928, Atlanta, GA, OKeh 45256

"Shear the Sheep Bobbie" (W 147647-1), Gatwood Square Dance Band, 12/15/1928, New Orleans, LA, Columbia 15363

"Take Me Back to Tulsa" (Dal 1180-1), Bob Wills & His Texas Playboys, 02/25/1941, Dallas, TX, OKeh 06101

Other versions in this book by Enos Canoy ("Possum and Coon"), W. E. Claunch ("Chicken Pie" and "Miss Sally at the Party"),
  Ruby Costello ("Want to Go to Meeting"), John Hatcher ("Old Miss Sally"), Charles Long ("Jones County"), and Hardy Sharp
  ("Great Big Yam Potatoes").

THEODOSIA LONG

Saltillo Lee Co.

From Abbott Ferriss's field notes:

Mrs. Theodosia Bennett Long was born 1856 at Guntown, Itawamba (now Lee) County, Mississippi, at which place she lived practically all her life. She married Andrew J. Long in 1872, had one daughter, Mary Ila Long, and one son, Claude E. Long, both of whom are still living. She has been a member of the Missionary Baptist Church since 1880.

Mrs. Long wore a gingham dress with a neat apron. Her black low-quarter shoes were well polished. Her shoulders were slightly bent and at her neck hung a heavy metal neckpiece. Her gold-rimmed glasses sat low on her nose. Her features were soft; her complexion, slightly pale.

But the thing you looked at first was the large white sunbonnet that shadowed her features. The edges were scalloped. It was embellished by needlework of flowers. Starching made the brim stand out over her Dutch features.

Her father and mother were born in Fairfield District, South Carolina, in 1815 and 1818 respectively. They moved to Alabama in 1827 and lived there until they moved to Neshoba Co., Mississippi, in 1847. The following year they came to Lee County where Mrs. Theodosia Bennett Long was born in 1856. Her ancestry is of Irish, English, Welsh and Dutch descent.

Mrs. Theodosia Long. Photo by Abbott Ferriss, 1939, Courtesy Mississippi Department of Archives and History.

Mrs. Long's voice is soft and carries a note of gentility. However, she carefully wets the frayed end of a match, applies it to the box, and tucks into her mouth a dip of snuff. From this, her teeth are slightly discolored.

When Mrs. Long removed her bonnet, her hair was grey, well kept, neat.

She learned to sing as a child. Hers was a singing family. They sang "anytime"—at home together, play songs, etc.

She says the old songs were based upon the truth. "Some act or some form of something caused them to compose the songs that way," she says. "To build a song they had something to start from. New songs are often made up. I like old songs best—because I'm older. I like songs because there are truth and sentiment to them. There was more reality in old songs—a feeling among people who composed songs was very fine. With a lot of people, this feeling has gone."

She has forgotten the words to a great many songs, although the tune still lingers with her. "The tune was with me, but I forgot the words. When I remembered them one day, I called the lady to put them down. One day I was making up biscuits and I remembered a verse to a love song."

"Once in a while," she says, "another song comes back to me."

When young, Mrs. Long's memory was good. "One day the teacher wrote a composition for me, and I memorized it. Another time we were practicing for a concert. I never got the book to learn the words I was supposed to say. But the teacher wrote it off for me and I remembered, not only my own, but every body's else."

Further facts about Mrs. Long's ancestry; Father and mother moved to south Alabama. Grandfather on mother's side was an Irishman. Grandmother on mother's side was Irish and English. Elija Ivy fought in the Revolutionary War and had four brothers who also engaged in that war. The family always celebrated July 4th. They accumulated a great deal of wealth, slaves, etc. in South Carolina. Her father's mother was Welsh and Irish.

Mrs. Long sings whenever moved. At work. Nights. A big crowd would gather at her father's house and "git in a big way." and sing a lot. "People done many things in older days they don't do now. I suppose they do many things now they never think to do then."

She is a lively old lady. She can dance and does occasionally. When singing she pats her foot. While listening to the others sing, she sits quietly and still in a straight-back chair.

The immediate family and the townspeople call her affectionately "Aunt Dosh."

Most of the songs she sang were read from a paper, which had been written out by her daughter, Miss Mary Ila Long. The texts included below are those used in recording.

Authors' comments: Mrs. Long was one of A. P. Hudson's informants. Many of her song texts are in *Folksongs of Mississippi and Their Background*, which led to her being recorded by Herbert Halpert.

Her Songs recorded 1939 by Herbert Halpert:

Barbara Allen
Johnny Doyle
King William
Lord Lovell
Mary Blain
Old Blind Drunk John
Old Napper
Pretty Jimmy
Snail, Snail
Song to President Lincoln
Sweet William
The Farmer or the Dogs and the Gun
The Frog Went a-Courtin
The King's Seven Daughters
The Old Man Lived in the West
The Rich Lady from London
The Sailor and the Soldier
The Temperance Ball
The Young Oyster-man
Three Little Babes
Under the Juniper Tree

Mary Blain

I wish I was in Ire - land, A - sitting on my chair, And

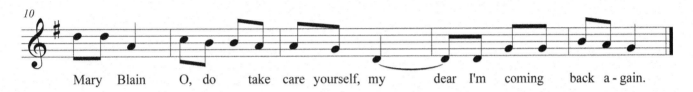

in my hand a glass of wine and by my side, my dear O, then Farewell, poor

Mary Blain O, do take care yourself, my dear I'm coming back a - gain.

Her eyes were like the bright corn meal
Made out of flint and steel
And when she rolls them eyes at me
My gizzard danced a reel
O, then Farewell, poor Mary Blain
O, do take care yourself, my dear
I'm coming back again.

Recording comments: Herbert Halpert asked, "What kind of song did you say that was?" Mrs. Long replied, "It must be Irish, he said wished he was in Ireland." She added that she had learned the song from her mother.

Authors' comments: "Mary Blane" was one of the more popular minstrel show tunes, judging by the many published pieces of sheet music which can be seen on the Library of Congress website. This 1940 transcription is on deposit at the Archive of American Folk Song at the Library of Congress.

Comparable versions:
"Mary Blane," J. C. Scherpf (New York: Wm. Vanderbeek, 1846) www.loc.gov/item/sm1846.060080/
"Mary Blane," William Whitlock (New York: C. G. Christman, 1846) www.loc.gov/item/sm1846.410560/
"New Mary Blane polka" (New York: Wm. Hall and Son, 1850) www.loc.gov/item/sm1850.130400/

JIM MEYERS

McGee, Simpson Co.

Old Field Rabbit

Authors' comments: This tune is made up of three phrases. After the above, Myers plays A', A, B, and first two measures of A'.

HARDY C. SHARP

Meridian, Lauderdale County

From Abbott Ferriss's field notes:

He is slightly gray-haired, wrinkled, and tired. He is 55 years old, a W.P.A. worker.

He started fiddling (he says he is no violinist) after watching other fiddlers play, at the age of 15 in Newton County where he was reared. He used his brother's fiddle, which wasn't very good, and "I had to steal it whenever I wanted to play."

Sharp moved to Meridian from Chunky about 18 years ago.

He says he let other people sing, but he never did. In his day they "had what they call a 'caller.'" When he was 21 he remembers that the guitar was used as "second" for fiddle, taking the place of the straw. He recalls some fiddlers singing, but he does not sing. "Have too much respect for neighbors to sing."

Since living in Meridian, he has helped organize bands. He does not play a great deal now, but broadcasts from the Meridian station with the band.

"Seconding" Sharp was Douglass Williams, guitar, 1709 11th St., Meridian, a house painter. His father had a band in Clarke County with which he played.

Played the bass fiddle when he was so small he had to stand on a cracker box. About 18 years ago he began playing the guitar. In the old days most pieces were played with in D chord and in A chord. He is 44 years old.

Authors' comments: Mr. Sharp was born in Newton County in 1884.

Recording location: Meridian, Lauderdale Co.
Tuning: GDAE. Sharp uses this for all of his pieces.

Eighth of January

Field notes: "This is one of Kinard's favorites. He says he has a good swing on it."

Comparable versions of "Eighth of January":
Ford, Ira, *Traditional Music of America* (New York: Dutton, 1940), 63
Arkansas Barefoot Boys (W 400229-B), 02/11/1928, Memphis, TN, OKeh 45217
Fox Chasers (W 5404166-A), 06/11/1930 San Antonio, TX, OKeh 45496
Ted Gossett's Band (GN 17041), 09/16/1930, Richmond, IN, Champion 16160
Other versions of "Eighth of January" in this book by Enos Canoy, W. E. Claunch, Charlie Edmundson, John Hatcher, and
    J. A. Moorman.

Great Big Yam Taters

Field notes: Mr. Sharp said, "I don't remember where I picked it up."
Authors' comments: Also known as "Mammy's Chimney Corner"; * indicates a bow rock.

Comparable versions:
Belden, H. M., and Arthur Palmer Hudson, *Frank C. Brown Collection of North Carolina Folklore; Vol. 3: Folk Songs* (Durham, NC: Duke University Press, 1952), 510, 565
"Been to the East Been to the West")W 146208-2), Leake County Revelers, 04/27/1928, New Orleans, LA, Columbia 15318-D
"Share 'Em" (W 402127-A), Scottsdale String Band, 08/10/1928, Atlanta, GA, OKeh 45256
"Shear the Sheep Bobbie" (W 147647-1), Gatwood Square Dance Band, 12/15/1928, New Orleans, LA, Columbia 15363
"Take Me Back to Tulsa" (Dal 1180-1), Bob Wills & His Texas Playboys, 02/25/1941, Dallas, TX, OKeh 06101
Other versions in this book by Enos Canoy ("Possum and Coon"), W. E. Claunch ("Chicken Pie" and "Miss Sally at the Party"), Ruby Costello ("Want to Go to Meeting"), John Hatcher ("Old Miss Sally"), and Charles Long ("Jones County" and "Steamboat").

Leather Britches

Little boy, little boy
Who made your breeches?
Mammy cut 'em out
And daddy sewed the stitches.

Comparable versions:

"Lord McDonald's Reel," Niel & Nathaniel Gow, *Third Collection of Niel Gow's Reels* (ca. 1792), 9

M. M. Cole, *One Thousand Fiddle Tunes* (Chicago: M. M. Cole, 1940; reprinted from *Ryan's Mammoth Collection*, 1883), 22

"Leather Breeches" (N 839-), Carter Brothers & Son, 11/22/1928, Memphis, TN, Vocalion 5295

"Leather Breeches" (W 143968-2), Leake County Revelers, 04/13/1927, New Orleans, LA, Columbia 15149-D

Other versions of "Leather Britches" in this book by John Hatcher, Stephen B. Tucker, and J. H. Wheeler ("Leather Breeches").

Liza Jane

Field notes: The title is "Raccoon up the 'possum tree."

Recording notes: Mr. Sharp announces but does not play "Sally Ann," which he learned from Blind Joe Mangrum who made two 78rpm recordings with Fred Schriver on 10/06/1928 in Nashville, TN: Victor 40018, "Bill Cheatham" (BVE 47154-3) and "Bacon and Cabbage"
(BVE 47153-3).

Authors' comments: Sharp plays the repeats as A, B, B', then A, B"

Comparable versions:

"Cindy in the Meadows" (81706-1), Samantha Bumgarner & Eva Davis 4/22/1924, NYC, Columbia 167-D

"Cindy" (W 143867-), Riley Puckett & Clayton McMichen, 04/02/1927, Atlanta, GA, Columbia 15232-D

"Get Along Home, Miss Cindy" (BVE 41853-2), Pope's Arkansas Mountaineers, 02/06/1928, Memphis, TN, Victor 21577

Other versions in this book by Charlie Addison ("Want to Go to Meeting"), John Brown ("Cindy"), W. E. Claunch ("Cindy"), Enos Canoy ("Where'd You Get Your Whiskey"), Mrs. R. C. Clifton ("Miss Cindy"), B. M. Guilette ("Liza Jane"), Frank Kittrell ("Cindy Jane"), Mrs. Joe McCoy ("Her Cheeks Are Like the Cherry"), Rev. J. E. Williams ("Cindy Waltz"), and Thaddeus Willingham ("Miss Cindy").

Mississippi Sawyer

Manuscript comments: "All four feet were keeping time."

Comparable versions:

"Love from the Heart," George P. Knauff, *Virginia Reels*, vol. 4, no. 4 (Baltimore, 1839)

"Mississippi Sawyer" (W 148200-1), Gid Tanner and His Skillet Lickers, 04/08/1929, Atlanta, GA, Columbia 15420-D

"Mississippi Sawyer" (E 29271-), Kessinger Brothers, 02/05/1929, NYC, Brunswick 309

"Old Time Corn Shuckin' pt. 1" (BVE 39270-2), Ernest Stoneman & the Blue Ridge Corn Shuckers, 07/27/1927, Victor 20835

Other versions of "Mississippi Sawyer" in this book by W. E. Claunch, Sinclair Crocker, J. E. Shoemaker, Stephen B. Tucker, Rev. J. H. Wheeler, and Rev. J. E. Williams.

Puncheon Floor

Field notes: Mr. Sharp said, "They had puncheon floors in those days."
Authors' comments: In the second strain, note the fine example of shuffling over a double stop.

Comparable versions:
"Lost Train Blues" (87676-1), Arthur Smith, 01/22/1935, New Orleans, LA, Bluebird B 5858
"White Mule" (41898-2), Floyd (Hoyt) Ming and His Pep Steppers, 02/13/1928, Memphis, TN, Victor 21534

STEPHEN BENJAMIN TUCKER

(12/12/1858–7/28/1945)
Collinsville, Lauderdale Co.

From Abbott Ferriss's field notes:
A friend who knew Mr. Tucker said, "Whenever that man walks in the bank, the bankers sit up and take notice." But to look at Mr. Tucker one would not think he had a bank account. He is an eighty-year-old man with thinning gray hair and a white mustache. He was dressed in a cotton suit and wore heavy-polished black shoes. "I am not used to wearing a coat," he said.

Mr. Tucker has lived on the same farm all of his life. From his father he acquired eighty acres. He now lives in his father's log cabin. On the same place, which Mr. Tucker has enlarged to two hundred acres (he sold forty acres not long ago) lives one of Tucker's sons. Tucker has eight children, six girls and two boys.

All of the daughters are married except one, who is a seamstress in Meridian, using an "electric machine." One daughter and one son have been working in the Meridian powder factory. Tucker's wife is living.

Mr. Tucker's father did not play the fiddle. "I just picked it up myself." One of his two brothers, both of who were in the Civil War, played the fiddle.

"I was nine or ten years old when I learned. So little I had to put the fiddle on my shoulder."

The first fiddle Tucker played was an old one left behind by a man who moved to Texas. Someone whittled pegs for it; strings were made of horsehair. "I fooled with it and they saw I wanted to play. They bought me strings."

The present fiddle was bought by Mr. Tucker when he was fifteen from an old fiddler. "Bought from a fellow named Thompson right after the Civil War. I have had it since he got shet of it." About this time Tucker whittled an apron out of bone. This apron is still on the fiddle. He says that the old finger bowl "wore out on it" and not long ago he had it replaced. It is not satisfactory and he intends to have it whittled down.

Tucker learned to play from hearing other fiddlers play. "To play you just have to have an ear for sound."

"Oh, I have spent some of my happiest hours playing just this way. Love to play." He says he has played in many old fiddlers contests. "I commenced going to old fiddlers contests and most always I won the prize. Reason I did this is I was the oldest and ugliest man."

He says he hadn't played much in the last ten years. He has forgotten many of the old pieces. He has played only two or three times this year. Once he learned a piece he could play it easily, although

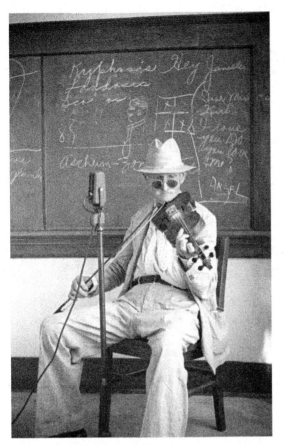

Stephen B. Tucker. Photo by Abbott Ferriss, 1939, courtesy Mississippi Department of Archives and History.

At one time when he was practicing, he said, "I was just sort of sawing." Most of his tunes were played in what he calls the "Cross note" which is E, A, E, A.

"My fingers are old and untrained. I miss my notes sometime."

Most of these tunes were learned by Tucker shortly after the Civil War from old fiddlers. He does not recall their sources.

Authors' comments: Mr. Tucker was born in Lauderdale County in 1859. His granddaughter, Mary Tucker Conner, remembers him playing mandolin as well as fiddle.

Mr. Tucker also played this tune but it was not collected:
Dutchman's Dog (a.k.a. Oh Where Oh Where Has My Little Dog Gone? Or the Lauterbach waltz)

Recording location: Collinsville, Lauderdale Co.

he sometimes forgot the title. Probably he could remember a great many more selections than those recorded were he to practice them. He says he played occasionally in local bands, for picnics, and frolics.

"I never did like to have straw beats," he said when asked about "knocking the straw." He explained that pieces were played on the first two or three strings. If the piece employs the last string, beating straws annoys him. However, he says that anything played on the first two strings can be accompanied by the straw. He has played with the straw "second," but doesn't like to.

Tucker also plays the guitar and at one time sang. It is interesting that all of his children play some instrument. One daughter and one son play the fiddle. "They can play the fiddle better than I can."

Arkansas Traveler

The Music Transcriptions

Comparable versions:

"The Arkansas Traveler," *The Arkansas Traveller's Songster* (New York: Dick & Fitzgerald, 1864), 5–9 imslp.org/wiki/
The_Arkansas_Traveler's_Songster_(Various)

"Arkansas Traveler" (B 26660-2), Henry C. Gilliland and A. C. "Eck" Robertson, 06/30/1922, NYC, Victor 18956

"Arkansas Traveler" (8613-A), Fiddlin' John Carson & His Virginia Reelers, 03/1924, Atlanta, GA, OKeh 40108

"Arkansas Traveler" (AL 228), Kessinger Brothers, 02/11/1928, Ashland, KY, Brunswick 247

Other versions of "Arkansas Traveler" in this book by W. E. Claunch and John Hatcher.

Bragg's Retreat

Comparable versions:
"Forked Deer," Knauff, George P., *Virginia Reels*, vol. 1 (Baltimore, ca. 1839)
"Forki Deer" (13319), Uncle Am Stuart, 06/1924, NYC, Vocalion 14846
"Forked Deer Hornpipe" (AL 207), Kessinger Brothers, 02/10/1928, Ashland, KY, Brunswick 247

Calico

Tuning: ADAE modal

Recorded comments: Mr. Tucker said, "Right after the Civil War the South was broke up. Didn't have nothin'. Picked up a little and the ladies started wearing calico. Ladies come out in new calico dresses." "Don't care where in the world I go, I can't get around for that calico"

Comparable versions:
Other versions in this book by John Brown ("A" part), W. E. Claunch ("A" part), and Stephen B. Tucker ("Calico," "B" part).

Chippy Get Your Hair Cut

Field notes: "I play it different from the way I learned it." After playing he said he should have started it in C. "That's the tune but I couldn't get it all in. It wasn't much to it when I heard it." He learned it about forty years ago.

Comparable versions:
O'Neil, Francis, *The Dance Music of Ireland: 1001 Gems* (Chicago: Lyon and Healey, 1907): "Mrs. Thorntons reel" (#534), 100, "That's How the Money Goes" (#620), 112.
"Grannie Will Your Dog Bite" (19102), Walter Family, 03/29/1933, Richmond, IN, Champion S-16643
"Gippy Get Your Hair Cut" (C 30199-), Kessinger Brothers, 06/29/1929, NYC, Brunswick 364

Christmas Time in the Morning

Christ-mas time will soon be ov-er
Christ-mas time will soon be ov-er
Christ-mas time will soon be ov-er
Then we'll join the band band.

Tuning: AEAE modal

Comparable versions:
"Christmas Time Will Soon Be Over" (W 81755-), Fiddlin' John Carson & His Virginia Reelers, 10/11/1927, Atlanta, GA, OKeh
   45273 (compare with "B" part of Tucker version)
"Cuckoo's Nest," Ed Haley, *Grey Eagle* (CD, Rounder 1133, 1998) (compare with "A" part of the Tucker version)

Circus Piece

Tuning: ADAE

Comparable versions:

"Strawberry Blossom," O'Neill, Francis, *O'Neill's Music of Ireland, Eighteen hundred and fifty Melodies* (Chicago: Lyon and Healy, 1903), 253

"Texas Quickstep" (DAL 689-), Red Headed Fiddlers, 10/18/1928, Dallas, TX, Brunswick 285

"Cherokee Polka," Ed Haley, *Grey Eagle* (CD, Rounder 1133, 1998)

"Mississippi Breakdown" (151123-2), Leake County Revelers, 12/18/1930, Jackson, MS, Columbia 15668-D

Cold Frosty Morning

Tuning: ADAE
Authors' comments: * Indicates a slight pulse in the upbow to divide the tied notes.

Devil's Dream

Tuning: AEAE

Comparable versions:
Howe, Elias *Howe's School for the Violin* (Boston: Oliver Ditson, 1851), 29
"Devil's Dream" (AL 213), Kessinger Bros, 02/10/1928, Ashland, KY, Brunswick 256
"Devil's Dream" (65713-A), Clayton McMichen, 06/01/1931, NYC, Decca 2649
Other versions of "Devil's Dream" in this book by W. E. Claunch and Mr. T. W. Cooper ("Untitled").

Fiddle Piece

Comparable versions:

"Run Nigger, Run," Allen, William Francis, *Slave Songs of the United States* (New York: A. Simpson & Co., 1867), #110, 89

"Crow Creek," Garry Harrison, Jo Burgess, *Dear Old Illinois* (Bloomington, IN: Pick Away Press, 2007), 253

"There's No Hell in Georgia" (M-828-), Luke Highnight & His Ozark Strutters, 11/22/1928, Memphis, TN, Vocalion 5325

"Run Nigger, Run" (8709-A), Fiddling John Carson, 08/27/1924, Atlanta, GA, OKeh 40230

"Run Nigger, Run" (667/668), Uncle Dave Macon, 04/13/1925, NYC, Vocalion 15032

"Run Boy, Run" (BVE 56361-2), Eck Robertson & Dr. J. B. Cranfill, 10/10/1929, Dallas, TX, Victor V40205

Other versions of "Run Nigger, Run" in this book by Mrs. M. B. Brister, W. E. Claunch, Mr. John McCartie, Jr., Stephen B. Tucker, Mrs. A. Tynes, Mrs. Louise Walker Wallace, and Thaddeus Willingham.

Fisher's Hornpipe

Tuning: ADAE

Authors' comments: So far this is the most challenging, most inspired reformulation of the "Fisher's Hornpipe" versions we have encountered.

Comparable versions:

"Fisher's Hornpipe," J. Fishar, *A New & Highly Improved Violin Preceptor* (ca. 1780) (Utica, NY: William Williams, 1817), 23

"Old Zip Coon and Medley Reels" (GE 13833), Doc Roberts & Asa Martin, 05/15/1928, Richmond, IN, Gennett 6495

"Fisher's Hornpipe" (E 3972W), The Hillbillies, 10/21/1926, NYC, Vocalion 5017

"Fisher's Hornpipe" (6713-), Clayton McMichen, Hoyt "Slim" Bryant & Jerry Wallace, 06/01/1939, NYC, Decca 2649

"Texas Breakdown" (W 404065-B), W. T. Narmour & S. W. Smith, 06/06/1930, San Antonio, TX, OKeh 45492 (has only the "A" part in common)

Other versions of "Fisher's Hornpipe" in this book by Billie Mansfield, Alvis Massengale, Mr. N. Odom, and "Unknown."

The Music Transcriptions

Haste To the Wedding

Tuning: ADAE

Comparable versions:
"Haste to the Wedding," *One Thousand Fiddle Tunes* (Chicago: M. M. Cole, 1940), 53
"Medley of Irish Jigs" (B 2366-1), Charles D. Alamaine, 03/13/1905, NYC, Victor 4336
"Mountain Rangers" (BVE 34340-3), Mellie Dunham & His Orchestra, 01/19/1926, NYC, Victor 19940

Hogeye

Tuning: ADAE modal

Field notes: He learned this song from his girl when he was a little boy. He has heard it on the banjo, has heard the words but does not recall it.

Authors' comments: As noted above, Tucker anticipates the downbeat of measures 3, 6, 26, and 29. He also anticipates the downbeat in measures 1, 6, 8, 10, 12, 14, 26, and 31. This technique is common to his playing in other tunes.

Comparable versions:

All four of the tunes in the collection that mention "Hog Eye" have a few measures that sound related. In Stephen B. Tucker's 1939 version, "Hog Eye" the "B" part is related to the measures marked "Chorus" in Mittie Lee Adams's 1936 "All I Wants A Hogeye," Charlie Addison's 1936 "Hog Eye," and Birmah Grissom's 1939 "Hog-eye."

Indian Eat a Woodpecker

Comparable versions:
"Village Hornpipe," Howe, Elias, *Musician's Omnibus*, vol. 1 (Boston: Elias Howe, 1863–82), 52
"The Gems of Ireland," M. M. Cole, *One Thousand Fiddle Tunes* (Chicago: M. M. Cole, 1940), 40
"Duck River," John Salyer, Magoffin County, KY, for the Library of Congress, 1941

Joke on the Puppy

Alt measure 1

Tuning: ADAE

Comparable versions:
"Rye Straw (The Unfortunate Pup)" (13329), Uncle Am Stuart, 06/1924, NYC, Vocalion 14843
"Rye Straw" (W 149290-2), Clayton McMichen & Riley Puckett, 10/29/1929, Atlanta, GA, Columbia 15524-D
"Rye Straw" (GE 16086), Doc Roberts & Asa Martin, 01/13/1930, Richmond, IN, Gennett 7221
Other versions in this book by Charles Long ("Alabama Waltz") and Frank Kittrell ("Rye Straw").

The Music Transcriptions

Leather Britches

Comparable versions:

"Lord McDonald's Reel," Niel & Nathaniel Gow, *Third Collection of Niel Gow's Reels* (ca. 1792), 9

M. M. Cole, *One Thousand Fiddle Tunes* (Chicago: M. M. Cole, 1940; reprinted from *Ryan's Mammoth Collection*, 1883), 22

"Leather Breeches" (N 839-), Carter Brothers & Son, 11/22/1928, Memphis, TN, Vocalion 5295

"Leather Breeches" (W 143968-2), Leake County Revelers, 04/13/1927, New Orleans, LA, Columbia 15149-D

Other versions of "Leather Britches" in this book by John Hatcher, Hardy Sharp, and J. H. Wheeler ("Leather Breeches").

Mississippi Sawyer

Tuning: ADAE

Comparable versions:

"Love from the Heart," George P. Knauff, *Virginia Reels*, vol. 4, no. 4 (Baltimore, 1839)

"Mississippi Sawyer" (W 148200-1), Gid Tanner and His Skillet Lickers, 04/08/1929, Atlanta, GA, Columbia 15420-D

"Mississippi Sawyer" (E 29271-), Kessinger Brothers, 02/05/1929, NYC, Brunswick 309

"Old Time Corn Shuckin' pt. 1" (BVE 39270-2), Ernest Stoneman & the Blue Ridge Corn Shuckers, 07/27/1927, Victor 20835

Other versions of "Mississippi Sawyer" in this book by W. E. Claunch, Sinclair Crocker, Hardy Sharp, J. E. Shoemaker, Rev. J. H.
  Wheeler, and Rev. J. E. Williams.

Pound Cake and Sugar

Tuning: AEAE

Comparable versions:

"The Twenty-Second of February," George P. Knauff, *Virginia Reels*, vol. 2 (Baltimore, 1839)

"John Sharp's Hornpipe," John Sharp Band, *Five Miles Out of Town: Traditional Music from the Cumberland Plateau*, vol. 2
(County Records, 1980; original recording from 1949)

Raker's Hornpipe

Comparable versions:

"Rickett's Hornpipe," *One Thousand Fiddle Tunes* (Chicago: M. M. Cole, 1940) 89

"Rickett's Hornpipe" (11922-), Tweedy Brothers, 06/14/1924, Atlanta, GA, Gennett 5613

"Rickett's Hornpipe" (GS 17036), Green's String Band, 09/15/1930, Richmond, IN, Champion 16489

"Rickett's Hornpipe" (W 151027-2), Gid Tanner & His Skillet Lickers, 12/04/1930

Other versions in this book by Charles Long ("Fisher's Hornpipe") and Reverend J. E. Williams ("Soldier's Joy Hornpipe").

Run, Nigger, Run

Nigger and white man playin' seven-up
Nigger turned the jack and picked money up
Run, Nigger, Run. Patter-roller git you
Run, Nigger, run. You better git away

Comparable versions:
"Run Nigger, Run," Allen, William Francis, *Slave Songs of the United States* (New York: A. Simpson & Co., 1867), #110, 89
"Run Nigger, Run" (8709-A), Fiddling John Carson, 08/27/1924, Atlanta, GA, OKeh 40230
"Run Nigger, Run" (667/668), Uncle Dave Macon, 04/13/1925, NYC, Vocalion 15032
"Run Boy, Run" (BVE 56361-2), Eck Robertson & Dr. J. B. Cranfill, 10/10/1929, Dallas, TX, Victor V40205
Other versions of "Run Nigger, Run" in this book by Mrs. M. B. Brister, W. E. Claunch, Mr. John McCartie, Jr., Mrs. A. Tynes, Mrs. Louise Walker Wallace, and Thaddeus Willingham.

Soldier's Joy

Tuning: ADAE

Authors' comments: After playing the above, Mr. Tucker ends with the second strain.

Comparable versions:

Aird, James, *A Selection of Scotch, English, Irish and Foreign Airs*, vol. 1, no. 109 (1778)

"Soldier's Joy" (9189-A), Fiddlin' John Carson & His Virginia Reelers, 06/30/1925, Atlanta, GA, OKeh 45011

"Soldier's Joy" (GE 12747), Taylor's Kentucky Boys, 06/27, Richmond, IN, Silvertone 5060

"Soldier's Joy" (E29273), Kessinger Brothers, 02/05/1929, NYC, Brunswick 341

Other versions of "Soldier's Joy" in this book by W. A. Bledsoe ("Farewell Mary Ann"), Dalton Brantley, W. E. Claunch, Charlie Edmundson, John Hatcher, W. E. Ray, and Rev. J. E. Williams ("Rickets Hornpipe").

Texas Wagon

Authors' comments: The famous Tennessee racing horse Wagner beat Grey Eagle in a race in 1839. Both horses have fiddle tunes named for them.

Comparable versions:
"The Hero," Knauff, II #5, 1839
"Waggoner" (13308), Uncle Am Stuart, 06/1924, NYC, Vocalion 14840
"Kentucky Wagoners" (10220), Allen Sission, 02/25/1925, NYC, Edison 51720
"The Waggoner" (10462-2), Fiddlin Doc Roberts Trio, 03/05/1931, NYC, Banner 32309
"Northeast Texas" (MEM 755-), Milner & Curtis with the Magnolia Ramblers, 02/1930, Memphis, TN, Vocalion 5246
Other version in this book by W. E. Claunch ("Wagoner").

Throw the Soap Suds Over in the Corner of the Fence

Tuning: ADAE

The Music Transcriptions

Tom & Jerry

Tuning: AEAE

Authors' comments: Alt m15 and 16 are played on the second passes through the part.

Comparable versions:
Elias Howe, *Musician's Omnibus* (Boston: Elias Howe, 1864), 46
"Tom and Jerry" (E 4959), Uncle Dave Macon & His Fruit Jar Drinkers, 05/09/1927, NYC, Vocalion 5165
"Tom and Jerry" (DAL 526-), Smiths Garage Fiddle Band, 10/29/1929, Dallas, TX, Vocalion 5375
Other versions in this book by John Hatcher and Stephen B. Tucker.

Untitled Jig

Tuning: AEAE

Authors' comments: Alt m15 and 16 are played on the second passes through the part.

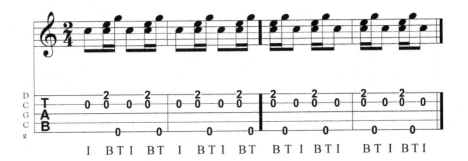

I BT I BT I BT I BT BT I BT I BT I BT I

Banjo Transcriptions from 1939

Notes on the Tablature

Tablature is a representation of the strings on a banjo and shows how they are played. The lower staff shows strings 1 thru 5, from top to bottom. The numbers on the lines of the tablature staff show where the fingers of the left hand fret each string.

The letters I, M, T, B seen under the tab staff indicate which finger of the right hand is used to strike or pluck the string, striking down in clawhammer style and plucking up in three-finger style.

Thaddeus Willingham's tunes are all in clawhammer style with the exception of "Who Will Shoe Your Pretty Little Foot," which is in three-finger style.

Willingham's style is a very basic old-time style. His playing is solid and clear. His tunes stand alone as solo tunes, but his style would work well as accompaniment to a fiddler or in a band setting. He learned his banjo from the playing of black tenants on the family plantation, and this is evident from the prominent use of syncopation in his playing.

He does not appear to drop his thumb to any noticeable degree, but uses various hammer-ons, pull-offs, slides, and syncopated phrasing to create melodic and rhythmic interest.

He will often use a ghost note in his playing, in which the 16th note before the thumb stroke is not struck, but the right-hand movement is made as if that note were being played—the finger

makes its stroke but misses the string in question, causing a subtle but useful change in the figure, which amounts to a tie of the preceding note.

Basic strum in Double C tab

Horace Kinard recorded two tunes. He had a straightforward clawhammer style with no more elements than Willingham. His banjo accompaniments with Sharp are beautiful examples of how a simple chordal approach is sometimes the ideal method for backing a fiddle tune.

Double C basic strum

Example 1 demonstrates the basic strum in double C tuning.

I = index finger (RH) strikes down on the second string.

B = brush down on the second and first strings with either the index or middle finger or any combination of index, middle, and third fingers (RH) (I usually prefer the middle with Willingham's settings).

T = pluck the fifth string with the RH thumb.

This gives the typical galloping rhythm of the banjo, or bum-diddy, bum-diddy. Measures 1 and 2.

This is the basis for all clawhammer banjo playing, and this rhythmic feel should be present at all times no matter what the melody is doing.

Interestingly, if one plays this persistently, the rhythm may seem to shift from bum-diddy to diddy-bum, which is both a useful way of *hearing* the rhythm and an alternative way of *playing* it that comes in handy at times. The piece or phrase you are playing or backing up will usually tell you which is most fitting, if you let it. Measures 3 and 4.

Hammer On

Hammering on is a method of sounding a string percussively with a finger of the LH without striking the string with the RH. In Example 2 in G tuning, the index finger strikes the open fourth string, and immediately afterward (in rhythm), the second finger of the left hand comes down crisply (like a little hammer) on the fourth string at the second fret.

The hammered-on note (E) will ring out like it has been plucked. This gives a different rhythmic figure—four 16th notes—which sounds like Chat-ta-noo-ga. H is the symbol for this in tab. The open and hammered notes are connected with a slur.

Pulling Off

In Example 3, I = index finger (RH) strikes down on first string, which is held down by second finger at second fret. Then the 2second finger (LH) immediately (in rhythm) pulls off of the first string. The

first string rings out as if it had been struck. B = brush down with the middle finger on the upper strings. T = Thumb plucks the fifth string. Again, this gives the Chat-ta-noo-ga rhythm.

The symbol for this in tab is P. The pulled and open notes are connected with a slur.

Slides

In Example 4, I = Index finger (RH) strikes down on the third string, which is held down with the second finger (LH) at the second fret. The second finger (LH) then slides up to the fourth fret (in rhythm). The slide across the frets makes the third string at the fourth fret sound out like it has been struck. B = brush down across the upper strings with the middle finger. T = Thumb plucks the fifth string.

The symbol for the slide is SL; the two notes are connected with an arrow or slanted line.

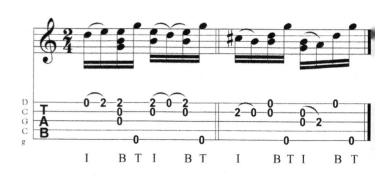

Complex combinations

Hammering on and pulling off can be combined to produce more complex rhythmic figures.

The Music Transcriptions

In m1 of Example 5, a simple hammer-on in the first half of the measure is combined with a sequential pull-off and hammer-on in the second half of the measure.

For the second figure, the first string is fretted at the second fret by the second finger (LH)

The index finger (RH) strikes down on open second string while the second finger (LH) pulls off the first string, and then hammers back on at second fret, while the middle finger simultaneously brushes down on the first and second strings.

In m3 a simple pull-off in the first half of the measure is combined with a hammer-on in the second half, in which the index finger (LH) strikes down on the open second string; the second finger (LH) hammers on to the third string at the second fret; the third string is not struck with the RH, but rings out as if struck.

HORACE KINARD

Meridian, Lauderdale Co.

Railroad Bill

Railroad Bill is a mighty bad man
Shot that lantern out the brakeman's hand
Railroad Bill, he got so fine
He's shoot them melons off the vine.

If I die a railroad man bury me under the ties
So I can hear that fast train when she come rat-
tlin' by
Lawdy Lord!

If I die a railroad man bury me under the floor
So I can hear my partner say, "I bet a hundred
dollars or more."

Railroad Bill went up on the mountain took his
stand

A Winchester rifle on his shoulder and a pistol in
his hand

Railroad Bill lyin' down to take his rest
Had a forty-four rifle across his breast

Mr. Brakeman, won't you just look back
Nineteen hoboes right beside your track
Mr. Brakeman, don't you look back again
All them hobos done caught your train

Railroad Bill got so mean, wouldn't wear no
shoes
He couldn't tell his track from a horse or mule.

Tuning: G
Recording comments: Kinard said, "I heard this piece thirty or thirty-five years ago from a fellow named Brown."
Authors' comments: Phrases vary in length, sample given here.

Comparable versions:
"Railroad Bill" (140023-2), Riley Puckett, 09/11/1924, NYC, Columbia 15040-D
"Railroad Bill" (W 402509-B), Frank Hutchinson, 07/09/1929, NYC, OKeh 45425

Liza Jane

I went to see miss Liza
She met me at the door
Shoes and stockings in her hands
And her feet all over the floor
Her feet all over the floor

I went up on the mountain
cut myself a cane
Every time I chew that cane
I think about Liza Jane
I think about Liza Jane

Went up on the mountain
And I give my horn a blow
I thought I heard my Liza say
Oh yonder come my Beau
Oh yonder come my Beau

I went down the new cut road
Miss Liza down the lane
Stuck my head through a crick in the fence
And there I kissed Miss Liza Jane
And there I kissed Miss Liza Jane

Tuning: C

Comparable versions:
"Old Liza Jane" (13302), Uncle Am Stuart, 06/1924, NYC, Vocalion 14846
"Liza Jane" (140018-1), Riley Puckett, 09/11/1924, NYC, Columbia 15014-D
"Goodbye Liza Jane" (9596-A), Fiddlin' John Carson & His Virginia Reelers, 03/11/1926, Atlanta, GA, OKeh 45049
Other versions in this book by Enos Canoy ("Where'd You Get Your Whiskey"), Everett Mitchell ("Liza Jane"), J. P. Reece ("I Ain't Gonna Leave Her by Herself"), and Thaddeus Willingham.

THADDEUS C. WILLINGHAM

Gulfport, Harrison Co.

Abbott Ferriss noted:

Thaddeus C. Willingham was born in Tuscaloosa County, Alabama. At about the age of fifteen years he began picking the banjo, playing by ear. He learned to play from "the boys."

He plays a five-string banjo. "I got more music out of five strings." For most pieces Willingham uses C and G chords. On certain of his pieces, however, he makes other changes in the tuning; for instance, "running the bass down." He uses three fingers and thumb in picking banjo. The thumb is used chiefly on the fifth string, but drops to others occasionally on certain pieces.

He has lived in Harrison County since his marriage. At present he is employed by the WPA, as a laborer. He is a squatter, living in a house on the edge of town constructed principally of tin. The mental condition of his wife is not sound. He has several children.

He is tall, wears clean overalls, heavy black work shoes. His shoulders are slightly stooped. His face tells you that his grip on life is infirm. His jaw is weak his mouth without determination, his eyes without expression. At no time during the interview did his occasional smile show merriment. He spoke in a low voice with little inflection.

For most pieces, Willingham both played and sang.

T. C. Willingham, 5-string banjo player of Gulfport, Miss., has resided in the vicinity of Gulfport since his coming to the Coast in 1902. He engaged in farming, principally in the nearby Long Beach trucking district, but alternated at times with work in logging operations for various sawmills.

Both his grandfathers, Willie Simeon Willingham and Grandfather Ward, migrated from South Carolina about 1840 to Tuscaloosa County, Alabama. Both were large slaveholders and prominent planters. Here his father was born and from here, enlisted in the Confederate Army; a faithful slave, Henry, accompanying him. Dixie, a Negro maid given to Mr. Willingham's mother at his mother's birth, married Henry and remained in the family till her death, long after freedom came. Here T. C. Willingham was born, Jan. 4th, 1884, attended school through the grades and high school and carried on his dead father's diminished plantings.

Mr. Willingham enjoyed a fair amount of success and prosperity for a number of years after coming to the coast at the age of eighteen. Twice married, he has one daughter aged twenty-five from his first marriage; she is a talented singer and

skilled fingers and the magic of his banjo playing and singing has helped to keep him and his family more cheerful in the face of disheartening circumstances.

Location: Gulfport, Harrison Co.

Thaddeus Willingham. Photo by Abbott Ferriss, 1939, Courtesy Mississippi Department of Archives and History.

deputy chancery clerk of Stone County at Wiggins, Mississippi. There are six children aged two to sixteen, from his second marriage. Harassed by ill health and the collapse of the trucking industry, logging and other available sources of income, they have become very poor. But the old plantation melodies still live in this man's memory and

Black Eyed Susie

Banjo

Bjo.

All I want in this creation
Pretty little wife and a big plantation

Love my wife and love my baby
Love my biscuits sopped in gravy

All I want to make me happy
Two little boys to call me pappy

Love my wife and love my baby
Love my biscuits sopped with gravy

Tuning: Double C

Field notes: "When he hears this song, Willingham is reminded of a man he knew in Alabama. The man played fiddle. He played only when drunk. Every Saturday Dave White went to town. Every Saturday, he got drunk, staggered home late at night.

It was only then that he played his fiddle; the tune was Black-Eyed Susie. Willingham remembers walking past Dave White's house late at night and hearing this tune."

Comparable versions:

"Black Eyed Susie" (81635-1), Gid Tanner and Riley Puckett, 03/08/1924, NYC, Columbia 119-D

"Black Eyed Susie" (GE 13040), Fiddlin' Doc Roberts, 09/1927, Richmond, IN, Gennett 6257

"Black Eyed Susie" (BVE 39747), J. P. Nestor, 08/01/1927, Bristol, TN, Victor 21070

Other versions of "Black Eyed Susan" in this book by John Brown, W. E. Claunch ("Black Eyed Susie"), John Hatcher, and J. A. Moorman.

Cripple Creek

Banjo

Bjo.

Roll my breeches to my knee
Chase the mussel to the Rigolets*

Going up to Cripple Creek, Going on run
Goin' up to Cripple Creek, See my hon

Roll my breeches to my knee
Wade old Cripple Creek, where I please

Tuning: G

Field notes: "It is an old breakdown, played on banjo and violin. Verse one was learned on the coast."

* The Rigolets (pronounced ric-o-lees) is a chain of islands and the mainland, joining Lake Pontchartrain and
  Mississippi Sound.

Comparable versions:

"Cripple Creek" (10616) Fiddlin' Powers and Family, 10/03/1924, NYC, Edison 51789

"Cripple Creek" (W 149283-2), Gid Tanner & Riley Puckett, 10/29/1924, Atlanta, GA, Columbia 15485-D

"Cripple Creek" (12125-A), Tweedy Brothers, 01/15/1925, Richmond, IN, Gennett 5635

Cross Eyed Gopher

Hey, cross-eyed gopher
Punch him in the ribs and he'll turn over

Oh, cross-eyed gopher
Punch him in the ribs and he'll turn over

_____

Tuning: G

Going On Down Town

I met a possum in the road
Possum where you gwine
Look out man, don't bother me
I'm huntin' muscadines

(Chorus)
I'm goin' on down town
Goin' on down town
Goin' on down town
Goin' on down to Mobile town
Hear my banjo sound

Somebody stole my old speckled hen
I wish they'd let her be
Every day she lays two eggs;
Sunday, she lays three.

Somebody stole my old black dog
I wish they'd bring him back
Run the big hogs over the fence,
Little pigs through the crack

Raccoon's got a ring round tail;
Possum's tail goes bare
Rabbit's got not tail at all
Jes' totes a bunch of hair,

If I had a scoldin' wife,
I'd whip her, shore you born.
I'd take her down to New Orleans
And trade her off for corn.

Raccoon up a 'simmon tree
Possum on the ground
Think I heard the Possum say
Shake them 'simmons down

Monday morning at four o'clock,
Boss man's got me gwine;
Saturday night at eight o'clock,
That yaller gal is mine.

Tuning: G
Field notes: "On the record a howl will be noticed.
This howl, usually coming at the end of each verse was as learned by Willingham from older banjo pickers. In some of these
    songs take note that this howl has been added to the verses."

Comparable versions:
"Turkey Buzzard," James Gray, *I'm the Man You Don't Meet Every Day Songster* (1883), 42
"Going Down to Lynchburg Town" (W 141856-1), Blue Ridge Highballers, 03/24/1926, NYC, Columbia 15096-D
"The Old Hat" (W 145016-), Leake County Revelers, 10/24/1927, New Orleans, LA, Columbia 15205-D
"Going Along Down Town" (W 148202-1), Gid Tanner & His Skillet Lickers, 04/08/1929, Atlanta, GA, Columbia 15420-D

Humpbacked Mule

(Chorus)
Ridin' the humped back mule
Ridin' the humped back mule
All the song that I can sing
Ridin' the humped back mule

I got on that ol' mule
Started off to town
Rode me across clothes line
Knocked all washin' down

I got on that ol' mule
You ought to heard him holler

Tied a slip knot on his tail
And jumped right through the collar

Time is a-gettin' hard
Money's a-gettin' scarce
Times don't git no better here
I'm a-gonna leave this place

If I could read my titles clear
The mansions in the sky
Bid farewell to meat and greens
And drink my hard liquor dry

Tuning: "kind of a cross-note." It is played with a low bass from G.

Field notes: "He does not recall all verses."

Authors' comments: In m3 the index finger of the right hand plays the C note on the second string. The second (or third) finger of the left hand then pulls off of the first string at the second fret, to sound the D note on the open first string. The index finger does not hit the first string during this process.

Comparable versions:

"Whoa Mule" (1487/8/9), Bill Chitwood and Bud Landress, 11/21/1924, NYC, Brunswick 2811

"Whoa, Mule" (S 73120-A), The Hillbillies, 01/15/1925, NYC, OKeh 40376

"Hold on to the Sleigh" (E 3720/21), Uncle Dave Macon, 09/09/1926, NYC, Brunswick 114

Other versions in this book by Mrs. R. L. Halberg ("Whoa Mule") and J. W. McDonough ("My Old Coon Dog").

Liza Jane

The Music Transcriptions

Oh, Liz Jane, po' gal
Oh, Liza Jane
Don't care where in the world you go
So long as you don't carry my name

Drinkin', gamblin'
Brought me so low
Soon as I git able
I'll pay that debt I owe
Who-who-ho

She went through the new-cut road
I went down the lane

Ask that gal to have me
Says, Oh, ain't you ashamed.

Mis' Sally went to meetin'
To hear them shout and squeal
Got so full of religion
Busted her stocking heel
Who-ho-ho
He-he-he

Tuning: Double C

Authors' comments: In m22 (indicated *), the right hand index finger strikes the second string, with a simultaneous hammer-on
to the third string with the second finger of the left hand.

Comparable versions:

"Old Liza Jane" (13302), Uncle Am Stuart, 06/1924, NYC, Vocalion 14846

"Liza Jane" (140018-1), Riley Puckett, 09/11/1924, NYC, Columbia 15014-D

"Goodbye Liza Jane" (9596-A), Fiddlin' John Carson & His Virginia Reelers, 03/11/1926, Atlanta, GA, OKeh 45049

Other versions of "Liza Jane" in this book by Enos Canoy ("Where'd You Get Your Whiskey"), Horace Kinard, Everett Mitchell,
J. P. Reece ("I Ain't Gonna Leave Her by Herself"), and Thaddeus Willingham ("Want A Little Water Johnny").

Miss Cindy

Went to see miss Cindy
She met me at the door
Shoes and stockings in her hand
And 'er feet all over the floor

———————

Tuning: Double C
Field notes: "An old violin piece, a breakdown."

Comparable versions:

"Cindy in the Meadows" (81706-1), Samantha Bumgarner & Eva Davis, 4/22/1924, NYC, Columbia 167-D
"Cindy" (W 143867-), Riley Puckett & Clayton McMichen, 04/02/1927, Atlanta, GA, Columbia 15232-D
"Get Along Home, Miss Cindy" (BVE 41853-2), Pope's Arkansas Mountaineers, 02/06/1928, Memphis, TN, Victor 21577
Other versions in this book by Charlie Addison ("Want to Go to Meeting"), John Brown ("Cindy"), W. E. Claunch ("Cindy"), Enos Canoy ("Where'd You Get Your Whiskey"), Mrs. R. C. Clifton ("Miss Cindy"), B. M. Guilette ("Liza Jane"), Frank Kittrell ("Cindy Jane"), Mrs. Joe McCoy ("Her Cheeks Are Like the Cherry"), Hardy Sharp ("Liza Jane"), and Rev. J. E. Williams ("Cindy Waltz").

Oh, My Little Darlin'

The Music Transcriptions

Oh, my little darlin'
Don't you weep and cry
Some sweet day a-comin'
Marry you and I

Oh, my little darlin'
Don't you weep and moan
Some sweet day a-comin'
Take my baby home

Up and down the railroad
'Cross the county line
Pretty girls a-plenty
But wife is hard to find

Nigger drive the wagon
Nigger walk behind
Kill yourself a-laughin'
See them horses flying.

————————

Tuning: G

Authors' comments: * ghost note. In m22 for the pull-off, the right hand index finger strikes second string; left hand second fin-
    ger pulls off first string, sounding open note, then comes back down and frets first string (at 2 pos.) as right hand index finger
    strikes first string.

Old Dan Tucker

Old Dan Tucker was a fine old man
He whipped his wife with a frying pan
Combed his head with the wagon wheels
Died with the toothache in his heel

Come too late old Dan Tucker
Come too late to git his supper

Come too late old Dan Tucker
Come too late to git your supper

Folks is gone, dishes washed
Ain't nothin' left but a piece of squash

Come too late old Dan Tucker
Come too late to git your supper
Folks is gone, Fire's all out
Nothin' in the pot but the old pig snout

Tuning: Double C

Authors' comments: Note that in m3 and m7 the index (RH) strikes second string. Second finger (LH) pulls off first string, sounding open note, then comes back down and frets first string (at 2 pos.) as index finger (RH) strikes first string.

Comparable versions:

"Old Dan Tucker," Dan Emmett, *Aldophous Morning Glory Songster* (1843), 14

"Old Dan Tucker" (669/70), Uncle Dave Macon, 04/13/1925, NYC, Vocalion 15033

"Old Dan Tucker" (S 73-039-A), Fiddlin' John Carson, 12/18/1924, NYC, OKeh 40263

Other versions of "Old Dan Tucker" in this book by C. M. Coursan ("Big Tom Bailey").

(right page)

Tuning: G

Comparable versions:

Sharp, Cecil J., & Maud Karples, *English Folk Songs from the Southern Appalachians*, vol. 2 (Oxford, UK: Oxford University Press, 1932), 259

"Fare Thee Well, Old Joe Clark" (S 72-016-B), Fiddlin' John Carson, 11/071923, NYC, OKeh 40038

"Old Joe Clark" (B 30582-1), Fiddlin' Powers & Family, 08/18/1924, Camden, NJ, Victor 19434

"Old Joe Clark" (S 73117-A), The Hillbillies, 01/15/1925, NYC, Victor 19434

Other version in this book by John Brown.

Old Joe Clark

I went down to Old Joe Clark's
Didn't go there to stay
Got my hand in the whiskey keg
Now I stayed all day

Flyin' around Old Joe Clark
Goodbye Betsy Brown
Flyin' around Old Joe Clark
I'm gonna leave this town

I went down to Old Joe Clark's
Old Joe, he was gone
Eat up all the meat he had cooked up
And left Old Joe the bones

Used to have old gray mule
Rode him once to town
Every tooth in that mule's head
Was a mile and a half around

I used to have an old grey mule
His name was old Joe Clark
Carried him down to the foot of the hill
Hitched him to my cart

If I was old Joe Clark
Sho' would be ashamed
Caught him down at Sally Ann's house
A huggin' Liza Jane
There I stayed all day

Roll On the Ground

The Music Transcriptions

Work on the railroad
Sleep on the ground
Eat soda crackers
And the wind blow 'em around

Roll On the Ground, Boys
Roll On the Ground
Roll On the Ground, Boys
Roll On the Ground

Work on the railroad
Work all the day
Eat soda crackers
And the wind blow 'em away

Tuning: C

Comparable versions:
"Roll on the Ground" (B-377/2), Billy Golden, 09/01/1903, Philadelphia, Victor 616 (www.loc.gov/jukebox/recordings/detail/id/253/)
"Big Ball in Town" (W 145049-1), Gid Tanner & His Skillet Lickers, 10/31/1927, Atlanta, GA, Columbia 15204
"Big Ball Uptown" (BVE 47022-1-2), Taylor Griggs Louisiana Melody Makers, 09/13/1928, Memphis, TN, Victor 21768
Other version in this book by Charley Goff ("Big Bill's in Jail").

Rove, Riley, Rove

Went up on the mountain
Give my horn a blow
Thought I heard my true love say
Yonder comes my beau

Rove Riley Rove
Rove Riley Rove
Rove Riley, poor boy
Got nowhere to go

If you want to marry
I'll tell you how to do
Every day wear you 'round and about
And Sunday wear your long-tailed blue

Sixteen pounds of meat a week
And whiskey here to sell
How can a young man stay at home
Pretty girl look so well

Masta had a great big house
Sixteen stories high
Every story in that house
Filled with chicken pie

Masta give me meat
Mistus give me bread

Pretty gal give me one sweet kiss
Like to been killed me dead

Mistus give me one drink
Ol' Masta give me two
Want another one so bad
I don't know what to do

Raccoon is mighty man
He rambles in the dark
Oughta see him hunt his den
When he hears old Ranger bark.

I went down to New Orleans
What do reckon I saw
Sixteen pottridges pullin' a plow
Jaybird hollering "Haw"

Miss Sally went to meetin'
To hear them shout an' squeal;
She got so full of religion
She busted her stocking heel.

Somebody stole my old black dog
I wish they'd bring him back.
He'd run the big hogs over the fence
An' the little pigs through the crack

Tuning: Double C

Run Nigger, Run

Banjo

Banjo

Run, nigger, run, the patter-roller git you
Run, nigger, run, you're almost day
Run, nigger, run, the patter-roller git you
Run, nigger, run, you better git away

Nigger run down through the field
Black snake bit him on the heel

Nigger run, higger flew
Nigger almost lost his Sunday shoe

Nigger run, Nigger flew
Nigger tore his shirt in two

Nigger run and run his best
Run right into a hornet's nest

Tuning: G

Field notes: "Willingham gave the following explanation of the term 'patter-roller.' The explanation, he learned from his father. On his grand father's pre-war plantation in Tuscaloosa County, Alabama, it was necessary for the slaves to carry a pass when going from one plantation to another, when on visits, and the like. To enforce this rule slave owners employed patrollers. When caught without a pass a slave was punished."

Comparable versions:

"Run Nigger, Run," Allen, William Francis, *Slave Songs of the United States* (New York: A. Simpson & Co., 1867), #110, 89

"Run Nigger, Run" (8709-A), Fiddling John Carson, 08/27/1924, Atlanta, GA, OKeh 40230

"Run Nigger, Run" (667/668), Uncle Dave Macon, 04/13/1925, NYC, Vocalion 15032

"Run Boy, Run" (BVE 56361-2), Eck Robertson & Dr. J. B. Cranfill, 10/10/1929, Dallas, TX, Victor V40205

And other versions of "Run Nigger, Run" in this book by Mrs. M. B. Brister, W. E. Claunch, Mr. John McCartie, Jr., Stephen B. Tucker, Mrs. A. Tynes, and Mrs. Louise Walker Wallace.

Sally Goodin

Love 'tater pie, love 'tater puddin'
Love that girl they call Sally Goodin

Huckleberry pie, blackberry puddin'
On my way to see Sally Goodin

Looked up the road and saw Sal comin'
Thought to my soul I'd kill myself runnin'

Blackberry pie, huckleberry puddin'
On my way to see Sally Goodin

I got a girl, name is Isabella
Had a hump on her back like a open umbrella

Tuning: G

Authors' comments: * Index finger plays a pull-off on the second fret to open on third string with simultaneous brush on the first and second strings and a thumb stroke on the fifth string. It is simple to do but difficult to convey in notation.

Comparable versions:

"Sally Goodwin," Ford, Ira, *Traditional Music of America* (New York: Dutton, 1940), 64, 209 (calls), 419 (verses)

"Sally Gooden" (B 26664-1), Eck Robertson, 07/01/1922, NYC, Victor 18956

"Old Sally Goodman" (S 72-015-A), Fiddlin' John Carson, 11/07/1923, NYC, OKeh 40095

"Sally Goodin" (E 29275-), Kessinger Brothers, 02/05/1929, NYC, Brunswick 308

Other versions of "Sally Goodin" in this book by John Brown, W. E. Claunch ("Sally Goodin" and the "A" part of "Bear Creek's Up"), and J. E. Shoemaker.

Shake That Little Foot, Sally Ann

Shake yo' little foot, Sally Ann
Shake yo' little foot, Sally Ann
I'm goin' home with Sally Ann

Makin my livin' on sandy land
Makin my livin' on sandy land

Tuning: G

Comparable versions:
"Mississippi Square Dance, Pt. 2" (404741-B), Freeny's Barn Dance Band, 12/16/1930, Jackson, MS, OKeh 45533
"Sandy Land" (GE 12464), Sam Long, 02/23/1926, Richmond, IN, Gennett 3255
"Sally Ann" (S 73-121-A), The Hillbillies, 01/15/1925, NYC, OKeh 40336
Other version in this book by Frank Kittrell ("Going to the Wedding to Get Some Cake").

Uncle Bud

The Music Transcriptions

Where shall the weddin' supper be, Uncle Bud
Where shall the weddin' supper be
Way down yonder in the hollow tree

Big cat, little cat playin in the sand, Uncle Bud
Big cat, little cat playing in the sand
Little cat yell like a natural man

What did the hen duck tell the drake, Uncle Bud
What did the hen duck tell the drake
No more crawfish in this lake

Hollow at the mule, mule don't mind, Uncle Bud
Hollow at the mule, mule don't mind
Hit him in the head with loaded line*

Hollow at the mule, mule won't ghee, Uncle Bud
Hollow at the mule, mule won't ghee
Hit him in the head with single-tree

What yo gonna' do when the crawfish is gone,
    Uncle Bud
What you gonna' do when the crawfish is gone
Move on down to another pond

What you gonna' do when the meat's all out,
    Uncle Bud
What you gonna' do when the meat's all out
Sit in the corner with your mouth poked out

Uncle Bud's got meat
Uncle Bud's got ham
Uncle Bud's got gals
That don't give a damn.

Tuning: C
Field notes: "An old Break down. He says he sings the old 'bad' verses when off to himself (cf. Salty Dog)."

Comparable versions:
"Crawdad Song" (15782-), Asa Martin and James Roberts, 08/1934, NYC, Banner 33180
"Getting into Trouble" (80016-A), Land Norris, 04/28/1926, NYC, OKeh 45058

* a loaded line, in the old days, was the line used to drive the mules. On it were tied strips of leather, which were used
    to pop the horses' flank.

Want a Little Water, Johnny?

Want a little water Johnny
Want a little water child
Want a little water Johnny
Little, ev'ry once and a while

Wish I had a nickel
All I want's a dime
Give me back my nickel
To give that gal of mine

Want a little water Johnny
Want a little water child
Want a little water Johnny
Little, ev'ry once and a while

Tuning: G

Comparable versions:
"Old Liza Jane" (13302), Uncle Am Stuart, 06/1924, NYC, Vocalion 14846
"Liza Jane" (140018-1), Riley Puckett, 09/11/1924, NYC, Columbia 15014-D
"Goodbye Liza Jane" (9596-A), Fiddlin' John Carson & His Virginia Reelers, 03/11/1926, Atlanta, GA, OKeh 45049
Other versions of "Liza Jane" in this book by Enos Canoy ("Where'd You Get Your Whiskey"), Horace Kinard, Everett Mitchell,
    J. P. Reece ("I Ain't Gonna Leave Her by Herself"), and Thaddeus Willingham ("Liza Jane").

Who Will Shoe Your Pretty Little Foot/
Mississippi Valley Waltz

The Music Transcriptions

Who will shoe your pretty little feet
Who will glove your hand
And who will kiss your rosy lips
While I'm in the foreign land

Papa will shoe my pretty little feet
Mama will glove my hand
You can kiss my rosy lips
When you come from the foreign land

Tuning: G
Field notes: "This is not a banjo piece. There are additional verses which Willingham does not recall. The tune is the same as the tune to 'Mississippi Valley Waltz', which Willingham has heard since he has lived in Mississippi."
Authors' comments: This piece is finger picked. The thumb (T) picks down and the middle (M) and index (I) fingers pick up.

Comparable versions:
"Green Valley Waltz" (W 147242-), McCartt Brothers & Patterson, 10/18/1928, Johnson City, TN, Columbia 15454-D
"Hyter's Favorite Waltz" (BVE 56437-2), Hyter Colvin, 10/21/1929, Dallas, TX, Victor 23815
"Green Valley Waltz" (14687-2), Walker's Corbin Ramblers, 01/25/1934, NYC, Decca 5102

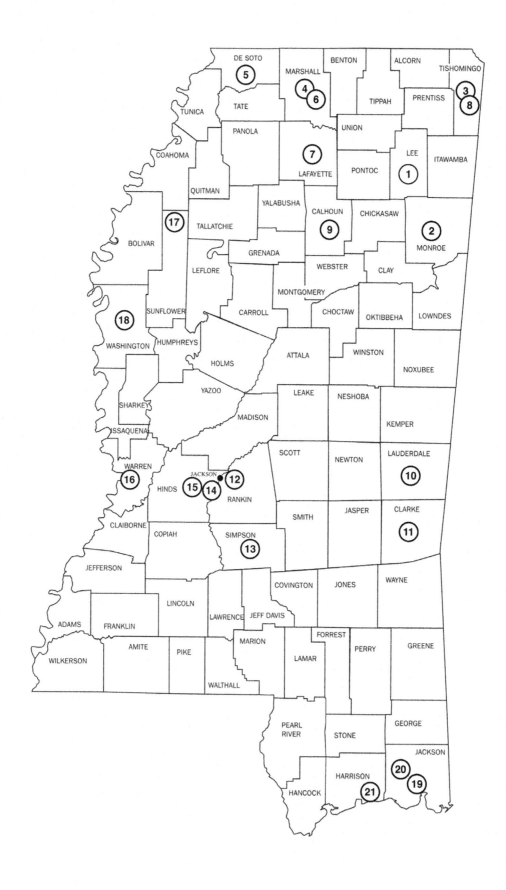

APPENDIX A
Maps

May 8–June 11, 1939: Herbert Halpert recording trip in Mississippi, list of informants and itinerary:

Sources represented in this collection in **bold**

1. May 8–9, Saltillo, Lee Co.: Maud McShan Wesson, Theodosia Long, Birmah Grissom

    May 9, Tupelo, Lee Co.: African Methodist Church, Lula Morris and children

    May 9–10, Saltillo, Lee Co: Mary Ila Long, Ruby and Laura Clifton

    May 10, Guntown, Lee Co.: **W. E. Claunch**

2. May 10, Amory, Monroe Co.: Monroe County Training School, pupils

3. May 11, Tishomingo, Tishomingo Co.: Bickerstaff family, Audrey Hellums, Mrs. Lillian Bickerstaff Pennington, Vivian Skinner

    May 11, Tishomingo, Tishomingo Co.: Dixie Puckett

    May 12, Iuka, Tishomingo Co.: Vivian Skinner, Ina Jones, Nellie Prewitt, Beatrice, Irene and Thelma Scruggs

    May 12, Iuka, Tishomingo Co.: **John Hatcher, John Brown**

4. May 13, Byhalia, Marshall Co.: Colored Methodist Episcopal Church, Mary, Katherine, Christine, Allison and Isaac Shipps

5. May 14, Mt. Sustin Church, Cockrum, Desoto Co.: Anne Mae Franklin, Annie Mae Tyson, Mary Clarke, Tennessee Spencer, Neda Glover, Henrietta Alexander, Mary Bailey, Anne Leonard, Eria Loving, Ella Cooper, Billy Flowers, Harris Mason, Lenus Williams, Sara Hasser, Tiny Parish, Jaybird Redding, Melvin Shoulders, Roseville Shipp, Edmund Phillips, Ben Rice

6. May 14, Holly Springs, Marshall Co.: 5 women, 7 men of Rust College choir

7. May 15, Oxford, Lafayette Co.: Mrs. Ada M. L. Mooney

8. May 17, Iuka, Tishomingo Co.: James D. Fairless, Mrs. Ossie Hanson, Miss Marie Floyd, Joe, E. Johnston, Will C. Thomas, Joe Walker, Miss Jewel Deaton, Mrs. Mildred Gravette

9. May 18, Bruce, Calhoun Co.: Mrs. G. V. Easley

    Pine Valley, Calhoun Co.: Mrs. Ollie Womble

10. May 20, Meridian Civic Center, Meridian, Lauderdale Co.: **Frank T. Kittrell and Mrs. Kittrell, Hardy C. Sharp, H. D. Kinard and Douglas Williams, W. A. Bledsoe**

    May 21, New Hope Baptist Church, Meridian, Lauderdale Co.: Sacred Harp singers led by Ed Griffin

11. May 21, Quitman, Clarke Co.: **Charles Long, and Sam Neal**

    May 23, Meridian Junior College, Meridian, Lauderdale Co.: **Stephen B. Tucker**, Ralph Bennett, singer

12. May 25, Brandon, Rankin Co.: Eva Grace Boone and children

13. May 26, McGee, Simpson Co.: Mrs. Sarah Jane Harvey, **Canoy Trio, Tim Canoy, Lola Canoy, Enos Canoy, Jim Meyers, and Lola Canoy**, Jessie Buchanan and Marguerite Bogan, Elgie Durr, Cora Strickland

    May 27, Magee, Simpson Co.: Mrs. Carrie Margaret Walker, Mrs. Liza White, Eva May White, Mrs. Bernie May, Mr. Dick Walker

14. May 27, Jackson, Hinds Co.: Eugene Dixon, Had Frazier, Lucille Dison, Thelma Dison, Fannie McGee, Leora Anderson

15. May 28, Southern Christian Institute, Mount Beulah College, Edwards, Hinds Co.: Sarah Ann Reed and young people's group, Samuel Brooks, T. J. Marshall

16. May 29, Vicksburg, Warren Co.: Jim Archer

    Vicksburg Co. Negro Baptist Academy: groups of Negro children, Falvia Woods, Thelma Williams, Susie May Miller, Lila May Stevens, Malinda Cooper, Laura Wilson

May 29, Baptist Academy, Vicksburg, Warren Co.: John Floyd, Morris "Shorty" Arnold

May 30, Colored YMCA, Vicksburg, Warren Co.: John Floyd and Emmet Jackson, Johnny Cook, Rhode Bailey

17. June 1, Women's Camp State Penal Farm, Parchman, Sunflower Co.: Mary James, Mary Alice Vanderson, Margarete Miller, Opal Brown, Elizabeth Moore, Mary James, Mattie May Thomas, Josephine Douglass, Beatrice Tisdale and Mattie May Thomas, Lucille Walker, Edna Taylor, Annie Bell Abraham, Elizabeth Moore, Hattie Goff, Beatrice Perry, Eva White, Betty May Bowman

Men's Camp State Penal Farm: John Henry Jackson, Norman Smith, Alexander Williams, Johnny Smith, Andy R. Guyton, Tricky Salmon

18. June 2–3, Greenville, Washington Co.: T. L. Williams, Edmund Jones, F. W. Lindsey, Prentiss Brown, Joe Shores, Sam Hazel, 12 Negro girls, D. Cook, Bessie Hoffman

19. June 10, New Era Baptist Church, Gautier, Jackson Co.: Theresa Smith, Adlin Bilbo, Laura Hatcher, Edwina Andrews, Louise Edwards, Washington H. Hatcher, Frank E. Bilbo, Julius C. Jacobs

20. June 10, Vancleave High School, Vancleave, Jackson Co.: Nol Carter, Q. Carl Roberts, Maud Roberts, Dr. C. L. Watkins, Eula May O'Neal, Carol Garter, Katherine Wilson

21. June 11, Gulfport, Harrison Co.: **Thaddeus C. Willingham**

Fiddler and Singer Sources by County

Alcorn:
Mrs. W. E. Wood (1936)

Attala:
Milner and Curtis (78rpm)

Benton:
C. M. Coursan (1936)
R. N. Hudspeth (1936)

Bolivar:
Mrs. M. B. Brister (1936)
Billie Mansfield (1936)
Mr. N. Odom (1936)
Mrs. Edwin Pease (1936)
Mrs. Ben Walker (1936)

Carroll:
Allen Alsop (1936)
Mrs. Louise Long (1939)
Gene Clardy & Stan Clements (78rpm)
Narmour & Smith (78rpm)

Choctaw:
William E. Ray (1936)
Hoyt Ming & His Pep Steppers (78rpm)
Ray Brothers (78rpm)

Clarke:
Charles Long (1939)

Coahoma:
Alice Cole (1936)
A. J. Howell (1936)

Copiah:
Dr. Ashley (1936)

Covington:
Berlon Flynt (1936)

Desoto:
Dave Holland (1936)
Holland Brothers (1936)
Mary Kirkwood (1936)

Forrest:
Mrs. Willie Davis (1936)
Charlie Edmundson (1936)
Mr. John McCartie (1936)
Gatwood String Band (78rpm)
Rainey's Old Time Band (78rpm)

George:
Charlie Goff (1936)

Greene:
Mrs. Ruby Costello (1936)
Mr. R. C. Clifton (1936)
Mrs. Joe McCoyt (1936)

Harrison:
Josephine Compton (1936)
Tom Redditt (1936)
E. Thomas (1936)
Thaddeus Willingham (1939)

Hinds:
Cleve Bass (1936)
Annie Lee (1936)

Holms:
Mrs. Betty Thornton (1936)

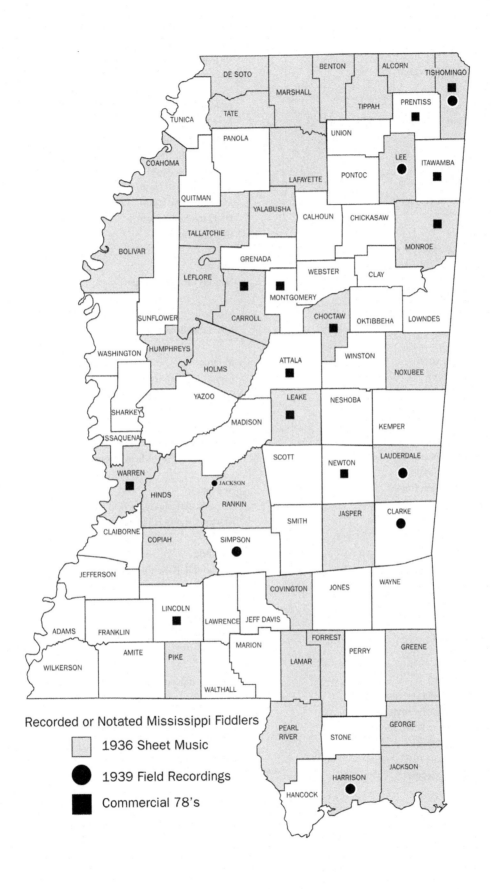

Recorded or Notated Mississippi Fiddlers

◻ 1936 Sheet Music

● 1939 Field Recordings

■ Commercial 78's

Humphreys:
Mrs. Della Patterson (1936)

Itawamba:
Mumford Bean & His Itawambians (78rpm)

Jackson:
Lee Holt (1936)
Richard Scovel (1936)
Mrs. Josie Gautier Winterton (1936)

Jasper:
J. E. Shoemaker (1936)

Lafayette:
Willie Campbell (1936)
W. S. Robertson (1936)

Lamar:
Mr. T. W. Cooper (1936)
Mrs. J. C. King (1936)
Elmer Ladner (1936)

Lauderdale:
W. A. Bledsoe (1939)
Narvelle Covington (1936)
Major D. M. Drye (1936)
Mrs. J. M. T. Hamilton (1936)
Horace Kinard (1939)
Frank Kittrell (1939)
J. P. Reese (1936)
Hardy Sharp (1939)
Wilbur Snowden (1936)
Mrs. E. J. Tartt (1936)
Stephen B. Tucker (1939)
Meridian Hustlers (78rpm)

Leake:
J. C. Foster (1936)
Collier Trio (78rpm)
Leake County Revelers (78rpm)
Freeny Harmonizers (78rpm)
Freeny's Barn Dance Band (78rpm)
Grover Russell (78 rpm)
Madden Community Band (78rpm)
Russell Brothers (78rpm)

Lee:
W. E. Claunch (1939)

Birmah Grissom (1939)
Theadosia Long (1939)

Leflore:
Mrs. P. F. Ezell (1936)
Florence Hoskins (1936)
Mrs. William Harrison (1936)
J. H. Johnson (1936)
Edward Kittrell (1936)
Mrs. R. S. Love (1936)
Dr. Frank Smith (1936)
Ben Wall (1936)

Lincoln:
Nations Brothers (78rpm)

Marshall:
Mrs. Ethel Bowen (1936)

Monroe:
Everett Mitchell (1936)
Carter Brothers & Son (78rpm)

Montgomery:
Mississippi Possum Hunters (78rpm)
Homer Grice (1970s field recordings)

Newton:
Alvis Massengale (1970s field recordings)
Newton County Hillbillies (78rpm)

Noxubee:
Reverend R. R. Keithley (1936)
Mrs. A. Tynes (1936)

Pearl River:
Mrs. J. Smith (1936)

Pike:
Charlie Addison (1936)

Prentiss:
Dutch Coleman (78rpm)

Rankin:
Reverend J. E. Williams (1936)

Simpson:
Enos Canoy (1939)

Claude Kennedy (1970s family recordings)
Jim Meyers (1939)

Tallahatchie:
W. M. Collum (1936)
Jim Gooch (1936)
J. E. Moorman (1936)
Mrs. Jeff Purcell (1936)
Mrs. E. M. Purcell (1936)
Mrs. J. H. Wheeler (1936)
Reverend J. H. Wheeler (1936)

Tate:
Dalton Brantley (1936)
C. Bronton (1936)
Babe Casey (1936)
R. H. Ellis (1936)
Mrs. Maude Freeman (1936)
Henry McClatching (1936)

Tippah:
J. W. McDonough (1936)

Tishomingo:
Mrs. W. J. Bonds (1936)
Mr. Jim Henry Boley (1936)
John Brown (1939)
John Hatcher (1939)
Miss Mae Belle Williams (1936)

Unknown location:
B. M. Guilette (1936)
Jerry Larco (1936)
Unknown (1936)
Mrs. Louise Walker Wallace (1936)
Magnolia Trio (78rpm)

Warren:
Ella Mae Berry (1936)
Mrs. R. L. Halberg (1936)
Mr. Jennings (1936)
Vertis McFarland (1936)

Yalabusha:
Sinclair Crocker (1936)
Mrs. Ernest Gonagill (1936)
Mrs. L. A. Walker (1936)

Alvis Massengale at the 1974 Smithsonian Folklife festival, Washington, DC. Photo courtesy Ralph Rinzler Archives and Collections, Smithsonian Institution.

APPENDIX B
Alvis Massengale (August 5, 1897–October 13, 1993)

Massengale recorded in the 1930s with the Newton County Hillbillies, played for radio stations WBKN in Newton, WMAG in Forrest, and WCOC in Meridian, and square dances for the American Legion. Late in his life he played with the Leake County String Band, but did not appear on their LP. He appeared at the 1974 Smithsonian Folklife Festival. The 1940 census lists his occupation as a laborer in the wood industry.

Fiddle Tunes played by Alvis Massengale, Union Co.
(List collected by Jerome Sage in 1939 just prior to Halpert's arrival)

After the Ball
Alabama Gal
Alabama Jubilee
Arkansas Traveler
Beautiful Texas
Billy in the Lowland
Blue Ridge Mountain Home
Bully of the Town
Careless Love
Carroll County Blues
Charleston No. 1
Charleston No. 2
Quaker Waltz
Chicken Reel
Chinese Rag
Climbing up the Golden Stairs
Combination Rag
Coming Around the Mountain
Correna, Correna
Creole Belle
Crow Black Chicken

Dark Clouds
Dark Town Strutters' Ball
Deep Ellum Blues
Devil's Dream
Dixie
Dixie Darling
Down Town Rag
Eighth of January
Fifty Cents
Fifty years Ago
Fire on the Mountain
Fisher's Hornpipe
Forked Deer
Gallop to Georgia
Give Me a Bottle
Good Ole Summertime
Goodnight Waltz
Goofer's Rag
Green Valley Blues
Happy Hour Breakdown
Hell After the Yearlings
Hen Cackle
Hi' Geared Daddy
Homebrew Rag
Hop Light Ladies
Hot Times
Howdy, Ladies, Howdy
Hump Back Mule
I Get the Blues When It Rains
I'm Goin' Crazy About You
Ida Red
Jake Walk Polka
John and Susie
Johnson Gal

Just Because
Kentucky Moon Waltz
Leake County Blues
Leather Breeches
Let Me Call You Sweetheart
Let Me Sleep in your Barn
Life On the Ocean Waves
Little Brown Jug
Little Princess Footsteps
Love Letters in the Sand
Maggie
Make My Bed on the Floor
Makes No Difference
Merry Widow Waltz
Mississippi Sawyer
Mockingbird
Monkey in a Dog Cart
More Pretty Girls
My Bonnie Lies Over the Ocean
My Little Girl
Negro in the Woodpile
Nellie Gray
Nettie Moore
Old Hat
Old Shanty Town
Ole Mollie Hare
Over the Waves
Peekaboo Waltz
Pass Around the Bottle
Rag Time Annie
Red Wing
Ricketts' Hornpipe
Run Nigger, Run
Sailing Down Chesapeake
Sallie Goodin
Saturday Night Breakdown
Shortnin' Bread
Show Me the Way to Go Home
Snow Deer
Soldier's Joy
Soldier's Dreams
Somebody Loves Me
Someone I Love
Speckled Bird
Sweet Bunch of Daisies
Sweetest of Flowers
Turkey in the Straw
Under the Double Eagle
Waltz You Saved for Me

Washington and Lee Swing
Wednesday Night Waltz
Who Broke the Lock
Wild Irish Rose
Wish You Was a Dead Rose (??)
Won't See Momma

Alvis Massengale recorded the following titles on December 16, 1930, with the Newton County Hillbillies in Jackson, MS, for OKeh Records: Alvis Massengale, fiddle, Marcus Harrison, mandolin, Andrew Harrison, guitar.

Little Princess Footsteps
Happy Hour Breakdown
Nine O'clock Breakdown
Going to the Wedding to Get Some Cake
Give Me a Bottle of I Don't Care What
Quaker Waltz

Field recordings of Alvis Massengale, fiddle, with unidentified guitar. Recorded at his home by Guthrie Meade in the 1970s.

Little Princess Footsteps (2 versions)
Happy Hour Breakdown
Going to the Wedding to Get Some Cake
Give Me a Bottle of I Don't Care What
Soldier's Joy
Ragtime Annie
Sebastopol
I'll Be All Smiles Tonight
The Goodnight Waltz
Leather Britches
Over the Waves Waltz
Make Me a Pallet on the Floor
Monkey in the Dogcart
Magnolia Waltz
Mississippi Sawyer

Alvis Massengale, field recording in preparation for 1974 Smithsonian Folk Festival; Rinzler Archive, Washington

(Lost Indian?)
Arkansas Traveler
Bilbo Rag
Chicken Reel
Durangs Hornpipe
Faded Love
Fisher's Hornpipe
Golden Slippers

Goodnight Waltz
Happy Hour Breakdown
I'll Be All Smiles Tonight
Leather Britches
Love Letters in the Sand
Magnolia Waltz
Mississippi Sawyer
Over the Waves
Peekaboo Waltz

Ragtime Annie
Rickett's Hornpipe
Saturday Night Breakdown
Soldier's Joy
Sweet Bunch of Daisies
Sweet Mama Every Night
The Old Hat
Turkey in the Straw

BILBO RAG

Collector: Howard Marshall, February 1974 (preparatory field tape for the Smithsonian Folk Festival in Washington, DC)
Location: Union, Newton Co.

m14 and m30 - the
second beat is anticipated

Authors' comments: Theodore Gilmore Bilbo was governor of Mississippi, 1916–20 and 1928–32, then U.S. Senator from Mississippi from 1935–47.

Comparable versions:
"East Tennessee Blues" (E 3976W), Al Hopkins & His Buckle Busters, 10/21/1926, NYC, Brunswick 103
"Huckleberry Blues" (E 21834), Dykes Magic City Trio, 03/10/1927, NYC, Brunswick 129
"Honeysuckle Rag" (11042-2), Blue Ridge Mountain Entertainers, 12/01/1931, NYC, Banner 32432
"Doughboy Rag," (C-634-1), Light Crust Doughboys, 10/11/1933, Chicago, IL, Vocalion 02633

FISHER'S HORNPIPE

Collector: Howard Marshall, February 1974 (preparatory field tape for the Smithsonian Folk Festival in Washington, DC)
Location: Union, Newton Co.

Authors' comments: As is usual there are sixteen measures in this tune. But notice that the "A" part has seven measures and the "B" part has nine measures.

Comparable versions:
"Fisher's Hornpipe," J. Fishar (ca. 1780), *A New & Highly Improved Violin Preceptor* (Utica, NY: William Williams, 1817), 23
"Old Zip Coon and Medley Reels" (GE 13833), Doc Roberts & Asa Martin, 05/15/1928, Richmond, IN, Gennett 6495
"Fisher's Hornpipe" (E 3972W), The Hillbillies, 10/21/1926, NYC, Vocalion 5017
"Fisher's Hornpipe" (6713-), Clayton McMichen, Hoy "Slim" Bryant & Jerry Wallace, 06/01/1939, NYC, Decca 2649
"Texas Breakdown" (W 404065-B), W. T. Narmour & S. W. Smith, 06/06/1930, San Antonio, TX, OKeh 45492 (only the "A" part in common)
Other versions of "Fisher's Hornpipe" in this book by Billie Mansfield, Mr. N. Odom, Stephen B. Tucker, and "Unknown."

GOODNIGHT WALTZ

Collector: Gus Meade, ca. 1970
Location: Newton Co.

Comparable versions:
"Good Night Waltz":
Leake Co Revelers (W 143970-1), 04/13/1927, New Orleans, LA, Columbia 15189-D
Kessinger Brothers (AL 219), 02/11/1928, Ashland, KY, Brunswick 220
Other version in this book by Edward Kittrell.

SEBASTAPOL

Collector: Gus Meade, ca. 1970
Location: Newton Co.

Authors' comments: Mr. Massengale said he learned "this little old Spanish tune" from his grandfather. Seems to have been named after the town in Mississippi.

Comparable versions:
"Walking in My Sleep," Haun, Mildred, "Cooke County Ballads and Songs" (M.A. thesis, Vanderbilt University, Nashville, 1937), 237–38 (Learned before 1900)
"Walking in My Sleep" (BS 07122-1), Arthur Smith Trio, 02/17/1937, Charlotte, NC, Brunswick B7043
"Walking in My Sleep" (MEM 51-), Roy Acuff & His Smoky Mountain Boys, 10/1939, Memphis, TN, Vocalion 05093
Other version in this book by Cleve Bass.

APPENDIX C
A 1936 Field Worker's Account of a Fiddle Contest in Hazlehurst

Unfortunately the most colorful of the tune titles listed here have unknown tunes.

Account of Fiddle contest
Hazlehurst, Mississippi, 1936, by Ruth Bass

Old Fiddler's Contests

In the early history of the state one of the most popular forms of recreation was fiddling. The "corn stalk fiddle and shoestring bow" was a prized possession and fiddles as well as fiddling tunes were preserved and handed down from one generation to another. Fiddle songs came to be true folk music of the backwoods. The very titles of these tunes were part of the every day life in cabins, fields and woods. The fiddlers played into them and the listeners heard and danced into these songs the sounds of the work-a-day world about them in such tunes as, "Three Nights in the Piney Woods," "Waggoner's," "Went Down to the New Ground," "Wild Horse in the Canebrake," "Cotton Chopin' Dick," "Indian at the Ferry" and perhaps a hundred others can testify.

Fiddling ability often "runs in the family," and fathers, sons, daughters and grandsons made up famous fiddling teams. Fiddling contests were a natural outcome, since Saturday night frolics could not possibly give the many expert fiddlers their proper chance for appreciation. In recent years these "Old Fiddling Contests" have been revived by various community recreation projects. At these fiddling contests prizes are often donated by local business houses or cash prizes are obtained by admission fees. Prizes are given for the best single fiddling, for pairs, quartets, quintets, etc. Often prizes are given to the oldest fiddler, the youngest, the largest fiddling family, the fiddler who has come the longest distance, the biggest wagonload of folks etc. The contestants usually draw for places and there is always a great deal of "aiggin" on, razzing, singing, shuffling and applause from the audience. It is also a custom for the audience to call out for favorite tunes and favorite fiddlers.

The fun usually begins with a number, some favorite such as "Money Musk" or "Mammy's Chimney Corner," played by the entire lot of fiddlers. About a dozen men and perhaps a boy or two, a young girl and occasionally a woman come to the platform carrying their fiddles. (The contests are usually held in a schoolhouse or crowd around an outdoors platform.) The fiddles are carried in cloth bags under their arms—perhaps one or two of the fiddlers boast a violin case with a handle. There is a great squeaking of pegs in rosined holes, trying of the A string and now and then a chord or a snatch of melody. At last all are properly tuned and the master of ceremonies calls out,

"Now folks when I say go, everybody all together on 'Arkansas Traveler.'" Each fiddler tucks his fiddle against his upper arm, settles back in his chair and sets his right foot forward in a position to pat out the rhythm. "Go!" They all start together, each playing the tune in his own particular way. Yells and shouts from the audience spur them on. "Bear down on 'hit, boys!" "Let 'er go!" "Git yo' partners!" "Play that cornstalk fiddle, Joe!" One of the fiddlers suddenly raises his fiddle up over his head, flips it behind his back or stands up and holds it between his legs, sawing away for dear life and keeping up with the tune, all the while. The crowd laughs and cheers, stamps and whistles. The bows mover faster and faster, the rhythm of the patting feet grows quicker and quicker—and "Arkansas Traveler" ends in a wild swift flourish.

"Well now thar's the way to start off a fiddlin' in style. I'd hate to be the judge 'er this here contest," the Master exclaims. "Now we'll hear Number one, Mister Bill Giles from Rocky Ford. Set out here, Bill. Whut you gonna give us, Mr. Giles?" Bill Giles from Rocky Ford brings his chair forward, sits and announces, "Sugar in the Coffee." He rosins his bow, sounds his A string, fixes his right foot and is off. When he has played for a few moments, his partner, a grey-headed old timer pulls out his chair and leans over the racing fiddle with a broom straw about a foot and a half long. He places this straw across the fiddle strings, then with the other end of the straw between his second and third fingers of his right hand he begins to bounce it up and down on the string, thus drumming out a rhythmic and altogether pleasing accompaniment to the melody.

The fiddling never stops but goes faster and faster while the straws knock swiftly and merrily. The audience whoops and roars. Everyone is warming up. Some one in the back of the house gets up and begins to shuffle, his heavy brogans raising the dust from the plank floor. Then quite suddenly the tune stops, and the fiddler and his grey-headed straw-knocker retire amid much applause.

Next comes a fiddling family, Old Man Polk and his two sons and young granddaughter. The granddaughter is a guitar picker and his son Dan Polk is a trick fiddler who plays the fiddle in almost every conceivable position and with many exaggerated and amusing muscular and facial contortions. They play "Mississippi Sawyer" and "Jim Along Josie" and the crowd goes wild. So the contest goes on for perhaps two hours then the judges retire to consider their decisions and the floor is cleared for a little swingin' and shufflin'. There is a hurried pairing off. The fiddlers will all take turns playing for the dancers. Suddenly the five Bowes brothers, playing like one man begin, "Take me back to Mammy, Mammy's Chimney Corner," Then, "Polly put the Kittle On."

"Polly put the kittle on
Jenny blow the fire strong,
Katie call the boys along
We'll all have tea"—
Somebody sings the words.
The Master calls "Swing four!"
"Hands in yo' pockets—back to the wall,
Take a chaw er' baccer and balance all!
Chicken in the bread tray, scratching out dough,
Lizard on the fence rail —all must go!
Promenade! Promenade!

Chicken in the bread tray, scratching out dough,
Mammy will yo' dawg bite? No, chile no!
Promenade! Promenade!

Swing your partner—
Ladies bow,
Gents know how—
All run away."

The five Bowes brothers stop suddenly and immediately, the Master calls up other fiddlers and begins rounding up the next dance.

"Tune up your fiddle.
Rosin up your bow
An' come knock the devil
out'n Cotton-eyed Joe."

And the fiddlers play on and on for a hundred tunes or more.

APPENDIX D
Tunes in Alternate Tunings

If a tuning is not given for a tune, it is standard fiddle tuning GDAE.

AEAE
John Brown 1936:
Molly Put the Kettle On 72
Old Joe Clark 74
John Brown 1939:
Cindy 227
Dusty Miller 229
Froggy Went A-Courtin' 230
Give the Fiddler a Dram 231
Sally Goodin 234
Wolves A-Howling 235

Enos Canoy
Poor Little Mary Settin' in the Corner 245

W. E. Claunch
Devil's Dream 256
How Old Are You My Pretty Little Miss 263
Oh Yes, Mammy Look at Sam 266
Sally Goodin 272
Wolves A-Howlin' 279
John Hatcher
Buffalo Girl 289
Farewell Whiskey 292
Pretty Little Girl 299
Tom and Jerry 304
Frank Kittrell
Cindy Jane 308
Corn Stalk Fiddle 309
Going to the Wedding 310

Indian War Whoop 312
Little Boy Went A-Courtin' 313
Charles Long
Drunken Hiccups 321
Hard Road to Texas 323
Jones County 324
My Little Dony 326
My Old Dog's Trailing up a Squirrel 327
Rock Candy 328
Sally-O 329
Stephen B. Tucker
Christmas Time in the Morning 349
Devil's Dream 352
Pound Cake and Sugar 361
Tom and Jerry 367

AEAC#
Enos Canoy
Pickin' the Devil's Eye 244
Where'd You Get Your Whiskey 247
W. E. Claunch
Drunken Hiccups 257
Texas Bells 274
Frank Kittrell
Want to Go to Meeting and I Got No Shoes 315

ADAE
W. E. Claunch
Arkansas Traveler 251
Black Eyed Susie 253
Cindy 255
Devils Dream 256
Eighth of January 258

[419]

RESOURCES

Abrahams, Roger D. "Mr. Lomax Meets Professor Kittredge." *Journal of Folklore Research* 37, no. 2/3, Special Double Issue: Issues in Collaboration and Representation (May–December 2000).

Bindas, Kenneth J. *All of This Music Belongs to the Nation: The WPA's Federal Music Project and American Society* (Knoxville: University of Tennessee Press, 1995).

Botkin, B. A. "WPA and Folklore Research: 'Bread and Song.'" *America's Folklorist: B. A. Botkin and American Culture* (Norman: University of Oklahoma Press, 2010), 269–70.

Gronow, Pekka. "Recordings: An Introduction." *Ethnic Recordings in America, A Neglected Heritage* (Washington: American Folklife Center, Library of Congress, 1982), 3.

Halpert, Herbert. "Coming into Folklore More Than Fifty Years Ago." *Journal of American Folklore* 105, no. 418 (Fall 1992).

Hamilton, M. "The blues, the folk, and African-American history." *Transactions of the Royal Historical Society* 11 (2001): 17–35 (quoting Memo from Eri Douglass to Jerome Sage ["Subject: Data for Mr. Alan Lomax"], 29 October 1942, Folder 10 [Correspondence October 1942–January 1947], Fisk University Mississippi Delta Collection, AFC-LC).

Heiman, Mark F., and Laura Saxton Heiman. Preface to the New Edition. *The English and Scottish Popular Ballads*, vol. 1 (Washington: Loomis House Press, 2001).

Hudson, A. P. *Folk Songs of Mississippi and Their Background* (Chapel Hill: University of North Carolina Press, 1936).

———. *Folktunes from Mississippi* (New York: DaCapo, 1977).

Lloyd, James B. *Lives of Mississippi Authors, 1817–1967* (Jackson: University Press of Mississippi, 2009), 241–42.

Malone, Bill C. *Music From the True Vine: Mike Seeger's Life & Musical Journey* (Chapel Hill: University of North Carolina Press, 2011), 24–25.

Mangione, Jerre. *The Dream and the Deal: The Federal Writer's Project, 1935–1943* (Syracuse: Syracuse University Press, 1996).

McCulloh, Judith. Introduction. Ira Ford, *Traditional Music in America* (Folklore Associates, 1965; reprint of Dutton, 1940), x–xi (quoting from *English Folk Songs from the Southern Appalachians* [New York and London: G. P. Putnam and Sons, 1932]).

Meade, Guthrie, Dick Spottswood, and Douglas Meade. *Country Music Sources: A Biblio-Discography of Commercially Recorded Traditional Music* (Chapel Hill: Southern Folklife Collection, University of North Carolina Press, 2002).

Meltzer, Milton. *Violins & Shovels: The WPA Arts Projects* (New York: Delacorte Press, 1976).

Morris, Alton C. *Folksongs of Florida* (Gainesville: University of Florida Press, 1950).

Patterson, Daniel W. *Sounds of the South* (Durham, NC: Duke University Press, 1991).

Pescatello, Ann M. *Charles Seeger: A Life in American Music* (Pittsburgh: University of Pittsburgh Press, 1992).

Porterfield, Nolan. *Last Cavalier: The Life and Times of John A. Lomax* (Champaign: University of Illinois Press, 1996).

Rankin, Tom. *Great Big Yam Potatoes: Anglo-American Fiddle Music from Mississippi* (Jackson: Mississippi Department of Archives and History, 1985) (Eri Douglas letter to Mrs. Charles Long in 1939 in answer to her question concerning the recordings made of her husband's fiddle music).

Szwed, John. *Alan Lomax: The Man Who Recorded the World: A Biography* (New York: Viking, 2010).

Taylor, Nick. *American Made: The Enduring Legacy of the WPA: When FDR Put the Nation to Work* (New York: Bantam, 2008).

Tick, Judith. *Ruth Crawford Seeger: A Composer's Search for American Music* (New York: Oxford University Press, 1997).

———. *Our Singing Country* (New York: Dover, 2000), xvi–xvii.

Websites

"California Gold: Northern California Folk Music from the 1930s." Library of Congress digital collection: memory.loc.gov/ammem/afccchtml/cowhome.html

Alan Jabbour, article from his website: www.alanjabbour.com/BenBotkinArchiveAmericanFolkSong.pdf

Andy Kuntz, The Fiddlers Companion: www.ibiblio.org/fiddlers/index.html

Lester S. Levy Sheet Music Collection, John Hopkins University: levysheetmusic.mse.jhu.edu/

19th Century American Sheet Music, University of North Carolina at Chapel Hill: www.lib.unc.edu/dc/sheetmusic

Southern Folklife Collection: www.lib.unc.edu/wilson/sfc/

Library of Congress, Music for the Nation, American Sheet Music: memory.loc.gov/ammem/mussmhtml/mussmhome.html

Library of Congress, African-American Sheet Music, 1850–1920: memory.loc.gov/ammem/collections/sheetmusic/brown/index.html

Mississippi Department of Archives and History Documents

Jerome Sage. "A Report of the Federal Music Project in Mississippi covering period from December 1, 1935 to April 1, 1936." Mississippi Department of Archives and History, Box 11074.

"Research Work of the Federal Music Project." Mississippi Department of Archives and History, Box AR 125.

"Types of Songs Desired" (handout sheet). Mississippi Department of Archives and History, 439 Box 11077.

"Outline Of Work of Folk Music Research Project." Mississippi Department of Archives and History, Box 11079.

Letter from Jerome Sage to Dr. Nikolai Sokoloff, January 4, 1937. Mississippi Department of Archives and History, Box 11074.

Letter from Jerome Sage to Mrs. Hugh E. Browne, September 10, 1936. Mississippi Department of Archives and History, Box 11074.

Letter from Jerome Sage to Dr. Nikolai Sokoloff, January 4, 1937. Mississippi Department of Archives and History, Box 11074.

Jerome Sage. "Notes trip May 1-3 Inclusive Miss Sage, Mrs. Browne." Mississippi Department of Archives and History, 439 Box 10911.

Recordings

Narmour and Smith, *Complete Recorded Works (1928-1930)*, Vols. 1 & 2. Document Records DOCD 8065 & 8066.

Mississippi String Bands, Vol. 1 (CO-3513-CD, County Records).

Mississippi String Bands, Vol. 2 (CO-3514-CD, County Records).

Mississippi String Bands, Vol. 1: 1928–1935 (Document Records DOCD-8009).

Mississippi String Bands, Vol. 2: 1928–1930 (Document Records DOCD-8028).

Leake County Revelers, Vol. 1: 1927–1928 (Document Records DOCD-8029).

Leake County Revelers, Vol. 2: 1929–1930 (Document Records DOCD-8030).

Due in print near the publication of this book, *Mississippi Fiddle Tunes and Songs from the 1930s*, the Halpert field recordings.

Harry Bolick: *Rediscovered*, recording of many of the 1936 tunes from this book, is available at www.mississippifiddle.com.

Harry Bolick: *Carroll County, Mississippi*

Harry Bolick with Brian Slattery: *Come on Over and See Us Sometime*: contains tracks of these tunes known in Mississippi: Poor Little Mary/Roll them Simmons/Little Black Train.

Harry Bolick with Joel Winnerstrom: *The Pleasure of Your Company*: contains tracks of these tunes known in Mississippi: The Shadow of the Pines/Louis Collins/Lincoln County Blues/Good Fellers.

Jack McGee: *Give the Fiddler a Dram*, Soundwagon, www.flossthefiddle.com/home.html

Out-of-print Recordings

Great Big Yam Potatoes: Anglo-American Fiddle Music from Mississippi (Jackson: Mississippi Department of Archives and History, 1985). Contains a selection of the best of the 1939 Halpert fiddle recordings.

Hoyt Ming and his Pep-Steppers, *New Hot Times!* (LP, Homestead 103, 1975).

Mississippi Sawyers (LP, Sawyer Productions, 1980).

Leake County String Band (Morgan and George Gilmer, Walnut Grove, Mississippi) (LP, privately pressed, probably from the 1970s).

Ode to Billy Joe (soundtrack, Warner Brothers, 1976), has tracks from Hoyt Ming and Morgan Gilmer.

Archived Recordings

All of Herbert Halpert's 1939 recordings at the American Folklife Center, Washington, DC: www.loc.gov/folklife/

Gus Meade's 1970s field recordings of Alvis Massengale of the Newton County Hillbillies in the Southern Folklife Collection, Warren Wilson Library, Chapel Hill, NC: www.lib.unc.edu/wilson/sfc/

Howard Marshall's February 1974 field tape made in preparation for the Smithsonian Folklife Festival, 1974 in Washington, DC. Rinzler Archive, Smithsonian Folkways Records cassette A74 (74-114-CT)(M9)

Tune books

Mississippi Echoes by Tim Avalon, paperback, 92 pages, Brandon, Mississippi 2012

The Milliner-Koken Collection of American Fiddle Tunes, Transcribed and Annotated by Clare Milliner and Walt Koken (Kennett Square, PA: Mudthumper, 2011) www.mudthumper.com/fiddletunesbook.html. While not primarily about Mississippi, there are quite a few great ones from 78s as well as from the Halpert recordings.

GENERAL INDEX

TUNE INDEX

Tunes with similar melodies but different titles are in
parentheses.

"Alabama Waltz," 319 (314, 358)
"All I Wants A Hogeye," 35 (*see* "Hog Eye")
"Arkansas Traveler," 251, 284, 344

"Baldin" (*see* "Long Eared Mule")
"Bear Creek," 204
"Bear Creek Waltz," 205
"Bear Creek's Up," 252 (*see* "Sally Goodin")
"Big Bill's in Jail, Boys," 108 (390)
"Big Eyed Rabbit," 320 (*see* "Black Eyed Susie")
"Big Footed Nigger in a Sandy Lot," 218
"Big Tom Bailey," 88 (*see* "Old Dan Tucker")
"Bilbo Rag," 413
"Bill Cheatum," 219
"Billy Boy Waltz," 138
"Billy in the Lowground," 43, 148, 286
"Black Eyed Susan [Susie]," 70, 149, 253, 287, 377 (320)
"Bonaparte's Retreat," 288
"Bonny Blue Flag," 193
"Bragg's Retreat," 346
"Buck Dancin' Charlie," 237
"Buckeyed Rabbit," 115
"Buffalo Girl [Gals]," 103, 120, 127, 199, 289 (76)

"Calico," 347 (*see* "Give the Fiddler a Dram")
"Carve That Possum," 63, 133
"Chicken in the Bread Tray," 183
"Chicken Pie," 254 (*see* "I Want To Go To Meeting")
"Chicken Reel Waltz," 75
"Chippy Get Your Hair Cut," 348
"Christmas Time in the Morning," 349

"Cindy," 227, 228, 255 (41, 79, 111, 142, 206, 247, 308, 339, 384)
"Cindy (Waltz)," 206 (*see* "Cindy")
"Cindy Jane," 308 (*see* "Cindy")
"Circus Piece," 350
"Cold Frosty Morning," 351
"Coon," 187
"Cornstalk Fiddle," 309
"Cotton Field Song," 208
"Cotton-Eyed Joe," 44, 207
"Couldn't Hear Nobody Pray," 45
"Crap Game," 64
"Cripple Creek," 378
"Cross-Eyed Gopher," 379

"Dan Tucker," 163 (*see* "Old Dan Tucker")
"Danville Girl" (*see* "Little Danville Girl")
"Darling I'm Crazy 'Bout You," 168
"Devil's Dream," 256, 352 (86)
"Do, Johnny Booker, Do," 200
"Down Yonder," 290
"Drunken [Drunkard's] Hiccups," 257, 321 (292)
"Dusty Miller," 229
"Dutch Waltz," 94 (136, 166, 210, 343)

"Eighth of January," 150, 238, 258, 291, 336 (95, 104)
"Eighth of January March," 95
"Eighth of January Waltz," 104
"Evening Star Waltz," 96

"Fannie Logan," 151
"Farewell Mary Anne," 220 (*see* "Soldier's Joy")
"Farewell Whiskey," 292 (*see* "Drunken [Drunkard's]
    Hiccups")
"Fiddle Piece," 353 (*see* "Run, Nigger Run")

"Fiddlers Reel (Mrs. McCloud's)," 90 (212)
"First Time I Saw Liza," 80
"Fisher's Hornpipe," 135, 157, 188, 322, 354, 414
"Flirtin' Song," 177
"Flop Eared Mule," 58 (107, 169, 297)
"Forked Deer," 46 (346)
"Froggy Went a Courtin'," 230

"G & C Schottische," 107 (see "Flop Eared Mule")
"Gee Whiz," 125
"Georgia Camp Meeting," 122
"Give the Fiddler a Dram," 231, 259 (347)
"Go Long Liza," 83, 93, 182 (see "Goodbye Liza Jane")
"Going From the Cottonfield," 89
"Going On Down Town," 380
"Going to the Wedding," 310
"Going up to Hamburg," 293
"Going Way to Memphis, Dolly-O," 47
"Good Bye Liza Jane," 62 (see "Liza Jane")
"Goodnight Waltz," 128, 415
"Goose Girl Waltz," 136 (see "Dutch Waltz")
"Grand Bay Schottische," 118
"Grasshopper Sitting On Sweet Tater Vine," 76 (see "Buffalo Girl")
"Great Big Taters" (270, 310)
"Great Big Yam Taters," 337 (see "I Want To Go To Meeting")
"Great Titanic," 260
"Grey Eagle," 261
"Grub Springs," 262, 294
"Gulfport," 169 (see "Flop Eared Mule")

"Hard Road to Texas," 323
"Hardy Smith," 78
"Haste to the Wedding," 355
"Hell After the Yearlings," 311
"Henry Holmes' Holla," 239
"Her Cheeks Are Like the Cherry," 142 (see "Cindy")
"Hog Eye [Hogeye or Hog-Eye]," 36, 281, 356 (35)
"Holland Waltz," 77 (see "Kiss Waltz")
"Honey Babe," 152
"Horseshoe of the Battle," 184
"How Old Are You My Pretty Little Miss," 263
"Humpback Mule," 381 (see "Whoa Mule")
"Hungry Confederate Soldier, A," 106

"I Ain't Goin' To Leave Her By Herself," 164
"I Love Somebody," 160

"I Want To Go To Meeting," 41, 87 (79, 246, 247, 254, 265, 298, 324)
"I'm Gwine Keep My Husband Workin' If I Can," 60
"I'm Gwine To My Shanty," 143
"Indian Eat the Woodchuck," 81
"Indian Eat the Woodpecker," 357
"Indian War Whoop," 312 (see "Dusty Miller")
"Irish Washerwoman," 84, 137, 194

"Jaybird, The," 119 (178)
"Jaybird Died," 178 (119)
"Jenny Lind Polka," 97
"Jewel Waltz," 69
"John Butter and the Fat," 71
"Johnny Get Your Hair Cut Polka," 214
"Joke on the Puppy," 358
"Jones County," 324 (see "I Want To Go To Meeting")
"Joplin Girl," 215

"Kiss Waltz," 98 (see "Holland Waltz")

"Ladies Fancy," 170 (see "Molly Put the Kettle On")
"Lazy Kate," 121, 153
"Leather Britches [Breeches]," 202, 295, 338, 359
"Little Boy Went A Courtin'," 313
"Little Danville Girl," 296
"Little Dog (Waltz)," 166 (see "Dutch Waltz")
"Little Star, (Twinkle, Twinkle)," 276
"Little Willie," 325
"Liza Jane," 37, 111, 146, 147, 339, 374, 382 (400) (see "Cindy")
"Liza Jane (Raccoon up the Possum Tree)," 339
"Long Eared Mule," 297 (see "Flop Eared Mule")
"Lost John," 240
"Loving Nancy," 61

"Make Me a Bed On the Floor," 189
"Mary Blain," 333
"Merry Widow Waltz," 131
"Miss Cindy," 79, 384 (see "Cindy")
"Miss Sally at the Party," 265 (298) (see "I Want To Go To Meeting")
"Mississippi Sawyer," 91, 171, 203, 209, 264, 340, 360
"Mississippi Valley Waltz," 402
"Mollie Bring the Kettle," 85 (see "Molly Put the Kettle On")
"Molly Put the Kettle On," 72 (85, 170)
"Money Musk," 163 (see Redditt's "Dan Tucker")
"Muddy Road to Texas," 57
"Murilla's Lesson," 190

CPSIA information can be obtained at www.ICGtesting.com
Printed in the USA
BVOW10*0439151015

422524BV00004BA/4/P

9 781496 804013